Reconciling the Deepening and Widening of the European Union

ASSER INSTITUTE COLLOQUIUM ON EUROPEAN LAW

SESSION 36 – 29 SEPTEMBER 2006

T.M.C. ASSER INSTITUUT
The Hague

Reconciling the Deepening and Widening of the European Union

edited by

Steven Blockmans

and

Sacha Prechal

T·M·C·Asser press

Published by T·M·C·Asser press
P.O. Box 16163, 2500 BD The Hague, The Netherlands
<www.asserpress.nl>

T·M·C·Asser press' English language books are distributed exclusively by:

Cambridge University Press, The Edinburgh Building, Shaftesbury Road,
Cambridge CB2 2RU, UK,
or
for customers in the USA, Canada and Mexico:
Cambridge University Press, 100 Brook Hill Drive, West Nyack, NY 10994-2133, USA
<www.cambridge.org>

ISBN 978-90-6704-264-2

T.M.C. Asser Instituut – Institute for Private and Public International Law, International Commercial Arbitration and European Law

Institute Address: R.J. Schimmelpennincklaan 20-22, The Hague, The Netherlands; Mailing Address: P.O. Box 30461, 2500 GL The Hague, The Netherlands; Tel.: +3170 342 0300; Fax: +3170 3420 359; Internet: www.asser.nl.
Over forty years, the T.M.C. Asser Institute has developed into a leading scientific research institute in the field of international law. It covers private international law, public international law, including international humanitarian law, the law of the European Union, the law of international commercial arbitration and increasingly, also, international economic law, the law of international commerce and international sports law.
Conducting scientific research, either fundamental or applied, in the aforementioned domains, is the main activity of the Institute. In addition, the Institute organizes congresses and postgraduate courses, undertakes contract-research and operates its own publishing house.
Because of its inter-university background, the Institute often cooperates with Dutch law faculties as well as with various national and foreign institutions.

FOREWORD

In the history of the European integration process, each enlargement since 1973 has emphasized the dilemma of the strain that widening puts on the deepening of the European Communities/Union. The need to reform the institutional architecture of the European Union has become even more pressing with the recent accession of twelve new Member States. This 'big bang' enlargement has stretched the operational capacity of the EU institutions to the maximum – and maybe even beyond that – in terms of their decision-making and the continued evolution, implementation, and enforcement of the Union's *acquis*. Moreover, the current legal framework, as provided for by the Treaty of Nice, does not cater for the absorption of any other states. The institutional arrangements to take in today's candidate countries – Croatia, Macedonia and Turkey – are still to be made.

An attempt at making the European Union more democratic, transparent and efficient, by way of the Treaty establishing a Constitution for Europe, was rejected in the French and Dutch referenda. It is striking to note that the 'no' votes in France and the Netherlands have been said to reflect, *inter alia*, the opposition to the ongoing enlargement of the Union, in particular the possible future EU membership of Turkey. Nevertheless, the European Council has reaffirmed that it will honour the existing commitments in the sphere of enlargement. Of course, it has also emphasized that the cohesion and the effectiveness of the Union should be protected. In view of the EU's unresolved 'constitutional' issues and the enlargement fatigue of a number of Member States, reconciling the deepening and widening agendas of the Union proves to be a bigger challenge than ever before.

At this important juncture, the T.M.C. Asser Instituut held its 36th Colloquium on European Law to debate aspects of further enlargements, including the absorption capacity and the final borders of the European Union, and methods for improving the quality of the institutional and substantive reform processes. The aim of the 2006 Colloquium was to identify ways and means to ensure that the enlarging European Union is able to function politically, financially and institutionally, thereby deepening Europe's integration project. Ideas were exchanged about the potential and limits of enhanced cooperation, future accession treaties and several forms concerning partnership.

The deepening and widening of the European Union is a topic which has been at the heart of the Asser Institute's activities for the last 25 years or more. The Institute was one of the first academic institutions in Western Europe to establish close contacts with universities in Central and Eastern Europe, in particular, starting with the University of Zagreb in the 1970s. Since 1989, the Asser Institute has successfully cooperated with Dutch universities and those from Central and Eastern European candidate countries, such as the Central European University, as well as universities from Croatia, Russia, Belarus and Ukraine, through its post-graduate training and research Programme 'Asser College Europe'. This Programme, which has been financed for many years by the Dutch Ministry of Foreign Affairs under its MATRA programme, is specifically designed to educate lawyers from Central and Eastern Europe in areas such as European law and WTO law. Additionally, since 1997 the Asser Institute has been active in technical assistance projects for candidate, potential candidate and ENP countries, often under the auspices of the European Commission. The Institute's experts have been advising governments on the adoption of the *acquis* and have been training judges, diplomats and others in applying EU law in practice.

Such practical work related to widening is combined with the deepening of academic knowledge of both the Institute's own researchers and those with whom it cooperates. As an interuniversity research institute with a strong focus on EU law the Asser Institute is proud that the Colloquium on European law sets an example for the unique tradition of cooperation with the Dutch law faculties and their specialists in EU law. In the 36th edition of the Colloquium, this was clearly visible in the cooperation with the University of Utrecht and more specifically Prof. Sacha Prechal as the co-organiser of the conference and the co-editor of its proceedings. Prominent professors and senior researchers from other Dutch universities, Prof. Christophe Hillion (Leiden); Dr. Andrea Ott (Maastricht); Prof. Fabian Amtenbrink (Rotterdam); and Prof. Monica den Boer (VU Amsterdam), as well as Prof. Norbert Reich (University of Bremen); Dr. Adam Łazowski (University of Westminster) and Dr. Steven Blockmans (T.M.C. Asser Institute), also contributed to the success of both the conference and this volume. Members of the Asser College Europe Steering Committee, Prof. Tibor Varady, Prof. Kresimir Sajko, Prof. Bernadette Bordas, Prof. Vladzimir Astapenka and Prof. Alexandru Farcas, and Prof. Jaap de Zwaan (Director of the Clingendael Institute) as discussants, and the participants of the Colloquium made sure that the debate was fruitful and of a high quality. Dr. Wybe Douma (Head of the EU law department of the T.M.C. Asser Institute) played an important role in finding the right speakers and commenting on some of the contributions in these proceedings.

I would like to express my gratitude to the Editors, Prof. Sacha Prechal (University of Utrecht) and Dr. Steven Blockmans (T.M.C. Asser Institute), who have editorially developed and produced this excellent volume in the Asser Institute Colloquium on European Law Series. I also would like to thank Mieke Eijdenberg for her sub-editing and Peter Morris for his language-editing of the book.

October 2007

Frans Nelissen
General Director
T.M.C. Asser Instituut

SUMMARY OF CONTENTS

Foreword by Frans NELISSEN V

Table of contents IX

List of abbreviations XV

Chapter 1
The European integration process: a continuum of 'deepening' and 'widening' 1
Steven BLOCKMANS and Sacha PRECHAL

Chapter 2
A diagnosis of the Area of Freedom, Security and Justice: remedies and reforms in the domains of immigration, terrorism and security 13
Monica DEN BOER

Chapter 3
'Widening' vs. 'deepening' the European Union: free movement vs. social rights in the *Laval* case before the ECJ 29
Norbert REICH

Chapter 4
Consolidating the enlargement agenda for South Eastern Europe 59
Steven BLOCKMANS

Chapter 5
Box of chocolates integration: the European Economic Area and the Swiss model revisited 87
Adam ŁAZOWSKI

Chapter 6
On the European Union's institutional capacity to cope with further enlargement 111
Fabian AMTENBRINK

Chapter 7
A flexible future for the European Union: the way forward or a way out? 133
Andrea OTT

Chapter 8
Widen to deepen? The potential and limits of accession treaties to achieve EU constitutional reform 157
Christophe HILLION

Keynote speech 167
Piet-Hein DONNER

Report of the discussions during the colloquium 175
Karolien PIETERS, Leonardo MASSAI and Tamara TAKÁCS

List of contributors 185

Index 187

TABLE OF CONTENTS

Foreword by Frans NELISSEN V

Summary of contents VII

List of abbreviations XV

Chapter 1
The European integration process: a continuum of 'deepening' and 'widening' 1
Steven BLOCKMANS and Sacha PRECHAL
1. Introduction 1
2. A short history of 'deepening' and 'widening' 2
3. The EU's final frontier – and beyond 4
4. The perceived need for further 'deepening' 6
5. A flexible future for the European Union? 8
6. The academic contribution: this volume 10

Chapter 2
A diagnosis of the Area of Freedom, Security and Justice: remedies and reforms in the domains of immigration, terrorism and security 13
Monica DEN BOER
1. Introduction 13
2. Diagnosing the Area of Freedom, Security and Justice: the positive symptoms 13
3. Diagnosing the Area of Freedom, Security and Justice: the negative symptoms 15
4. It's the decision-making rules, stupid! 20
5. Would the Constitutional Treaty have been a good remedy? 23
6. Finale 25
7. Conclusion 27

Chapter 3
'Widening' vs. 'deepening' the European Union: free movement vs. social rights in the *Laval* case before the ECJ 29
Norbert REICH
1. Introduction 29
2. The Swedish *Laval* case as a starting point 30
3. Social rights as fundamental rights exempted from EC free movement rules? 32
3.1 Possible exemptions from Article 49 and 43 TEC for labour unions 32

3.1.1 Article 137(5) TEC? 32
3.1.2 'Non-statutory exemption' for trade unions derived from competition law? 33
3.1.3 Freedom of contract? 33
3.2 The importance of the *Gustafsson* and *Rasmussen* judgment of the ECtHR 34
3.3 The *Werhof* judgment of the ECJ 35
3.4 Constitutional traditions of Member States concerning social action 35
4. The applicability of Article 49 TEC to social actions against the posting of workers in *Laval* 37
4.1 The origin of the industrial conflict 37
4.2 The posting of workers by *Laval* in Sweden as an exercise of the freedom to provide services 38
4.3 Restrictions on the provision of services 38
4.3.1 Obligations of the Swedish state 39
4.3.2 Effects of Article 49 TEC against Byggnads, et al.? 40
4.4 Preliminary results of the discussion 41
5. Justifications 41
5.1 The Lex Britannia 42
5.1.1 Industrial action against an undertaking established in the European Union 43
5.1.2 Equivalence of Swedish and Latvian collective bargaining agreements? 45
5.1.3 The discriminatory element of action inherent in the Lex Britannia 46
5.2 Directive 96/71 46
5.2.1 Objectives of the directive 46
5.2.2 Article 3(1) of the Directive 96/71 47
5.2.3 The option for collective agreements under Article 3(8) 48
5.2.4 Enforcement of eventual minimum pay obligations? 50
5.3 Public policy exceptions under Article 3(10) in conjunction with constitutional law 51
6. Effects of an eventual non-justification of industrial action 52
7. Annex: Opinion of AG Mengozzi of 23 May 2007 55

Chapter 4
Consolidating the enlargement agenda for South Eastern Europe 59
Steven Blockmans
1. Introduction 59
2. The state of affairs 61
2.1 Turkey 61
2.2 Stabilisation and Association Process 65
2.2.1 Raising the threshold 65
2.2.2 A graduated process 67
2.2.3 Croatia 68

2.2.4 Macedonia (FYROM) 72
2.2.5 The 'potential' candidate countries 73
3. Novelties in pre-accession conditionality 76
3.1 Multi-dimensional nature 76
3.2 The requirement of regional cooperation 77
3.2.1 Conundrum 77
3.2.2 Reconciling enhanced bilateralism with enhanced multilateralism 79
3.3 ICTY conditionality 81
4. The revised procedure for accession negotiations 82
4.1 Protecting the Union 82
4.2 Benchmarking 83
5. Concluding remarks 85

Chapter 5
Box of chocolates integration: the European Economic Area and the Swiss model revisited 87
Adam ŁAZOWSKI
1. Introduction 87
2. The basics: What do the enhanced multilateralism and bilateralism amount to? 89
2.1 General remarks 89
2.2 The institutional set-up 91
3. The conundrum: how to reconcile the prerequisite of uniform application and interpretation of EU law with the enhanced multilateralism and bilateralism? 93
3.1 Introductory remarks 93
3.2 The nature of the European Economic Area and EC/EU-Swiss legal frameworks 95
3.3 Legislative methods for securing homogeneity 99
3.4 Administrative and judicial methods for securing homogeneity 102
4. The conclusions: is there a future for enhanced multilateralism and bilateralism? 108

Chapter 6
On the European Union's institutional capacity to cope with further enlargement 111
Fabian AMTENBRINK
1. Introduction 111
2. Absorption, enlargement and integration capacity 112
3. In search of the limits of the institutional framework 116
3.1 Democratic legitimacy 117
3.2 Efficiency 120
4. In search of sustainable solutions 123
4.1 Treaty establishing a Constitution for Europe – an adequate response? 123

4.2 Towards an 'enlargement-proof' institutional structure? 127
5. Conclusion 129

Chapter 7
A flexible future for the European Union: the way forward or a way out? 133
Andrea OTT
1. Introduction 133
2. Supranationality versus disintegration? 134
3. Different forms of flexibility in EU law and policy 136
3.1 Constitutional flexibility: enhanced cooperation and voluntary withdrawal 137
3.2 Differentiation through international agreements 140
3.2.1 Extending participation in EU law and policy for EU members 140
3.2.2 Extending participation in EU law and policy to non-EU members 142
3.3 Differentiation through accession treaties 146
3.3.1 Excluding participation in EU law and policy for EU members 146
3.3.2 Constitutional principles limiting exclusion? 150
4. Flexibility in an enlarging Union: the way forward of a way out? 154
5. Conclusion 155

Chapter 8
Widen to deepen? The potential and limits of accession treaties to achieve EU constitutional reform 157
Christophe HILLION
1. Introduction 157
2. Can widening serve as a vehicle for deepening? 158
3. The role of accession treaties in bringing about institutional reform 160
3.1 Legal potential 160
3.2 Advantages in introducing reforms through accession treaties 161
3.3 Practice 162
4. Limits to the introduction of institutional reforms through accession treaties 163
5. Role of the court 164
6. Conclusion 165

Keynote speech 167
Piet-Hein DONNER
1. Introduction 167
2. General remarks 168
3. Deepening 169
4. New solutions 170
5. The judicial system 172
6. Conclusion 172

Report of the discussions during the colloquium 175
Karolien PIETERS, Leonardo MASSAI and Tamara TAKÁCS
1. Deepening 175
2. Widening 177
3. Reconciling deepening and widening 179

List of contributors 185

Index 187

LIST OF ABBREVIATIONS

A	
AA	Act of Accession
AFSJ	Area of Freedom, Security and Justice
Australian YIL	Australian Yearbook of International Law
B	
BBC	British Broadcasting Corporation
BiH	Bosnia and Herzegovina
Bull. EC/EU	Bulletin of the European Communities/Union
C	
CDDRL	Center on Democracy, Development and the Rule of Law
CDE	Cahiers de Droit Européen
CEECs	Central and Eastern European Countries
CEFTA	Central European Free Trade Agreement
CEPOL	European Police College
CEPS	Centre for European Policy Studies
CFI	Court of First Instance
CFSP	Common Foreign and Security Policy
CML Rev.	Common Market Law Review
COM	European Commission document
COREPER	Comité des Répresentants Permanents
COSI	Committee on Internal Security
E	
EA	Europe Agreement
EAEC	European Atomic Energy Community
EAW	European Arrest Warrant
EC	European Community/Communities
ECAA	European Common Aviation Area
ECHR	European Convention on Human Rights
ECJ	European Court of Justice
ECR	European Court Reports
ECSC	European Coal and Steel Community
ECtHR	European Court of Human Rights
EEA	European Economic Area
EEC	European Economic Community
EFA Rev.	European Foreign Affairs Review
EFTA	European Free Trade Area
EGV	Vertrag zür Gründung der Europäischen Gemeinschaft
EJIL	European Journal of International Law
ELJ	European Law Journal

ELR	Environmental Law Reporter
EL Rev.	European Law Review
EMCDDA	European Drugs Monitoring Agency for Drugs Addiction
EMU	European Monetary Union
ENP	European Neighbourhood Policy
ENU	Europol National Unit
EP	European Parliament
EPC	European Political Cooperation
ERTA	European Road Transport Agreement
EU	European Union
EUPM	European Union Police Mission
Eurojust	European Judicial Co-operation Unit
Europol	European Police Office
EUV	Vertrag über die Europäische Union
EuZW	Europäische Zeitschrift für Wirtschaftsrecht
F	
FYROM	Former Yugoslav Republic of Macedonia
G	
GAERC	General Affairs and External Relations Council
I	
ICLQ	International and Comparative Law Quaterly
ICTY	International Criminal Tribunal for the former Yugoslavia
IGC	Intergovernmental Conference
ILM	International Legal Materials
IMF	International Monetary Fund
IPA	Instrument for the Pre-Accession Assistance
J	
JCMS	Journal of Common Market Studies
JHA	Justice and Home Affairs
L	
LCWA	Latvian Construction Workers Association
M	
MEP	Member of the European Parliament
N	
NATO	North Atlantic Treaty Organisation
NTER	Nederlands Tijdschrift voor Europees Recht
NYIL	Netherlands Yearbook of International Law
nyp	not yet published
nyr	not yet reported
O	
OECD	Organisation for Economic Cooperation and Development
OJ	Official Journal of the European Communities/Union
OSCE	Organisation for Security and Cooperation in Europe

P

PJCC	Police and Judicial Cooperation in Criminal Matters

Q

QMV	Qualified majority voting

S

SAAs	Stabilisation and Association Agreements
SaM	Serbia and Montenegro
SAP	Stabilisation and Association Process
SEA	Single European Act
SEC	European Commission documents which cannot be classified in any of the other series
SFRY	Socialist Federal Republic of Yugoslavia

T

TCE	Treaty establishing a Constitution for Europe
TEC	Treaty establishing the European Community
TEU	Treaty on European Union

U

UNSC	United Nations Security Council

W

WTO	World Trade Organisation

Z

ZEuP	Zeitschrift für Europäisches Privatrecht
ZEuS	Zeitschrift für Europäische Studien

Chapter 1
THE EUROPEAN INTEGRATION PROCESS: A CONTINUUM OF 'DEEPENING' AND 'WIDENING'

Steven Blockmans and Sacha Prechal

1. Introduction

On 11 December 1999, on the eve of the new millennium, 15 Heads of State and Government agreed on the most comprehensive and politically far-reaching enlargement in the history of European integration. Confirming the importance of the enlargement process launched in Luxembourg in December 1997 for the stability and prosperity of the entire European continent, the European Council widened the accession process to comprise 13 candidate countries within a single framework. The accession of 10 of these states on 1 May 2004 finally marked the end of the division of Europe, which resulted from the tragic history of the continent in the 20th century. The concept of peace through integration runs like a *leitmotif* through the sometimes impenetrable integration process. Today, the political and economic fabric of Europe is so tightly woven that the countries involved are inextricably dependent on each other and share a common destiny.

There is an inherent tension between the two aspects of European integration, 'deepening' and 'widening', which are central to the present volume. By some, widening is believed to threaten the deepening in the sense that it becomes increasingly difficult to bridge the diversity in an European Union with many more Member States and, in particular, more heterogeneous Member States, with very different interests. Yet, as the history of European integration shows, widening and deepening may also go hand in hand. Since its creation in 1951, the European integration process has progressed through a mixture of closer integration in a growing number of policy domains and the expansion of the group of countries participating therein. Every enlargement round was in fact accompanied with an effort, first, to 'put the EU house in order'. In other words, there may be tension between widening and deepening but they do not necessarily contradict each other.

Can deepening also stimulate widening? To a certain extent the answer is probably yes.

The relative success, when compared with other international organisations, of integration within in the European Union, the high degree of the Member States being intertwined in the context of a constitutional framework, makes it for many

S. Blockmans and S. Prechal, eds., Reconciling the Deepening and Widening of the EU

outsiders less attractive to stay out. Joining the European Union is often sought even at high costs in economic and, above all, societal terms. This is what we have witnessed in the latest two rounds, with often harsh consequences which many people have to pay as a price for meeting the criteria for accession. The process of transition from a communist regime into a liberal economic order, in combination with the preparations for EU membership set these pre-accession rounds apart from all previous ones.

2. A short history of 'deepening' and 'widening'

All previous enlargements of the European Communities/Union have been accompanied by a parallel (substantive and/or institutional) reform of the integration process. In 1973, the first widening of the European Communities (EC) with Denmark, Ireland and the United Kingdom was accompanied by significant deepening. A regional policy was created which initially comprised just 5% of the budget, but which grew steadily in later years. A common fisheries policy was established, controversially just before the United Kingdom joined. There were increased powers for the European Parliament (EP) and in 1979 there were the first direct elections to the EP. A Court of Auditors was also established. The 'southern' enlargements with Greece (1981) and Spain and Portugal (1986) were accompanied by the first major treaty reform since 1957. The Single European Act (SEA) of 1987 prepared the ground for the completion of the single market in 1992. It introduced the principle of cohesion and included two significant institutional changes: the greater use of qualified majority voting (QMV) in the Council in order to ensure policy output and the greater involvement of the EP in legislative and other decision-making procedures, in order to strengthen the EC's democratic legitimacy. The SEA also laid down in the form of a treaty the procedures for European Political Cooperation (EPC) in the field of foreign policy. It also included new policies with regard to the environment, economic and social cohesion, research, technology and social affairs.

Prior to the fourth enlargement with Austria, Finland and Sweden (1995), the Treaty on European Union (TEU) was signed at Maastricht in February 1992. The TEU included provisions for Economic and Monetary Union (with a clear timetable for the introduction of a single currency), subsidiarity, EU citizenship, the establishment of a Common Foreign and Security Policy (CFSP) and closer cooperation concerning Justice and Home Affairs (JHA). It also established a Committee of the Regions with an advisory role. Furthermore, the Treaty marked the first officially sanctioned moves towards a multi-speed European Union. The United Kingdom negotiated so-called 'opt-outs' from the provisions on the Euro, the Social Charter (which became the 'Social Protocol' to the Maastricht Treaty) and later refused to join the passport-free area known as 'Schengen'. After the failure of the first referendum to ratify the TEU in June 2002, Denmark also obtained opt-outs in the fields of defence and JHA. The Danish 'no' also effectively ended the debate on institutional reform that the then Commission President Jacques Delors sought to promote prior to the EU's enlargement with Austria, Finland and Sweden. Given the wide disagreements over the Treaty of Maastricht, it was decided to hold another IGC in 1996 to review the operation of the European Union, and in particular CFSP. The membership applications by a host of Central and Eastern European Countries (CEECs) in the mid-1990s strengthened the case for institutional reform before further enlargement. Specifically, the debate about reform covered the size and composition of the European Commission, the extent and modalities of QMV and how to facilitate closer cooperation among more integration-minded Member States.

The Treaty of Amsterdam (1997) led to a number of important changes. The EP was given additional powers, including the right to dismiss the Commission and to give its assent to the conclusion of international agreements, including Accession Treaties. The constitutional framework was further strengthened by asserting, in Article 6 TEU, the normative foundations of the Union, namely respect for human rights, democracy and the rule of law. Respect for these principles was not only a matter for the European Union alone, but also for the Member States and the candidate countries. The new treaty also incorporated 'Schengen' and introduced the concept of 'closer' cooperation. The UK's social policy opt-out was brought to an end and the Social protocol was incorporated into the text of the EC Treaty. Parts of the Third Pillar (JHA) were integrated into the First Pillar's community framework, leaving only police and judicial cooperation in criminal matters apart. Much attention was also centred on the measures to strengthen CFSP, especially the creation of the position of the High Representative with a supporting staff. But with the next wave of enlargement unlikely to take place for at least another five years, Member States were not under immediate pressure to bite the bullet of institutional reform.

The so-called 'leftovers' from Amsterdam were the focus of the IGC which led to the conclusion of the Treaty of Nice (2001). The negotiations were confused and bad tempered. Against the background of accession talks with 10 candidate countries, EU Member States were reluctant to contemplate a reduced size for the Commission in advance of enlargement and to accept any significant extension of QMV. Although a number of institutional changes were agreed, including a ceiling for the number of Commissioners (27) and MEPs (732), plus a complicated reform of the weighted voting system of the Council, the changes did nothing to improve the transparency of the Union. The provisions on 'closer' cooperation, under the Nice Treaty renamed as 'enhanced' cooperation, were amended, with probably the most significant change being the fact that only a minimum of eight Member States is necessary to embark upon this type of action. One of the few more positive outcomes of the IGC was a number of significant changes to the judicial system of the European Union. In typical fashion, the disagreements at Nice were covered up by an agreement to hold yet another IGC in 2004 that would be prepared by a Convention modelled on the body that had prepared the Charter of Fundamental Rights of the European Union. Like its predecessor, the Convention on the Future of Europe included, *inter alia*, national parliamentarians, European parliamentarians and national government representatives. In view of the 'big bang' enlargement of the Union, its mandate was to revise the existing treaties in such a way so as to make the European Union more transparent, democratic and efficient. After 16 months of debate and deliberation, and more than 7,000 proposed amendments, the efforts of the European Convention resulted in a draft Constitutional Treaty which was submitted to the President of the European Council in July 2003. On 18 June 2004, six weeks after the European Union expanded with ten new Member States, the IGC approved a consolidated text of the Treaty establishing a Constitution for Europe. The Constitutional Treaty was signed in Rome on 29 October 2004 by the Heads of State and Heads of Government of the 25 Member States and of Bulgaria, Romania and Turkey in their capacity as candidate countries and observers to the IGC. The Constitutional Treaty was ratified by 18 Member States, but rejected by two in popular referenda (France and the Netherlands). The further eastern enlargement of the Union, with Bulgaria and Romania (2007) has stretched the operational capacity of the European Union, as prescribed by the Treaty of Nice, to the maximum, prompting the Member States to review the framework of primary law on the basis of the Treaty establishing a Constitution for Europe (see below, section 4).

At this stage of the Union's development, further integration and enlargement are once again taking place simultaneously. Reconciling the desire to deepen European integration in several policy fields with the promises made to widen the European Union with the current candidate countries (Croatia, Macedonia (FYROM) and Turkey) once they meet all the criteria for membership is a big challenge, especially in view of the EU's ambitions to match the United States in economic growth, connect with its own citizens and claim its role as a global player. Institutional reform is the means through which the Union can continue to act effectively, consistently and in solidarity and thereby secure its further 'deepening' and 'widening'.

3. The EU's final frontier – and beyond

In tune with the increasing difficulty to reach agreement on institutional reform between an ever-growing group of Member States, the call for a discussion on the EU's final shape and borders has become louder. According to Article 49 TEU, 'any European state' which respects the principles set out in Article 6(1) TEU (liberty, democracy, respect for human rights and fundamental freedoms and the rule of law) may apply to become a member of the Union. But what is Europe and where does its final frontier actually lie?

In geographical terms, Europe is a continent which is difficult to define. In the north, south and west, this is still relatively easy. The Arctic Ocean, the Mediterranean Sea and the Atlantic Ocean almost form Europe's 'natural' borders. Europe's eastern frontier, however, is difficult to discern because Europe and Asia form one single land mass. Today, it is commonly agreed that the Urals and the Bosphorus form the border between Europe and Asia. Belarus, Moldova and Ukraine therefore fall within the geographical parameters for EU membership. The question whether the same holds true for Turkey and the three countries from the southern Caucasus (Armenia, Azerbaijan and Georgia) is a more contentious one.

While Russia's eligibility for EU membership is a purely hypothetical issue, normative history has somehow accepted that Russia – with its Indo-European, Slavic and orthodox roots – is historically anchored in Europe. The bloody legacy of four centuries of Ottoman rule in Europe, however, has shaped a widely accepted 'European' point of view to deny the legitimacy of the Ottoman past. The pressing question of EU enlargement with secular but overwhelmingly Islamic Turkey has intensified the ongoing debate on Europe's identity and *finalité*. In objective terms, the arguments of those who claim that Turkey is not European are not very convincing. Like Russia, the Western-most part of the country geographically belongs to Europe. Moreover, its Islamic identity is no different from that of Albania, Bosnia-Herzegovina and Macedonia (FYROM), whose European credentials have not been questioned on this ground when they were granted (potential) candidate country status. By analogy, the decision to grant candidate country status to Turkey is therefore justified. Of course the consequences of this decision are not just limited to the interpretation of the foggy term 'European'. They are potentially grave in view of both the functioning of the EU institutions and the instability that might result from pushing the Union's borders to countries with volatile regimes such as Syria, Iraq and Iran.

The bottom line is that the European Union can neither integrate all of its neighbours nor exclude all of them on principle. Geopolitical factors will in the end define the future size of the Union and the nature of its relations with neighbouring countries. It is in the Union's interest that countries on its borders are well governed so that problems are kept out and the import of vital resources (energy, labour, etc.) is guaranteed. Neighbours who are engaged in conflict, weak states where organised crime flourishes, dysfunctional societies or exploding population growth on its borders all pose problems for the European Union: the influx of refugees, the importation of organised crime, the fall-out from environmental disasters, the disruption of the flow of gas and oil, etc. Hence the need for the European Union to prevent conflicts, to spread good governance, to support social and political reform, to deal with corruption and abuse of power, and to establish the rule of law and protect human rights in the neighbouring countries. Arguably, extending reform to a Europe which is wider than that represented by the Member States of the European Union and its candidate countries is the best way of strengthening the European order, *inter alia*, because it blurs the new dividing lines in Europe after each new enlargement.

The creation of the European Neighbourhood Policy (ENP) was the European Commission's response to the wish of Member States to develop a new strategy ahead of the EU's enlargement of May 2004 to mitigate the exclusion effects for countries like Ukraine, Belarus and Moldova, and to prevent the Mediterranean countries pooled together in the so-called 'Barcelona Process' from being disadvantaged by the expansion of the Union with ten CEECs, Cyprus and Malta. The three countries from the southern Caucasus were later incorporated in the ENP. While, at first sight, it is true that some of the neighbouring countries involved (Armenia, Azerbaijan, Georgia, Morocco, Tunisia) seem attracted to the idea of converging more closely on European identity and standards, the whole package of the ENP does not seem to be a particularly strong leverage for a sustained process of all-encompassing transformation of the Union's outer periphery. On the one hand, this is due to the fact that the ENP does not offer the prospect of EU membership, the 'pull' needed in European countries like Ukraine and Moldova that wish to accede. On the other hand, it is because the disincentives which the European Union applies are not strong enough to force long-ruling political elites into the tracks of progressive democratic reform (Belarus, Egypt, Syria). The question is whether the European Union can go further in developing links with its partners that go beyond the current ENP yet fall short of accession agreements.

4. The perceived need for further 'deepening'

The deepening of the integration process is an often used but not clearly defined concept. Broadly speaking, it refers to three closely related aspects. In the first place, it concerns the level and scope of action, i.e., the intensity of EU action – integration as opposed to loose collaboration arrangements – and the increasing number of policy areas which are included in the EU's scope of action. What once started as the European Economic Community evolved far beyond that into the European Union dealing with a very broad panoply of subjects. In the process of subsequent treaty changes new objectives and tasks were listed and new heads of competence were added to the treaties, including, for instance, the environment, immigration, consumer policy, the EMU and judicial cooperation in civil and criminal matters. Characteristic of this process is the semi-automatic spill-over from one sector into another, increasingly making inroads into politically more charged areas. A clear example of this is the creation of an 'area without internal frontiers', which triggered more intensive cooperation in relation to immigration from outside the European Union, as well as cooperation in the field of civil and criminal law and which became the Area of Freedom, Security and Justice. A more discrete illustration of the dynamics of the process is the liberalisation of the service markets which, in turn, seems to entail the need for EU legislative involvement with services of general interest.

Secondly, and perhaps more importantly, deepening requires institutional reform in order to manage the dynamic of the European integration process in an adequate manner. In order to have the necessary capacity to act with 27 or more Member States in an ever broader range of policy areas, including justice, foreign policy and defence, the institutional set-up, the institutions themselves and the decision-making mechanisms have to be adjusted and strengthened. One may even go a step further. As the construction of the European Union gradually shifts away from its initial focus, i.e., the single market, towards more sensitive issues of high politics, the need for 'government' is becoming more critical. The latest rounds of EU enlargement (2004/2007) have accelerated this trend. In the case of the single currency, the Maastricht Treaty came up with a solution: monetary policy was entrusted to an independent central bank. But solutions are still required for other areas. The question is what sort of governance is needed and by whom.

In any case, it is striking that over the last few decades the Member States have added, without too much hesitation, new substantive policy areas to the treaties, apparently accepting the necessity to explicitly include these areas in the European integration process . Similarly, the domains to which qualified majority voting applies were gradually extended. Overall, however, the institutional changes, needed in terms of efficiency and effectiveness, have been lagging behind, as agreement on power-sharing has been very difficult to reach during the previous IGCs, even with the prospect of new countries joining the Union.

To this one may add the third aspect of deepening. As deepening concerns also the intensity of action, this will have a considerable and direct impact on individuals' lives in ever broader areas. This, in turn, requires appropriate democratic and rule of law guarantees that should enhance the legitimacy of the whole project. Therefore, the institutional reform should respond to two closely related concerns, namely the efficiency of the institutional arrangements and the legitimacy of the European Union, including questions of democracy and accountability.

In both respects, the Constitutional Treaty went for an important part in the right direction. However, despite its failure to enter into force and in anticipation of the new reform treaty, certain deepening processes do go on. Interestingly, certain elements from the Constitutional Treaty that, arguably, will improve the capacity to act and enhance the Union's legitimacy, are becoming reality little by little, not only through the adoption of secondary legislation but also due to the case-law of the ECJ. To the latter belong in particular the discrete rapprochement of the First and Third pillar, the enhanced protection of human rights, with the Charter of Fundamental Rights as a central source of inspiration and the involvement of national parliaments in controlling the subsidiarity principle. Proposals to extend the jurisdiction of the ECJ, at least in Title IV of the EC Treaty, have been made. Another proposal, namely to abolish unanimity in the area of criminal law, has failed, however.

An important factor that may contribute to the process of incremental changes is the fact that in a number of areas, such as immigration, energy, the environment and security, EU citizens are expecting the Union to act. This may form both the stick and carrot for the Member States to accept measures which may seem to encroach too much on the latter's sovereignty.

In the ongoing IGC there is general agreement that the adaptations to the EU system as initiated by the Constitutional Treaty should be adopted, except for its name and symbols. References to the flag, anthem and currency will disappear, as well as a reference to the primacy of EU law. There will be no Minister for Foreign Affairs – the person in charge will remain the 'High Representative of the Union for Foreign Affairs and Security Policy'. It is indeed too early to speculate about the exact content of the new treaty. However, on the basis of the detailed mandate for the IGC, as agreed in June 2007 under the German Presidency, one may observe that, *inter alia*, the following features from the Constitutional Treaty are not called into question: the merger of the Union and the Community, the formal disappearance of the pillar structure and the legal personality of the Union. The supervision by national parliaments in relation to subsidiarity will be strengthened. The difficulties with the voting system, which were a major concern for the Polish government, have been resolved in the well-tried fashion: postponement, in combination with the 'Ioannina compromise'. Disquieting, but apparently politically unavoidable, is the removal of the Charter of Fundamental Rights from the main text and its integration into the body of primary EU law by a mere reference in Article 6 TEU. A special opt-out will again be created for the United Kingdom in relation to both the Charter and the police and judicial cooperation in criminal matters.

The new reform treaty should, in principle, facilitate the deepening of the integration process and secure future institutional cooperation in view of the next round of enlargement. However, the British opt-outs are in a way illustrative of another problem: a much larger and more heterogeneous Union is, arguably, in need of more flexible arrangements.

5. A flexible future for the European Union?

The European Union is based on a mix of supranationalism and intergovernmentalism. In the medium term it is unlikely that this mix will significantly change. The EU's budgetary and resource limitations, agreed by the Member States, mean that the Union will remain almost entirely dependent on its Member States in this respect. Also as far as the application, control and enforcement of the EU rules is concerned, the Union will continue to depend on the Member States' legislative, executive, administrative and judicial authorities. Given the different interests involved, it is unlikely that there will be a fundamental re-balancing in power between the Member States and the institutions. However, increased social and economic divergences resulting from successive enlargement rounds will sooner or later bring important changes in political culture to the Union and its institutions. This, in turn, will further undermine a 'one size fits all' kind of policy-making. Flexibility, it is argued, should then be the answer. By some, it is considered as the beginning of disintegration. However, from an integrationist perspective, there is nothing wrong with a multi-speed European Union, provided that it is kept within certain limits. Indeed, different regimes for the Euro, Schengen and defence already exist. The temporary opts-out for the free movement of workers from the CEECs are another example. Other regimes may develop in the future.

Despite this optimistic tone, it is also useful to point to certain dangers. One of them is that democracy can hardly work in a complicated, if not impenetrable, system of multi-speed arrangements run by an ever-changing group of unidentified and unaccountable people. Democracy requires transparency, simplicity and a sense of belonging to a defined community and these are difficult to acquire in a diversified and open-ended European Union. Also from this perspective a set of well-defined procedures and conditions is crucial. However, a striking feature of flexibility within the European Union is that until now the provisions of the Treaties made for closer or enhanced cooperation have not been used. Rather, the Member States seem to prefer to set-up arrangements outside the scope of the EU treaty, such as initially the Schengen regime and the more recent Treaty of Prüm, comprising the cooperation of seven Member States. Obviously, in relation to the latter form of cooperation, mechanisms must be devised which will prevent EU policies from diluting into a form of traditional intergovernmental arrangements and they should be brought back within the EU framework as soon as possible.

Another danger, of a somewhat different nature, is a negative perception of flexibility, not least due to the vocabulary used. While the discussion about the terms 'flexibility', 'variable geometry', 'multi-speed EU', 'vanguard Europe', 'hard core', 'centre of gravity', 'directoire' and 'Europe *à la carte*' is still largely rhetorical, its potential practical implications are not. After all, the concept of 'avant-garde' – and all forms of flexibility translated in this idea – goes hand-in-hand with the concept of 'laggards'. They form two sides of the same coin. To make things even murkier, the discussion about the pros and cons of an avant-garde is usually conducted from a Western European perspective. In Central and Eastern Europe, the idea of a Western European avant-garde is viewed as a threat because it condemns 'new Europe' to an inferior status. Whereas the United Kingdom fears an avant-garde because access to the integrated system of decision-making is at stake, most of the CEECs, who might be willing to join the vanguard, may be unable to do so for many years to come because they do not have the ability to catch up with the advance group of prosperity and effective government. Of the twelve states that joined the Union in 2004 and 2007, only three have managed to jump onto the next level of closer cooperation by meeting the requirements to join the Euro zone (Slovenia, Cyprus, Malta). Conversely, at least two of the new Member States have serious problems in continuing to meet the Copenhagen criteria of reform of the judiciary (Bulgaria) and eradicating corruption (Bulgaria and Romania). This is clearly in contrast with opts-out which are based on deliberate political choices. One could easily argue that the idea of an avant-garde is largely about perpetuating the division of Europe between an affluent and stable core and a poorer and/or unstable periphery. The creation of a Western European avant-garde would undo the greatest benefit of the enlargement project, namely allowing the less advanced countries of Central and Eastern Europe to join their more prosperous and stable neighbours in Western Europe on equal terms.

Turning away from the EU Member States as such, there is an even broader and patchier area of differentiated cooperation, namely between the European Union and the outsiders, an area governed by a range of international agreements of a different nature and concluded with different purposes. The result is an extremely complex texture of arrangements in which only specialists seem to find their way.

6. The academic contribution: this volume

Further enlargement will continue to enhance the diversity within the Union and result in an ever greater disjunction between the EU's geographic and functional boundaries. The European Union will increasingly act in overlapping circles and along a variable geometry resembling what has been famously dubbed as a neo-medieval empire.[1] If this is unavoidable, then the Union should try to find ways to improve the functioning of the emerging patchwork organisation, rather than attempting to reconstruct a neo-Westphalian federal state. A multi-speed European Union does not need to be seen as a recipe for chaos and paralysis. Today, effective governance is about recognising complexity, flexibility and dispersion. As EU academic lawyers, we should work hard to find ways to mitigate the negative effects of the new diversified Europe while utilising positive aspects for the benefit of the entire continent.

The contributions to this volume provide an attempt to clarify the legal possibilities and limits to reconcile wishes for the further 'deepening' and 'widening' of the EU project. Many of the questions briefly raised in this chapter are discussed in much more detail. Yet, this treatise by no means pretends to tackle the topic in a comprehensive and exhaustive manner. Rather, these proceedings of the 36th Asser Colloquium on European Law encompass most of the papers which were presented by seasoned scholars from different EU law backgrounds at the Kurhaus Hotel in Scheveningen, near The Hague, on 29 September 2006.

The first two contributions address a number of aspects of deepening the European integration process in fields where great challenges need to be confronted.

Monica den Boer's contribution focuses upon considerable substantive law and policy developments that take place in the Area of Freedom, Security and Justice, the former JHA. An impressive flood of decisions and arrangements of a very different nature, which are scattered over various regulatory and decisional frameworks, characterise the 'Area'. The implementation record of the Member States is rather poor, judicial protection of individuals' rights is weak and democratic input is very limited. The Area of Freedom, Security and Justice is typically a field where there is a clear mismatch between substantive law and policy deepening and an appropriate institutional framework. The author reflects, partly on the basis of the impact which the Constitutional Treaty could have had in this field, on a number of crucial improvements that are necessary for adequately responding to the difficulties which this area is facing.

Central to Norbert Reich's contribution is the tension that occurs as a consequence of a different understanding of the free movement of services and the freedom of establishment between the 'old' and the 'new' Member States. In view of the former, the limits to liberalisation should in principle lie in the protection of social rights and in particular of the right to take collective action in order to oppose

---

[1] See J. Zielonka, *Europe as Empire: the Nature of the Enlarged European Union* (Oxford, Oxford University Press 2006).

what is perceived as a case of social dumping. In the view of the new Member States, they merely benefit from the comparative advantage of cheaper labour. The clash between the – fundamental – social rights, on the one hand, and the equally fundamental treaty freedoms, on the other, comes very clearly to the fore in the *Laval* and *Viking* cases, pending before the ECJ, which are meticulously analysed by the author.

On the widening side of the spectrum, it would be good to clarify which of the neighbouring countries are going to join the European Union, why, when and how. Such steps would inject a degree of order, predictability and legal certainty into a highly diversified and sometimes chaotic patchwork of European cooperation and would also enhance the Union's legitimacy. Steven Blockmans looks at the state of affairs in the pre-accession processes with the candidate and potential candidate countries and argues that, despite the difficulties in finding a political compromise on institutional reform and agreement about the geometry of participation in the 'deepening' of the project, this is not and should not be the end of the road for EU enlargement. The European Union should not step down from its role as a 'reform promoter', especially not *vis-à-vis* the candidate and potential candidate countries which it has earmarked for future accession if and when these states comply with all the membership conditions. In recognition of the fact that further widening cannot weaken the fabric of the Union, the author offers ways and means to consolidate the enlargement agenda so as to prevent the European Union from importing problems that it cannot solve or that it can address more powerfully in the pre-accession phase.

For those states that will – for now – remain outside the ambit of the European Union, new ways and means should be found to enhance relations and induce reform in return for stability on the Union's periphery. In his contribution, Adam Łazowski analyses the potential and limits of the legal models provided by the relations between the European Union and European Economic Area, on the one hand, and the European Union and Switzerland, on the other, for organising the Union's relations with the rest of its geographical neighbours. The author compares those complex models of enhanced bilateralism and multilateralism to a box of chocolates, where third states agree to swallow a few delicious pieces of the internal market but otherwise remain outside the EU framework. Łazowski concludes that, for various legal, economic and political reasons, these models will probably not serve as alternatives to the European Neighbourhood Policy for those countries wishing to accede to the Union, but may well offer elements for organising relations with states that will remain outside of the EU's framework.

The book then turns to ways to reconcile the deepening and widening agendas of the European Union. Fabian Amtenbrink concentrates on the procedural modalities to enhance the Union's internal functioning. First he examines, from an institutional perspective, the highly fashionable but poorly defined notion of absorption (or integration) capacity. Are we confronted with new terminology for old problems in the sense that the institutional design should guarantee democratic legitimacy, efficiency and transparency? Next, the author analyses the institutional framework, in particular the one existing between the European Parliament, the Council and the Commission. In Amtenbrink's view, the system as such is no longer appropriate to accommodate further enlargement. In fact, it was already flawed in 2004 and 2007. Nowadays, the most relevant question is whether a more drastic system change should not be preferred over another round of institutional reforms, which are necessarily constrained by the existing institutional framework.

In her contribution, Andrea Ott points out that the internal capacity to absorb new Member States has become closely linked with the external capacity to implement and apply EU institutional requirements and policies by new members. The characteristics which enable such a complex and ongoing process to work have been found in the elements of internal and external EU law instruments and policies. As a consequence, certain lines between the EU's ins and outs become blurred as, for instance, the Schengen *acquis* shows. Ott takes a closer look at the main instruments to reconcile the widening with the deepening, namely flexibility or differentiation with its manifold features. The author addresses the risks and limits which lie in the use of such a tool or, in other words, whether it is a way forward or a way out of a common legal order of the Union.

Finally, Christophe Hillion brings us back to the point of departure, namely the fact that widening the EC/EU has often been used as a vehicle for the deepening of the European integration process, although not specifically through accession treaties. Hillion argues that while there might be good reasons for introducing reforms to the EU framework and legal order on the basis of a treaty of admission, it should be done within limits. In particular, the author contends that institutional reform through accession treaties is limited notably by the Member States' and the institutions' observance of the fundamental principles underpinning the Union's constitutional order, the prohibition of discrimination on the ground of nationality in particular. Arguably, the ECJ could have a role to play to ensure that such limits are observed.

The volume concludes with Piet Hein Donner's keynote speech at the 36th Asser Colloquium. In his presentation, the former Minister of Justice of the Netherlands concentrates on the development of the Area of Freedom, Security and Justice and offers suggestions to move forward in this domain. The gist of the lively debate that followed the oral contributions is reflected in a report on the discussions during the colloquium. It is hoped that this modest academic collection will contribute to the debate that the European Union so much needs to reconcile its deepening and widening agendas.

Chapter 2
A DIAGNOSIS OF THE AREA OF FREEDOM, SECURITY AND JUSTICE: REMEDIES AND REFORMS IN THE DOMAINS OF IMMIGRATION, TERRORISM AND SECURITY

Monica den Boer

1. Introduction

A reflection on the substantive reforms in the domains of immigration, terrorism and security is intricately related to the journey through the various treaties. Although the institutional chronology starts with the inception of Justice and Home Affairs Cooperation in Title VI of the Maastricht Treaty on European Union, the hot spots during this journey are to be found in the Amsterdam Treaty and the inception of the Area of Freedom, Security and Justice in 1997, as well as in the subsequent Tampere and The Hague Programmes. Various policy plans have intersected with these transformative moments, including the European Neighbourhood Policy and the European Security Strategy, as well as the more specific ones on drugs, organised crime, crime prevention, illegal immigration and terrorism, and the Commission Green Papers (e.g., on migration, the European Public Prosecutor). Most of these legislative programmes and action plans contributed to amplification and convergence, but occasionally also to diversion, differentiation and confusion.

This chapter seeks to present a diagnosis of the Area of Freedom, Security and Justice (AFSJ), in particular the results of legislation, the system of decision-making and governance, as well as the positioning of the Area of Freedom, Security and Justice in the wider debate on security and surveillance. Secondly, a number of remedies and possible reforms will be looked at, including the value which an EU Reform Treaty may have for a further development of the Area of Freedom, Security and Justice. Throughout the article, we will use the perspective of the past and future enlargement of the European Union, including the JHA dimension of the European Neighbourhood Policy.

2. Diagnosing the area of freedom, security and justice: the positive symptoms

Looking back at 15 years of JHA cooperation, a consecutive number of treaties have had a transformative effect on the character, scope and procedural aspects of

S. Blockmans and S. Prechal, eds., Reconciling the Deepening and Widening of the EU

this relatively new policy terrain in the European Union. Before the institutionalisation of JHA cooperation in the Maastricht Treaty on European Union, many did not even dare to dream about a comprehensive set of policies that are geared around the facilitation of the free movement of persons and the complementary actions that were deemed necessary in order to compensate for the expected security deficit. But amongst the rubble of the failed External Borders Convention, and the tediousness with which the free movement of persons area was under construction, a need was also felt to bring matters under the umbrella of the European Union, thereby facilitating more rational, comprehensible and accountable decision-making. Even though Third Pillar matters, ranging from asylum cooperation to police cooperation, were not immediately brought under the Community sphere, it was already considered a significant step forward that Member States agreed to cooperate on sovereignty-sensitive matters (information exchange, border controls, immigration procedures) in an intergovernmental manner. Views about how much sovereignty was 'lost to Brussels' vary from Member States gaining strength by profiting from the rearticulation of national politics on the one end of the continuum to Member States (and their national jurisdictions in particular) gradually falling prey to standards of harmonisation at the other end.

Before the geographical widening of the European Union took place, first through accession of Austria, Sweden and Finland in 1995, and then by the 'big-bang accession' of ten new Member States on 1 May 2004 and the accession of Romania and Bulgaria on 1 May 2007, a substantial widening of the *ratione materiae* took place in the sphere of JHA cooperation. If this was intended to be a conscious strategy, it was a clever one, because the most contentious aspects of internal security policy-making had been ironed out before the system of unanimous decision-making was overcome by semi-paralysis due to the rapidly growing size of the JHA Council. Especially the Tampere Programme of 1999 gave rise to a deepening of JHA policy-making by means of institutionalisation (or the bolstering of already existing agencies such as Europol). Aided and formalised by the Amsterdam Treaty on European Union in 1997, the Area of Freedom, Security and Justice was carved out and initiated by this programme, which included various policy objectives, ranging from migration to criminal justice cooperation.

The Tampere Programme was regarded as a vision document for the measures that had to be taken in the years up to 2004. The policies it covered included the intended creation of a common EU asylum and migration policy, which was to be based on four elements, namely partnership with countries of origin, a Common European Asylum System to be gradually established, fair treatment of third-country nationals, and the management of migration flows at all their stages.[1] Furthermore, a key component in the Tampere Programme concerned the establishment of

[1] A. Sorel, 'Asylum, Migration and Border Controls in the Hague Programme', in J.W. de Zwaan and F.A.N.J. Goudappel (eds.), *Freedom, Security and Justice in the European Union. Implementation of the Hague Programme* (The Hague, T.M.C. Asser Press 2006) pp. 11-16, at pp. 11-12.

an area of justice in which legal decisions are mutually accepted in the Member States, with better access to justice and uniform standards in civil law. Another principal chapter in the Tampere document concerned the Union-wide fight against crime: especially the tackling of organised crime – such as organised trafficking in human beings – was prioritised and agencies were either created or boosted to deal with this challenge. A speculative question is whether institutionalised establishments such as Eurojust, the European Police College (CEPOL) and the European Task Force of Chiefs of Police would have been created after the enlargement of the Union. It seems as if this institutional deepening of the Union was deliberately achieved before the geographical widening of the Union was going to be accomplished. An important element added by the Tampere Programme to the JHA field was external action, which was the cooperation with neighbouring countries and countries of transit and origin of illegal migration, drugs, smuggled and stolen goods. Finally, the Tampere Council established a high-level body for the drafting of a Fundamental Rights Charter, which was adopted by the Nice Council in December 2000.

The implementation of the Tampere Programme was assessed in June 2004[2] and was basically seen as a glass which was half full, half empty. Helped by the Eurobarometer,[3] the European Commission was of the opinion that much had been achieved, in particular the support for JHA policies and the underlining of firm priorities. In view of specific challenges following from EU enlargement, the Commission was proud to announce a positive evaluation of the progress made on the external border control and the establishment of a next generation Schengen Information System. Moreover, the enlarged European Union was portrayed as the ideal context for boosting mutual trust and recognition, particularly in the area of justice.[4]

3. Diagnosing the Area of Freedom, Security and Justice: the Negative Symptoms

When the implementation of the Tampere Programme was subjected to an assessment,[5] the European Commission seized the opportunity to point its finger at a number of weaknesses. The Commission particularly blamed the institutional constraints and the frequent lack of political consensus. This can be illustrated by a number of observations.

First, the amount of work that had been done in the field of migration, security and anti-terrorism looked impressive, at least when taking the number of legal in-

[2] Communication from the Commission to the Council and the European Parliament, Area of Freedom, Security and Justice: Assessment of the Tampere Programme and future orientations (SEC (2004)680 et SEC (2004)693), COM (2004) 401 final, 2.6.2004.

[3] COM (2004) 4002 final, Brussels, 2.6.2004, p. 3, fn 3.

[4] Id p. 5.

[5] Id.

struments that have been adopted as a point of departure. The JHA record has been one of extensive deepening, with a strong development of its *acquis* (not least because of the incorporation of the Schengen *acquis* by virtue of the Amsterdam Treaty in 1997) and a noticeable emphasis on the creation of several agencies, ranging from Europol[6] and Eurojust[7] to the European Drugs Monitoring Agency for Drugs Addiction (EMCDDA)[8] and FRONTEX[9] (the agency which coordinates operational cooperation between Member States in the field of external border control). Probing behind this successful façade, however, tells us more about the lamentable implementation record of the Member States, and about the level of political symbolism that has crept into the agreement on non-binding instruments. The Scoreboard[10] of the European Commission is quite revealing in that sense, because it shows that several Member States fail to stick to the deadlines which have been agreed upon. The consequence of this feeble time-keeping is that some instruments fail to enter into force on the dates that had been set, or that instruments such as Framework Decisions only enter into force after having been ratified by a minimum number of eight Member States, thereby encouraging a piecemeal implementation of new legislation. Jörg Monar, a specialist in EU Justice and Home Affairs matters, has studied the implementation of JHA instruments and sees the 'poor implementation of agreed objectives and measures' as one of the main problems:

> 'The member states are in fact much better at agreeing on common objectives than at transforming them into effective measures afterwards. This is caused by weaknesses in both the decision-making capacity and implementation at the national level.'

In the field of EU anti-terrorism, for instance, by May 2006,

> 'the 2002 *Framework decision on combating* terrorism, arguably the most important measure of EU action in the field, had still not been fully implemented by three member states; the decision of February 2002 to establish Eurojust, crucial for the cross-border prosecution of terrorist offences, had still not been fully implemented by four member states; and the *Framework decision on the execution of orders freezing property or* evidence of July 2003 had not been implemented by 14 member states. All these lapses are in spite of repeated deadlines set by the Council.'[11]

---

6 <www.europol.europa.eu>.

7 <www.eurojust.europa.eu>.

8 <www.emcdda.europa.eu>.

9 The European Agency for the Management of Operational Cooperation at the External Borders of the Member States of the European Union, established by Council Regulation (EC) 2007/2004 *OJ* 2004 L 349/1.

10 Communication from the Commission to the Council and the European Parliament – Scoreboard to review progress on the area of 'Freedom, Security and Justice' in the European Union, COM (2000) 167 final, 13.4.2000.

11 J. Monar, 'The EU's approach post-September 11: global terrorism as a multidimensional law enforcement challenge', 20 *Cambridge Review of International Affairs* (2007), pp. 267-283, at p. 279. In footnote (36) Monar refers to Council document 9589/06 ADD 1 of 19 May 2006 on these and other missed implementation deadlines.

The effect is that there are unequal entitlements between the Member States and that citizens are potentially subjected to a different set of rules. Even though this is often a temporary situation, it may be considered undesirable when viewed from the perspective of the equal justice principle.

Second, what is striking is the incremental character of JHA decision-making, which is marked by step-by-step progress, apparently by dispensing the wider policy horizons on the way in which the European Union can achieve a satisfactory balance between the free movement of persons and the compensatory measures in the form of enhanced security and law enforcement cooperation. Whereas the '1992' objectives pointed in the direction of a *finalité*, the Area of Freedom, Security and Justice has been characterised as supplying 'a menu of compensatory measures concerning the control of movements across the EU's external borders and the development of new capacities for the internal monitoring of populations in light of the supposed "security deficit" attendant upon the completion of an internal market in which goods, persons, services, and capital should in principle move freely', and which has 'no other *finalité* other than continuing adherence to a highly abstract triumvirate of values.'[12] The neo-federalist ideology, which has been proclaimed by Fischer, Cohn-Bendit, and several others, presupposed an explicit and constitutionally-anchored view about the division of competences between the different levels of governance and authority. In the eyes of others, however, the need for 'end terms' of 'finality' within the European Union may be a rather pointless exercise, as European integration will follow its own incremental logic: this 'Schuman-Monnet' approach views the process of integration as more important than the final objective.[13]

Especially the terrorist attacks that took place on 11 September 2001 had a firm impact on the number of legal instruments announced by the European Council and the speed of their adoption.[14] These instruments generally intended to support the convergence between criminal law systems.[15] Long as Europe's regulatory list in the area of law enforcement cooperation may seem, it is interesting to observe that the Member States have not yet established deep institutional cooperation in the

---

[12] N. Walker, 'In Search of the Area of Freedom, Security and Justice: A Constitutional Odyssey', in N. Walker (ed.), *Europe's Area of Freedom, Security and Justice* (Oxford, Oxford University Press 2004), pp. 3-37, at p. 5.

[13] J.Q.Th. Rood, *Een einde aan de Europese integratie? Kanttekeningen bij het staatscentrisch paradigma in het integratiedebat*, Notitie 16 (The Hague, Clingendael Institute 2001) p. 14.

[14] M. den Boer, 'The EU Counter-Terrorism Wave: Window of Opportunity or Profound Policy Transformation?', in M. van Leeuwen (ed.), *Confronting Terrorism: European Experiences, Threat Perceptions and Policies* (The Hague, Kluwer Law International 2003) pp. 185-206; P. Norman, 'The Evolution of European Policing Strategies in Response to Transnational Crime', in J. Sheptycki and A. Wardak (eds.), *Transnational and Comparative Criminology* (Milton Park, Routledge-Cavendish 2006), pp. 316-334.

[15] J. Monar, 'Specific Factors, Typology and Development Trends of Modes of Governance in the EU Justice and Home Affairs Domain', ref. no. 1/D17, NEWGOV (New Modes of Governance), Integrated Project Priority 7, *Citizens and Governance in a Knowledge-based society*, 2006.

law enforcement area, thereby indicating that they prefer to stay in the driving seat when it concerns the governance of internal security.

Previous research has demonstrated that the impact of the European Union on the structure, organisation and governance of law enforcement is varied but generally light. This may imply active resistance from national and sub-national actors against Europeanization, but it may also be the effect of the generally non-binding regulation in which coercion is practically absent as a mode of governance. Yet, in combination with the effect of legal regulation, intergovernmentally agreed instruments in the area of criminal justice cooperation have culminated in a new dynamic, such as the redistribution of political, administrative and professional authority in national arenas of internal security governance.

Third, the JHA arena, which is epitomized in the Area of Freedom, Security and Justice, is established on the basis of policies that are occasionally inherently incompatible, at least to the extent that there are several underlying tensions between inclusion and exclusion, between allowing immigration for the benefit of the European labour market and making it more difficult for 'third-country citizens' to enter Europe. Symbiotic as the abolition of internal border controls and the reinforcement of security within Member State territories and at external borders may be, the Area of Freedom, Security and Justice as we have it now is marked by a profound ambiguity. In a radical interpretation, it may even be the case that the realisation of a common immigration and asylum policy in the European Union is hindered – perhaps even paralysed – by the securitisation of those very issues in another corner of the Area of Freedom, Security and Justice.[16]

Fourth, the incorporation of ten new Member States on 1 May 2004 was ambivalent and particularly difficult to realise in the area of JHA cooperation. Not only have several 'old' Member States introduced (temporary) restrictions on entrance to the labour market by employees from some of the Central and East European states,[17] they have also imposed tough demands on the Member States when it concerns the quality of external border controls, implying a systematic surveillance of each individual passing the external border as well as exercising effective border surveillance at authorised border-crossing points;[18] the reform of legal and law

[16] E.g., M. den Boer, Crime et immigration dans l'Union européenne, special issue of *Culture et Conflits,* 'Sécurité et Immigration', sous la direction de Didier Bigo (Paris, l'Harmattan, n°31-32, 1998), pp. 101-123. See also M. den Boer, 'Moving between bogus and bona fide: the policing of inclusion and exclusion in Europe', in Robert Miles and Dietrich Thränhardt (eds.), *Migration and European Integration. The Dynamics of Inclusion and Exclusion* (London, Pinter Publishers 1995) pp. 92-111.

[17] For instance, the European Commission even decided to formally request the Netherlands to review its rules whereby Community businesses had to obtain work permits for staff from certain new Member States before they could temporarily be posted to the Netherlands to perform services; the Commission considered this to be a violation of the rules of the Treaty regarding the freedom to provide services (Art. 49 EC Treaty).

[18] E.g., S. Lavenex, 'EU External Governance in "wider Europe"', 11 *Journal of European Public Policy* (2004), pp. 680-700; A. Niemenkari, 'EU/Schengen Requirements for National Border Security Systems', DCAF, Geneva, Working Paper Series No. 8, March 2002.

enforcement institutions, and anti-corruption measures. As such, the new Member States were compelled to adopt and implement the full Schengen *acquis* without the possibility to renegotiate its terms.[19] The same demand was not imposed on Switzerland, which negotiated an opt-out clause on the anti-money laundering measures before its accession to Dublin/Schengen, because the extension of judicial assistance in criminal matters to taxation would heavily affect its financial services industry, and hence it secured the maintenance the bank-client confidentiality.[20] Physically, almost four years after the accession of ten new Member States, the European Union is still segregated in two parts as the external border still runs between the old and the new Member States for as long as the Schengen *acquis* has not been fully operationalised. It is currently foreseen that the new Member States will only be allowed to fully implement Schengen by the end of 2007. Thus, the widening process has not been a balanced and neutral process. Moreover, the opt-outs which were negotiated by the United Kingdom, Ireland and lately also Switzerland have set a trend for further differentiation, leaving Europe between pioneering cooperation between seven Member States outside the EU framework (the Treaty of Prüm)[21] and the sheer criterion of a minimum of eight Member States in the form of enhanced cooperation.[22] It is also interesting to observe that the deepening process, in the form of creating new JHA agencies, predominantly took place prior to the accession of the ten new Member States. With hindsight, this may be interpreted as a move which anticipated a lack of consensus on sovereignty-sensitive issues in a larger Europe.

Drawing these observations together, like threads in a string, we cannot but conclude that poor implementation, incremental and ambivalent decision-making, and the one-sidedness of the enlargement process was governed by proactive anxiety. The Member States were caught in a genuine prisoner's dilemma: if they would have moved ahead to liberalise immigration, national electorates would be ready to punish them; if they would have introduced a nuanced anti-terrorism policy, political and diplomatic criticism from the United States would have been the price to pay; if they would have laid down a blueprint for a future European criminal justice arena, a loss of control over their national legal systems and selective harmonisation would have been the consequences.

A number of these weak symptoms were addressed by the European Commission, which cunningly translated them into new priorities for the (near) future. Hence, the Hague Programme,[23] which was adopted during the JHA Council meeting on 4-5 November 2004, contained a number of these 'Tampere leftovers'. An interest-

[19] M. den Boer, 'Mirror, Mirror on the Wall…Who's the Fairest of Them All? The Double Logic in the Imposition of JHA Instruments of Control on Candidate Countries', 2001, EUI Working Paper, Schuman Institute, European University Institute, Florence.

[20] Swiss banking media conference, 10 March 2005.

[21] However, in the Presidency Conclusions of 20 July 2007 (11177/1/07 REV 1) it is noted that there has been a recent decision to integrate the essential provisions of the Prüm Treaty into the Union's legal framework, which still leaves some intergovernmental provisions outside the EU.

[22] The Draft Reform Treaty changes this threshold into a minimum of nine Member States.

[23] Brussels, 13 December 2004, JAI 559, 16054/04.

ing item, already heralded in the Tampere assessment document, was the 'principle of solidarity', which was initially mainly viewed from the perspective of 'burden-sharing', but later extended to contingency planning and crisis management. The legal framework for the improvement of information exchange between law enforcement services was also announced in the Tampere assessment document, but was transformed into the 'principle of availability' in the Hague Programme, which will turn information-sharing between law enforcement sharing into a more direct process of exchange.

4. It's the decision-making rules, stupid!

If one takes a cynical view, the Area of Freedom, Security and Justice which has hitherto been constructed resembles a patchwork of 'rolling ratification' clauses, *ad hoc* projects, temporary clauses, mutual recognition applications, scoreboard mechanisms, opt-out clauses, soft law instruments, pilot groups, variable geometry, evaluation teams, network agencies, provisional arrangements, expanded mandates, and intergovernmental management boards, the latter composed of 27 Member States. Against this backdrop, the European Commission has gradually started to build its plea for a different system of decision-making, which was already expressed in diplomatic terms on the occasion of the evaluation of the Tampere Programme in the summer of 2004.[24]

From the perspective of the European Commission, an intergovernmental circus must be difficult to manage and coordinate, despite the fact that the brunt of this responsibility is carried by the General Secretariat of the Council, because they are – together with the Committee of Permanent Representatives (COREPER) – the principal intermediaries between the capitals of the Member States and the EU administration. The burden on the European bureaucracy is no doubt considerable, but this is probably the less worrying side of it all. One tends to get lost in the Area of Freedom, Security and Justice when taking into account the administrative layers and the differentiated functioning of agencies and applicable procedures. Moreover, it is also not easy to convince citizens that their security benefits from the abolition of the Third Pillar by virtue of a communautarisation of decision-making procedures.

The Area of Freedom, Security and Justice is supposed to be a project which corresponds with 'frequently expressed concerns of citizens' (para. 2). This is fully in line with the objective of Article 29 TEU that the Union shall 'provide citizens with a high level of safety' within the Area of Freedom, Security and Justice. Although this political project has taken a prominent stance on the EU agenda, the decision-making process still tends to be largely exclusionary and the surrounding discourse is technical and sterile. In particular, Title VI of the TEU has suffered from a chronic lack of transparency, which is due to the patchwork of different

[24] COM (2004) 4002 final, Brussels, 2.6.2004.

decision-making procedures,[25] the incomprehensibility of its legal order, its predominant culture of shielded decision-making, and the lack of public consultation in policy agendas.[26]

This calls into question whether democracy and citizens' participation can be enhanced if the rules become more understandable and if the policy-making process becomes more open. To a large extent, the flawed decision-making process is blamed for the incremental and hurdled progress in substantive policy-making. It is precisely because Member States know this very well that they have resisted the proposal by the former Finnish EU Presidency, endorsed by the European Commission, to change unanimity voting over police and judicial cooperation in criminal matters into qualified majority voting, by the application of Article 42 TEU. (This would have been made possible by applying the *passerelle* to certain JHA policies which have not yet been elevated to Title IV). Such a procedure, however, demands that Member States take action in accordance with their respective constitutional requirements, which – in some Member States – would have meant a referendum before the decision to allow it to take effect.[27]

However, if we turn this argument around, why does decision-making in matters related to immigration, asylum and external borders still tend to be cumbersome despite the introduction of QMV on the 1st of May 2004? Communautarising certain policies can help to remedy some of the shortcomings, but should certainly not be seen as a panacea for solid substantial progress. A more profound question is whether the Member States want to achieve this progress at all. We may wonder whether they are perhaps anxiously looking for ways to stop a moving train without compromising their credibility in other EU dossiers?

The Member States acknowledge that they must face the challenge to introduce reforms to the JHA decision-making system. A few scenarios have been under discussion. These include the rather minimalist, but probably most pragmatic option that some matters affecting the core of the legal order of the Member States, such as the harmonisation of penalties, can still be left subject to unanimous decision-making. Other scenarios include the taking into practice of a new decision-making system after a transition period, a more cautious drafting and assessment of the consequences of JHA legislation, and a more efficient monitoring of the implementation of the acts adopted in the JHA area.[28]

From the list of possible reforms,[29] it can be concluded that some of them can easily be introduced alongside one another. They do not necessarily represent alter-

[25] F. Pastore, 'Visas, Borders, Immigration: Formation, Structure, and Current Evolution of the EU Entry Control System', in N. Walker (ed.), *Europe's Area of Freedom, Security and Justice* (Oxford, Oxford University Press 2004) pp. 88-142, at p. 137.

[26] M. den Boer, C. Hillebrand and A. Nölke, forthcoming, 'Legitimacy Under Pressure: The European Web of Counter-Terrorism Networks', *Journal of Common Market Studies* (2008).

[27] E. Guild and S. Carrera (2005). 'No Constitutional Treaty?' Implications for the Area of Freedom, Security and Justice (CEPS Working Documents). Paris: CEPS, p. 15.

[28] <http://www.eu2006.fi/news_and_documents/>.

[29] Press Release, Finland's EU Presidency: EU's operating conditions in matters of justice and home affairs must be guaranteed, 22 September 2006.

native or incompatible scenarios. The latter two proposals are actually a perpetuation of one of the priorities in The Hague Programme,[30] and will particularly benefit the quality of the legislation. From the perspective of legal and democratic legitimacy, a better screening prior to and following legislation should always be the norm for a good governance framework in Justice and Home Affairs, hence it could also be seen as a late repair of a hitherto flawed legislation process.

The concern about the loss of sovereignty seems to dictate limited margins within which the solution will be sought. It could thus be expected that the majority of Member States would therefore opt (once again) for a partial approach, thereby seeking to improve the quality and procedure of decision-making, but in a piecemeal fashion. That being the case, Member States still face a dazzling puzzle of complex options. The enhancement of the effectiveness, efficiency and legitimacy of the Area of Freedom, Security and Justice by means of a genuine common policy based on Community decision-making, requires from the Member States that they are genuinely prepared to pool their national sovereignty on those matters. The Member States realise that without implementation, it will take a long time before the Area of Freedom, Security and Justice will be claimed as a real success, and hence they might want to find an answer to improving the implementation of legal instruments. Furthermore, the Member States will have to accelerate the incorporation of extra-EU cooperation into the European Union, knowing that multilateral cooperation outside the European Union has to be in accordance with principles of democratic and legal legitimacy

Perhaps these strategic options ought to be represented in a different manner, but it does not alter the complex positioning by the Member States. On the one hand, there is the strongly growing impact of the European Union on anything related to immigration, terrorism and security. It only takes a few examples to demonstrate that the EU instruments which have been adopted thus far can have a deep-reaching effect on domestic policies. The implementation of the Schengen *acquis* has demanded from the signatory states the introduction of technical infrastructures to allow a common standard of external border control. The introduction of the EU Arrest Warrant introduces a transfer system for suspects of 32 different offences which replaces the former EU extradition system; it is based on mutual recognition and it is binding upon national law. Had the JHA Council not adopted a Framework Decision on Terrorism, the introduction of anti-terrorism legislation in the Netherlands would not have been mandatory, for instance.[31] The ratification of the Europol Convention demands from the participating Member States that they create a Europol National Unit (ENU) to correspond with the headquarters in The Hague.[32] These

[30] 1.1. Setting up of a system for objective and impartial evaluation of the implementation of EU measures in the field of freedom, security and justice – Communication on and proposal for the creation of an evaluation mechanism, as envisaged by Article III-260 of the Constitutional Treaty (2006).

[31] M. den Boer, 'Wake-Up Call for the Lowlands: Dutch counterterrorism from a comparative perspective', in 20 *Cambridge Review of International Affairs* (2007), pp. 285-302.

[32] M. den Boer and P. Doelle (2000) (eds.), et al., 'Controlling Organised Crime: Organisational Changes within the Law Enforcement and Prosecution Services in the EU Member States', Report for

are just a few relatively arbitrary examples that illustrate the effect which the European Union has had on national law and the national institutional architecture.

On the other hand, there is the image of an Area of Freedom, Security and Justice which, despite its power and speed, fails to be firmly anchored in the Member States, leading to perpetual expressions of frustration by the European institutions about a lack of commitment from the Member States. Do European institutions perhaps exaggerate the lack of progress and the miserable implementation speed in order to amplify their own justifications for a fully communautarised Area of Freedom, Security and Justice? Until now, the attempts of the EU institutions to create a consensus in favour of the communautarisation of Title VI have failed to impress the Member States.

5. Would the Constitutional Treaty have been a good remedy?

Significant progress had already been achieved with the Treaty of Amsterdam, when the Area of Freedom, Security and Justice was called into being. Qualified majority voting was already introduced, albeit conditionally, for certain policy areas, such as migration, asylum, visa policy and external border control. The most welcome impact of an EU Constitutional Treaty would have been that Title VI would have been abolished, and that it would introduce a more integrated system of decision-making (rules, procedures, instruments) which applies to interrelated policy areas. This measure would have been beneficial to the extent that the intergovernmental procedure that has hitherto applied has proved to be cumbersome because of the unanimity that had to be reached within the Council.

The abolition of Title VI would have reduced the policy-overlap between areas affecting the whole Community, such as drugs, fraud and data protection. A positive effect of an EU Constitutional Treaty would also have been that the basic ingredients for the construction of a European Rule of Law would be introduced, especially by laying the basis for the creation of a European Prosecutor's Office from Eurojust. Note that the EU Constitutional Treaty did not provide a supervisory function of the European Prosecutor's Office over Europol. In addition, the Articles on Judicial Cooperation in Criminal Matters and Police Cooperation remain vague about the organisational-institutional architecture of a properly functioning European criminal justice system.

The Draft Reform Treaty,[33] which may be regarded as a kick-start for the EU Constitutional Treaty, has been the subject of discussion during an Intergovernmental Conference in the course of 2007, and has left most of the new provisions for JHA cooperation intact. Like the EU Constitutional Treaty, the draft Reform Treaty seeks to delineate the competence of the European Union with regard to criminal law interventions, which provides that a European framework law may

the European Commission, Falcone Programme (98/FAL/145), Maastricht, European Institute of Public Administration.

33 <www.consilium.europa.eu>.

establish minimum rules concerning the definition of criminal offences and sanctions in the areas of particularly serious crime with cross-border dimensions resulting from the nature or impact of such offences or from a special need to combat them on a common basis. The direction of a European criminal justice space remains unclear, however: to what extent will the national criminal law systems of the Member States be affected by legislative approximation? This is certainly not a trivial question given the tremendous differentiation between the criminal law systems in the European Union, which will become greater as a consequence of the incumbent enlargement. It is in this regard disappointing that the reform project has thus far failed to make a hard choice in favour of harmonisation, although there is ample emphasis on mutual recognition.

The former EU Constitutional Treaty as well as the current draft Reform Treaty provide an improvement to the legislative competence of the European Parliament, although it does not relate to operational matters.[34] Significant in this regard is that the role of the European Parliament has been subject to gradual dilution in successive drafts of the former Constitutional Treaty. The draft of 14 March 2003 (CONV 614/03) spoke of the fact that the European Parliament and the Council could adopt framework laws according to the legislative procedure. A later draft (CONV 725/03) put forward the provision that '(t)he Council shall act unanimously after receiving the approval of the European Parliament' (Section 4, Art. III-166 (ex Art. 15), Judicial Cooperation in Criminal Matters), and that '(t)he Council shall act unanimously after consulting the European Parliament' (Section 5, Art. III-171 (ex Art. 21), Police Cooperation). Then, to make things more complicated, the draft of 9 July 2003 (CONV 848/03) mentioned the consent of the European Parliament with regard to judicial cooperation in criminal matters. It is a consoling thought that the national parliaments will gain more influence through a stricter application of the principle of subsidiarity (Part I, Title III, Art. I-9-3).

In general terms the former EU Constitutional Treaty as well as the current draft Reform Treaty are the result of masterly compromises. This is demonstrated by the fact that state sovereignty is preserved through a shared right of initiative: the European Commission will not be trusted with an exclusive right of initiative in the area of police and judicial cooperation in criminal matters.

In summary, despite its dormant status, the EU Constitutional Treaty can be considered as a courageous project because it proposed a rather radical departure from the intergovernmental perspective in the issue of enlargement. The communautarisation project is potentially far-reaching, expressing itself in QMV, co-decision and a shared right of initiative. The legislative competence of the European Parliament is significant, although it does not relate to operational (law enforcement) matters. If a realistic time-path can be agreed upon, the development of

---

[34] Art. 65 – 3 of the draft Reform Treaty provides that 'The Council, acting in accordance with a special legislative procedure, may establish measures concerning operational cooperation between the authorities referred to in this Article. The Council shall act unanimously after consulting the European Parliament', CIG 1/07, p. 68, <www.consilium.europa.eu>.

an integrated European criminal justice area may well be a possible perspective. This could be paralleled by a consolidation of democratic control at all levels, to the extent that all national parliaments involved acquire adequate and timely information (in the form of an 'early-warning' system); the reinforcement of inter-parliamentary cooperation between the national parliaments and the European Parliament on JHA matters (this could go back to former proposals concerning the establishment of 'Parlopol'); the introduction of a co-decision as the general procedure for all AFSJ matters. Moreover, one may wish to consider the increase in the parliamentary control of institutions which exchange sensitive information, such as Europol and Eurojust. In this regard, it could be worthwhile to explore the application of national models for the parliamentary control of policing activities at the EU level, such as the establishment of a special supervisory agency for sensitive matters.

Furthermore, the enhancement of judicial control could be taken into consideration, for instance by widening the competencies of the European Court of Justice with regard to Title VI matters. Although sensitive in view of the maintenance of national sovereignty, the expansion of EU competencies in the field of internal security may be complemented by the gradual establishment of a European *Rechtsstaat*. This can be done by promoting the construction of a European Criminal Justice Area (or: European Judicial Space) which includes core elements such as a European Criminal Court, a European Public Prosecution Service, and a European Criminal (Procedure) Law. These elements may be considered complementary to a future extension of Europol's mandate with a (semi-)operational one.[35] If it is the case that the European Union is currently building a disproportionally large Big Brother and an exclusive Fortress Europe, the Member States may individually be too small to counter this development. Hence, a joint movement in favour of good governance and sound legislation at EU level may be the only feasible way forward.

6. Finale

Although it looks as if the draft Reform Treaty is still set to abolish the intergovernmental Title VI and replace it by a set of new articles, police and judicial cooperation in criminal matters may be 'trapped in a legal limbo' because a separate set of provisions will apply to the form of decision-making.[36] However, the quality of the legislation will improve by introducing a single regulatory framework and by allowing the European Parliament to (largely) scrutinize legislative proposals. The enhanced role of national parliaments on legislation in this area is essential, through the early-warning mechanism and the consistent application of the subsidiarity prin-

---

[35] M. den Boer, 'From Networks to Institutions...or Vice Versa? Opportunities for "Good Governance" in EU Police Cooperation'. *Collegium No. 22, XII.2001: Integrated Security in Europe, a democratic perspective,* College of Europe, Bruges, pp. 36-43.

[36] This would also have applied to the former EU Constitutional Treaty, see Guild and Carrera, *supra* n. 27, p. 7.

ciple, but we should be mindful of the vast differences between the scrutiny procedures of the national parliaments.[37] Finally, while the former EU Constitutional Treaty would have subjected the rights of citizens in the sensitive JHA arena (think of investigatory powers, surveillance, intelligence, the role of visas in entering the European Union) to an integrated and binding Fundamental Rights Charter, it has been decided during the German Presidency summit in June 2007 that the Charter will be included by means of a Protocol. Although this does not affect the binding character of the Treaty, it has already provided some Member States with the possibility to opt out, such as the United Kingdom. Key issues in the improvement of the Area of Freedom, Security and Justice include the introduction of a human rights framework for criminal justice issues, a data protection framework, democratic control mechanisms, judicial control mechanisms, and good governance measures.

The respect for human rights remains the fundamental normative basis for each practice, (legal) instrument, institution and process within the Area of Freedom, Security and Justice. In line with the proposals of the European Convention, the EU Charter of Fundamental Rights ought to become a fully binding text. It was inserted into the EU Constitutional Treaty, but due to its incomplete ratification it has not (yet) been turned into a binding legal framework for the whole European Union. Had it been ratified, it would have compensated for the unacceptable situation concerning the weak protection of citizens' rights,[38] certainly 'considering the impact' of the policy area on internal security on individual rights.

The emergence of a European surveillance society raises the prominence of fundamental rights and freedoms, and democratic rights.[39] In the eyes of many, data protection issues become pivotal as interference with personal privacy is (likely to be) increased: the application of uniform standards of protection throughout countries that participate in international data-exchange systems might be considered. To this end, the European Commission submitted a proposal for a Council Framework Decision on the protection of personal data processed in the framework of police and judicial cooperation in criminal matters.[40] This proposal was discussed by the European Council on 12 and 13 June 2001, and it was decided that the new Framework Decision will be based on the Council of Europe established minimum protection principles set by the Convention of 28 January 1981 for the protection of individuals with regard to automatic processing of personal data and its Additional Protocol of 8 November 2001, including Recommendation (87) 15 regulating the use of personal data in the police sector. Moreover, it would examine the solutions suggested by the European Parliament, which argued in favour of stronger data protection.

---

[37] See, e.g., H. Born and M. Caparini (eds.), *Democratic Control of Intelligence Services. Containing the Rogue Elephants* (Aldershot, Ashgate 2007).

[38] European Policy Centre, 2003, p. 8.

[39] D. Lyon, *Surveillance Society. Monitoring Everyday Life* (Buckingham, Open University Press 2001).

[40] COM (2005) 475 final, 4.10.2005.

Taking advantage of its stronger legislative role in the Area of Freedom, Security and Justice, the European Commission should claim a leading role in the debate on a future security governance in the European Union, which is not only substantive-strategic in nature, but which also seeks to address criteria of good governance (transparency, accountability, participatory debate and social legitimacy – in line with the Lisbon recommendations on the promotion of democracy). Hence, long-term planning is pivotal. An important element may not be overseen, which is the guarantee of internal and external accountability, as well as a sound assessment of input and output legitimacy, particularly with respect to the latest series of EU anti-terrorism measures.[41] Even if the Reform Treaty will succeed, it lacks the scope to reach within the EU agencies and institutions, but it will certainly improve the external accountability of agencies such as Europol and Eurojust.

Although there always seems to be a need for new agents in the field of internal security cooperation, it is not always clear from the onset what the precise competencies of new agencies are and to what extent they may overlap with already existing ones. In order to avoid institutional rivalry, and thus a lack of efficiency, it would be preferable if there would be proactive tuning between these agencies, and an inter-institutional arrangement could be established, which can possibly be achieved under the auspices of the Committee on Internal Security (COSI).

7. Conclusion

Representing one of the newest policy domains within the European Union, the Area of Freedom, Security and Justice has experienced a gradual maturation of its policies, legal instruments and decision-making procedures. Within the leading institutions of the European Union, but also within the national governments of the Member States, reflections on forms of internal security governance have been continuous. But in an arena where political views differ significantly between EU Member States, it is difficult to design an integrated blueprint that imposes the finalities of an internal security area within the European Union. In the evolution from a purely intergovernmental to a common framework for internal security governance, progress has thus far mainly been an aggregate of individual proposals from the Member States. For the time being, the anxiety about sharing sovereignty and legal harmonisation is flanked by the reluctance of EU Member States to create a pan-European infrastructure for law enforcement cooperation. A blueprint might therefore be regarded as a strait-jacket by the Member States, while it could also – more positively – provide a strategic policy horizon to the principal policy-makers in this area.

One of the governance characteristics of the JHA arena is its organisational complexity: despite the neat hierarchical Council structure, the gradual multiplication of forums has made the decision-making process less transparent. This is aggra-

[41] Den Boer, Hillebrand and Nölke, 2008, forthcoming.

vated by the fact that some new forums, created in the wake of the Tampere Summit which was held in 1999, have no clear mandate, let alone an institutional structure that supervises their activities. The construction of the Area of Freedom, Security and Justice seems to be exposed to contrasting dynamics. On the one hand, there is a deepening process in the sense of institution-building and consolidation of (binding) regulatory frameworks. On the other hand, there is a widening process in the sense of the expansion of mandates, flexible responses to new security challenges, and the transposition of normative expectations to candidate countries.

Another dominant governance feature of the Area of Freedom, Security and Justice is its incremental growth, marked by *ad hoc* decision-making which is often inspired by (perceived) international security crises, such as sheer unmanageable flows of asylum-seekers and transnational terrorism. Some argue that there is a need for profound benchmarks which function as navigation pointers for the future development of the European Union, which may have a strong impact on the development of the Area of Freedom, Security and Justice.

From a good governance point of view, the incremental and *ad hoc* decision-making process has been marked by imperfections, because it effectively excludes public and parliamentary scrutiny of the effects of legislation. The Hague Programme, for instance, introduced far-reaching powers for law enforcement agencies (such as the exchange of biometric data and the principle of availability which encourages autonomous exchange of data across the border), without introducing countervailing powers of institutions to control the integrity of the data-exchange process. Calls for the improvement of the legislative process and the introduction of good governance should not merely be the subject of a one-sided expectation which is imposed on candidate Member States, or even on the 'Ring of Friends'. By means of a more critical reflection on its own governance system, the current 27 Member States of the European Union may wish to bring themselves on a higher plane, turning the governance of the Area of Freedom, Security and Justice into a rich asset of which the European Union can be proud.

Chapter 3
'WIDENING' VS. 'DEEPENING' THE EUROPEAN UNION: FREE MOVEMENT VS. SOCIAL RIGHTS IN THE *LAVAL* CASE BEFORE THE ECJ*

Norbert Reich

1. Introduction

'Reconciling "deepening" and "widening" of the European Union' is the general topic of the Asser Conference, and it refers to such important areas as the relationship of the European Union to its neighbours,[1] citizenship in an enlarged Union,[2] institutional arrangements for this widening and deepening which are necessary after the failure of the Draft Treaty on a Constitution for Europe, and similar questions. The aim of this paper is more modest but at the same time more realistic. It refers to conflicts currently before the ECJ regarding the free movement of persons, respectively service providers from new Member countries with lower wage levels to 'older' EC countries with a higher level of social protection and a particularly strong position of labour unions which is guaranteed in their constitutional traditions. This conflict has a social and a legal dimension. This author is not qualified to discuss the social dimension; the paper will be restricted to the legal issues which show that enlargement ('widening') provokes new conflicts on 'deepening' the Union which must be settled in the existing framework of EC law demanding a particularly sensitive assessment by the ECJ which functions here as a true constitutional court. The main question will be how the widening of the European Union with 12 new members in 2004 and now in 2007 can be reconciled with an overall deepening in the sense of improving social standards in the European Union. Will the result be a win-win situation for both 'new' and 'old' member countries, reconciling 'free movement' in which 'new' member countries are interested, with 'high social standards' of 'old' member countries which is said to be the centre of the 'European

* The oral hearing of this case before the Grand Chamber of the ECJ took place on 9 January 2007; the opinion of AG Mengozzi was delivered on 23 May 2007, but could only be referred to in an annex to this paper (VII), the judgment is expected at the end of the year. This author was involved on the preparation of the case for the Latvian government. Any opinion voiced in this paper only commits the author.

[1] S. Blockmans and A. Łazowski (eds.), *The European Union and Its Neighbours – A Legal Appraisal of the EU's Policies of Stabilisation, Partnership and Integration* (The Hague, T.M.C. Asser Press 2006).

[2] See my paper: 'The Constitutional Relevance of Citizenship and Free Movement in an Enlarged Union', *ELJ* (2005), p. 675.

social model',[3] or will it lead to a 'win-loose' zero-sum game, either in the form of 'social dumping' on the labour market of 'old' member countries by the cheaper labour force from 'new' member countries, or inversely to a closure of the labour market of 'old' countries for economic citizens from new member countries?

The paper will take as a starting point the *Laval* case now before the ECJ, with some reference to the similar *Viking* case (section 2). Before discussing the applicability of the free movement provisions, some remarks should be made with regard to the position of fundamental social rights (e.g., right of collective bargaining and social action of labour unions) within the constitutional arrangements of the EC/EU Treaties (section 3). The paper will defend the opinion that EC law is also applicable in this area (section 4), subject to a delicate balancing and justification test which can refer to secondary law (section 5). Finally, the civil consequences of social actions violating free movement rules will briefly be mentioned: *ubi ius, ibi remedium* (section 6). An Annex will refer to the recent opinion of AG Mengozzi (section 7).

2. The Swedish *Laval* case as a starting point

The two references concern the compatibility with EU law of industrial disputes and collective actions against EU companies exercising their free movement rights. The Swedish case, referred to the European Court by the Arbetsdomstolen (Swedish Labour Court) on 15 September 2005 and concerning litigation between *Laval un Partneri Ltd* (hereafter: *Laval)* and *Svenska Byggnadsarbetareförbundet, Avdelning 1 of the Svenska Byggnadsarbetareförbundet, Svenska Elektrikerförbundet* (hereafter: *Byggnads*),[4] posed the question whether industrial action by Swedish labour unions against a Latvian company which wanted to perform a work contract under Swedish procurement rules by posted Latvian workers falls within the freedom to provide services rules of Article 49 TEC and if this is the case whether this action can be justified either under the posted workers' Directive 96/71/EEC[5] or under a specific Swedish law exempting labour unions from liability when taking action against foreign-based companies (the so-called *Lex Britannia*, see below section 5.1). A parallel case which will not be studied in detail here forms the basis of the reference from the English Court of Appeal of 23 November 2005 in the *Viking* case.[6] It concerns the question in how far labour unions can take social

---

[3] The debate has centred on 'European social rights'; for a recent overview see J.Th. Petersen, *Der Schutz sozialer Grundrechte in der EU* (Würzburg, Univ. Diss. 2006).

[4] Case C-341/05; the order for reference was published in *OJ* C 281/10 of 12.11.2005; the author could make use of a provisional English translation of 18.10.2005. The order is based on a prior judgment 49/05 case A 268/04 of 29 April 2005.

[5] Directive 97/71/EC of the EP and the Council of 16 December 1996 concerning the posting of workers in the framework of the provision of services, *OJ* L 18/1 of 21.1.1997.

[6] Case C-438/05, *The International Transport Workers' Federation (ITWF) & the Finnish Seamen's Union versus 1) Viking Line ABP 2) OU Viking Line Eesti*, *OJ* C 60/16 of 11.3.2006; the oral hearing

action against a reflagging by a shipping company from a 'high-wage' country (Finland) to a 'low-wage country' (Estonia); the ECJ was also asked to decide on the applicability of Article 43 TEC to the litigation, including possible justifications. Both Courts did not ask about the existence and extent of an eventual civil liability of labour unions should their actions have violated EC law without being able to be justified by social policy reasons.

Both references concern delicate matters of how to balance social policy objectives with economic freedoms which have become apparent in the European Union after the accession of 10 new member countries. Most of these new member countries still have much lower wages which give them a competitive advantage in the internal market, but which may easily be challenged (and have been challenged by social action in the host countries) as provoking 'social dumping' on the more elaborate wage policies in old, in particular Scandinavian member countries. The *Laval* case has given rise to strong political reactions in the Member States concerned which will however not be dealt with here. The aim of this paper is more modest: it wants to provide a legal analysis under existing EU law on how to solve these conflicts. It takes as a starting point the existing case-law of the ECJ which, however, has not yet really solved the new types of conflict which arose in *Laval* and, to a lesser extent, in *Viking*. Therefore, in deciding on the references, the Court will have to give a truly constitutional answer to how to solve the existing – and possible future – conflicts between existing social structures in Member States which still belong to their own competence, and the dynamics of EC law seemingly favouring the liberal spirit of free movement against the existing social arrangements in particular in Scandinavian countries with a strong welfarist tradition, based upon the central role played by autonomous labour unions enjoying far-reaching rights of action.

The analysis starts from the premise that the particular type of conflict which is before the ECJ has not been regulated by the rather elaborate transitory arrangements in the accession treaties. It must also be remembered that the actions are not directed against a Member State – which is the usual setting in free movement cases, but against labour unions which are governed by private, not public law and which enjoy, in the traditions of all Member States – whether old or new – a substantial amount of autonomy guaranteed by national and European constitutional provisions. Therefore, it must first be analysed how far this constitutional autonomy extends within the system of the EC free movement rules (section 3). Only then should the question be answered whether the relevant free movement provisions, namely on services (Art. 49 EC), regarding *Laval,* can be applied to social action by labour unions restricting the free movement of posted workers (section 4). Should

before the Grand Chamber took place on 10.1.2007. It is not known to this author why the case was taken to an English and not a Finnish court; the reason may have been that ITWF has its headquarters in London and therefore jurisdiction was conferred on the English Court under Art. 2 Reg. 44/2001, without the English Court being able to raise 'forum non convenience' objections, see ECJ case C-281/02, *Andrew Owusu* v. *N.B.Jackson et al.* [2005] *ECR* I-1383. AG Poiares-Maduro also gave his opinion on 23 May 2007.

the answer be in the positive, one has to look for possible justifications which in *Laval* must refer to the existence of the posted workers' Directive 96/71 (section 5). Finally, some remarks should be added with regard to an eventual civil liability of labour unions should their actions violate EU law – a question to be answered first by national tort law, but which must be applied in conformity with EU law principles (section 6).

3. Social rights as fundamental rights exempted from EC free movement rules?

3.1 Possible exemptions from Article 49 and 43 TEC for labour unions

3.1.1 *Article 137(5) TEC?*

It could be argued – and indeed has been argued by Byggnads and most governments from 'old' member countries having given written opinions in Laval – that labour unions taking social action in industrial disputes are exempted from the application of Community law in general and particularly from Article 49 TEC which is directed against states only. A collective action by labour unions is, according to such an opinion, not meant to restrict the freedom to provide services, but to ensure adequate conditions of work and pay. Under Article 137(5) TEC, the European Union does not have jurisdiction in matters of strikes, lock-outs and pay.[7] This seemingly implies the non-applicability of the fundamental freedoms to take industrial action.

The exclusion of Community legislation in the field of industrial action on the other hand does not preclude, however, that the general principles of Community law must always be respected, as the Court has frequently held with other prerogatives of Member States, e.g., with regard to direct taxation,[8] health provision,[9] social security,[10] higher education stipends and loans,[11] war pensions[12] or property regimes.[13] Article 137(5) TEC only excludes Community legislation in the area of strikes and lock-outs, but not the effects of primary law on industrial action.

[7] The extent of this exception with regard to indirect regulations on pay has been debated in the recent opinion of AG Poiares Maduro in case C-307/05, *Yolanda Del Cerro Alonso* v. *Osakidetza*, [2007] n.y.r. (10.1.2007).

[8] Case C-544 and 545/03, *Mobistar and Belgacom Mobile* [2005] *ECR* I-7723.

[9] Case C-372/04, *Yvonne Watts* v. *Bedford Primary Care Trust et al* [2006] *ECR* I-4325 para. 92.

[10] Case C-158/96, *Kohll* v. *Union des Caisses de Maladie* [1998] *ECR* I-1931 para. 20.

[11] Case C-209/03, *The Queen* (on the application of Dany Bidar) v. *London Borough of Ealing* [2005] *ECR* I- 2119 para. 42.

[12] Case C-192/05, *K. Tas Hagen, R.A. Tas* v. *Raadskamer WUBO* [2006] *ECR* I-10451.

[13] Case C-350/92, *Spain* v. *Council* [1995] *ECR* I-1985.

3.1.2 *'Non-statutory exemption' for trade unions derived from competition law?*

One could also refer to the limited application of Community competition rules to collective bargaining and industrial action, which should be taken over by analogy by the EU freedoms. With regard to competition law, it is debated, under the influence of US-American anti-trust law, whether there is an inherent 'non-statutory exemption' for collective action in industrial relations.[14] The ECJ, in its *Albany* judgment, took a somewhat more restrictive view:

> 'Under an interpretation of the Treaty as a whole which is both effective and consistent ... agreements concluded in the context of collective negotiation between management and labour in pursuit of such objectives (*i.e., social policy, NR*) must, by virtue of their nature and purpose, be regarded as falling outside the scope of Art. 81...' (para. 60).

This argument must however be limited to competition law where business and labour organisations are negotiating for a pension fund for the employees of a particular sector, as in the *Albany* case. The case did not concern industrial action as such, and therefore is not a precedent for the limitation of actions by labour unions with regard to fundamental freedoms. Where collective action by labour unions confronts individual businesses from other Member countries by rendering their market access impossible or more difficult, there is no 'non-statutory exemption' from the application of the EU free movement rules.

3.1.3 *Freedom of contract?*

It might finally be argued that Laval could have avoided the restriction of its freedom to provide services by simply concluding the demanded agreement with Byggnads. On other occasions the Court has held that, if there is freedom of contract and bargaining, there is no restriction of free movement.[15]

This argument holds true in individual negotiations, but not with regard to industrial action by collective entities where the service provider, legitimately exercising its freedom to provide services in another Member country, is placed in a 'take it or leave it' situation. The *Laval* case shows that the provider is in a dilemma which implies a restriction of his freedom whatever decision he takes:

- If he refuses to subdue he will be boycotted, the most absolute form of restriction.

---

[14] See the detailed comparative discussion of AG Jacobs in his opinion of 9.1.1999 in case C-67/96, *Albany International* v. *Stichting Bedrijfspensioenenfonds Textielindustrie* [1999] *ECR* I-5751 paras. 98-107 with regard to US law.

[15] E.g., case C-339/89, *Alsthom Atlantique* v. *Compagnie de construction mécanique Sulzer SA* [1991] *ECR* I-107 para. 15.

- If he yields he cannot profit from his competitive advantage by using the different wage levels existing in the European Union (Sweden/Latvia).

Both alternatives imply a severe restriction of his freedom to provide services under competitive conditions which cannot be counteracted.

3.2 The importance of the *Gustafsson* and *Rasmussen* judgments of the European Court of Human Rights

An important argument in proposing to exempt collective action by labour unions from the applicability of the fundamental freedoms could be based on Article 11 of the European Convention on Human Rights (ECHR). Since the European Union, according to its Article 6(2), has to 'respect' fundamental rights, and since the ECJ, in its case-law concerning fundamental freedoms, refers to judgments of the European Court of Human Rights (ECtHR),[16] it is helpful for the *Laval* case to look at precedents from the Strasbourg Court. The ECJ is of course not formally bound by the case-law of the ECtHR, but will usually respect it if questions of fundamental rights in the sphere of the application of law, in particular with regard to the exercise of fundamental freedoms, are at stake. This is the more true in areas where no consistent case-law of the ECJ exists, as with regard to the conflict between industrial action and fundamental freedoms.

Article 11(1) ECHR guarantees the freedom of association, subject to limitations spelled out in paragraph 2. This right can be invoked by labour unions in collective bargaining and action. It contains a positive element, and therefore it may conflict with the fundamental freedoms of the EC if such actions necessarily restrict the free movement of goods or services.

On the other hand, this 'positive right of association' which can be invoked by Byggnads in the *Laval* case is not without limits. It must respect the rights of other individuals to freely associate or *not to associate*. This problem was raised before the ECtHR in the case *Gustafsson/Sweden.* In its judgment of 25 April 1996,[17] the Court faced the question of how far industrial action against an entrepreneur who did not want to join a collective bargaining agreement was permitted or, vice versa, limited by Article 11 ECHR.

Even though the action was directed against Sweden, not against a labour union taking industrial action against Mr Gustafsson who refused to sign a collective agreement proposed by the relevant Swedish labour union and therefore was subject to industrial action including a boycott of his premises which finally forced him out of business, the ECtHR made important clarifications concerning the right of association protected under Article 11 ECHR. This judgment recognised that 'freedom of association' also has a 'negative side' which Sudre calls 'droit d'assocation négatif'.[18] This right is also enjoyed by *Laval* in offering its services

[16] See case C-112/00, *Eugen Schmidberger* v. *Austria* [2003] *ECR* I-5659 at para. 79.

[17] *Recueil* 1996, 637.

[18] Sudre et al., *Les grands arrêts de la Cour Européenne des droits de l'homme* (Paris, Thémis 2003), at 482.

in Sweden. It is made impossible by the industrial action of labour unions. Article 11 of the ECHR therefore does not exclude the application of Article 49 TEC law, but, on the contrary, it must be read together with Article 11 in protecting both the free movement and the negative right to association.

This case-law was confirmed by the recent *Sorensen/Rasmussen* judgment delivered against Denmark[19] where it was clearly stated that the requirement to join a certain trade union violates Article11 ECHR as such a requirement has an effect on the very freedom of assembly and association. Therefore, the state must avoid measures violating this 'negative right of coalition', even though it enjoys a certain margin of appreciation. Obviously, the primary addressees of such an obligation are the unions themselves which must avoid an infringement of the 'negative right to coalition'. Their actions will have to be balanced against the two components of Article 11 ECHR, namely their 'positive right' to association and the 'negative right' of social partners who do not want to adhere to a system of collective bargaining. In the EC context, this balancing must be accomplished within the free movement provisions of the Treaty which will be analysed in sections 4 and 5.

3.3 The *Werhof* judgment of the ECJ

In its *Werhof* judgment[20] the Court derived from Article 11 of the ECHR as interpreted by the ECtHR the principle that '(f)reedom of association ... includes the right not to join an association or union ...'. This 'negative right to association' must be respected when interpreting secondary Community law, e.g., in the case before it the directives on the transfer of undertakings. The Court expressly referred to the *Gustafsson* judgment of the ECtHR, thus indicating that it takes the same view on the limitations of the right to take collective action. This demonstrates clearly the concerns of the ECJ that social action rights of labour unions are not 'outside' EC law (whether primary or – as in the *Werhof* case – secondary law), but must be balanced in particular against existing free movement rights. This will be analysed in the next sections regarding the freedom to provide services (section 4).

3.4 Constitutional traditions of Member States concerning social action

According to Article 6(2) European Union, the Union will also respect fundamental rights as they are common to the constitutional traditions of the Member States. There is agreement that one of these traditions concerns the rights of social partners – labour unions and business organisations – to take social action to defend their legitimate interests in industrial disputes; but this right is not without limits. This right has been recognised in the Charter of Fundamental Rights in the European Union, namely its Article 28 (now Art. II-88 of the Draft Constitution of 29 October 2004) with the following words:

---

[19] Judgment of 11 January 2006, para. 58, applications 52656 and 52620/99.

[20] Case C-499/04, *Werhof* [2006] *ECR* I-2397 para. 33.

> 'Workers and employers, or their representative organisations, have, (*in accordance with Community law and national laws and practices emphasis added, NR*), the right to negotiate and conclude collective agreements at the appropriate levels and, in cases of conflict of interest, to take collective action to defend their interests, including strike actions.'

In particular the Scandinavian states defend their specific social model which is based on a large degree of autonomy granted to social partners by their constitutions without the state necessarily interfering in social action.[21] It is feared that this autonomy of the 'Scandinavian social model' is endangered if EC law interferes in its working by imposing its specific rules on free movement or – as had been discussed in *Albany*[22] – on competition to social action.

In the context of this discussion it suffices to remember that even in the Scandinavian model of industrial relations there are certain inherent limits to social action which are spelt out by the law. The most important and common one is the so-called 'peace obligation' (*Friedenspflicht*) which forbids industrial actions once a valid collective agreement has been concluded between social partners. Of course the extent of this 'Friedenspflicht' and the consequences of its beach may be very different, but they are in any case determined by law, not by the social partners themselves, as can be shown very clearly in the Swedish case of the 'Lex Britannia' which will be discussed below (section 5.1). This is exactly what is said in Article 28 of the Charter of Fundamental Rights whose indirect legal importance was recently recognised by the Court.[23]

The text of Article 28 makes it very clear that the right to take industrial action only exists within the limits of the law, including EC law. Of course, these limitations must respect the principle of proportionality, as is spelled out in Article 52(1) of the Charter. But it cannot be said that industrial action as recognised by Member State law is completely outside the cope of Community law. This has also indirectly been recognised by the Court in *Albany* where it defined, on the one hand, the existence of an exemption of social partners from the competition rules in order to attain legitimate social policy objectives, but implicitly rejected any extension of this exemption beyond matters of social policy. It is therefore a matter of balancing the different objectives of the EC Treaty on the one hand – free movement – and of social action on the other, namely the adequate social protection of workers as mentioned in Article 136 TEC. Exactly this balancing is now before the Court in the *Laval* cases. Any one-sided approach to solve this question must be rejected – either by giving absolute precedence to social rights, or by formally insisting on the supremacy of free movement without taking account of legitimate social policy objectives pursued by the Member States, even when delegated to social partners as

---

21 For a discussion see N. Bruun et al., *The Nordic Labour Relations Model* (Dartmouth, Aldershot 1994) at pp. 250-252; R. Fahlbeck, *Labour and Employment Law in Sweden* (Lund, Acta Societatis Juridicae Ludensis 1999), pp. 26-33; A. Ahlberg and N. Bruun in 56 *Bulletin of Comparative Labour Relations* (2005) (ed. R. Blanpain), pp. 117-124.

22 See *supra* n. 14.

23 Case C-540/03, *EP* v. *Council* [2006] *ECR* I-5769, para. 38.

in Sweden and Finland. The following sections will attempt such a balancing approach.

4. The applicability of Article 49 TEC to social actions against the posting of workers in *Laval*

4.1 The origin of the industrial conflict

Laval is a company established in Latvia and it provides building services both at home and abroad in other EU countries. In order to extend its business, it participated in a tender in the Swedish city of Vaxholm for the restoration of a school building and eventually won this tender because it had offered the 'economically most advantageous offer'. This was to some extent possible because the wages paid to the Latvian workers to be posted in Sweden were below Swedish rates as negotiated by Byggnads, which at this time were about 145 SKR; the wages to be paid were at first 80 SKR, later 109 SKR, plus free accommodation, transport and meals.

The legality of both the tender and the awarding of the contract is not in doubt; it has not been challenged, as far as we know. The industrial conflict with the defendant arose when it learned of the wages promised to the Latvian workers, thus fearing 'wage dumping' and 'unfair competition' with Swedish construction workers which it wanted to prevent. In the summer of 2004, its local unit demanded the conclusion of a collective agreement under Swedish conditions which Laval refused. On 14 September and again on 20 October 2004, Laval however decided to conclude a collective agreement with the Latvian Construction Workers Association (LCWA). The legality of this agreement is not in question; whether it was a 'circumvention' of Swedish law to 'pre-empt' the conclusion of a (Swedish) collective agreement as has been maintained by Byggnads will be discussed later (section 5.1.1).

Further negotiations between the parties failed, and on 2 November 2004, some 5 months after the initial contact with Laval, Byggnads instituted industrial action in the form of a boycott and picketing in front of the building site which continued until September 2005.[24] Svenska Elektrikerförbundet joined in a solidarity boycott on 3 December 2004 which resulted in electricity being interrupted on the building site. Laval had to remove its workers from the site and sent them back to Latvia where they received unemployment benefit. Laval itself had to apply for bankruptcy proceedings. The further fate of the building site is not known and is of no relevance here.

---

[24] See the order of the president of the Court of 15.11.2005, para. 5.

4.2 The posting of workers by *Laval* in Sweden as an exercise of the freedom to provide services

With regard to applicable Community law ever since *Rush Portuguesa,*[25] it is without doubt that the posting of workers of a company established in one EU country is a (cross-border) service to which Article 49 TEC is applicable. The workers employed by Laval were not seeking access to the Swedish labour market but would be removed once the construction work, as contracted, had been completed.[26] In principle they remained under Latvian jurisdiction. Therefore, the provisions on the free movement of workers (Art. 39) and on non-discrimination (Art. 12 TEC) can be disregarded in this context.

It should also be mentioned that Sweden did not make use of the possibility to invoke a transitory regime against the posting of workers, as had been conceded to Germany and Austria during the accession negotiations with the new Member countries, including Latvia.[27] Sweden entirely liberalised its transitory regime with regard to free movement *vis-à-vis* the new Member States, probably with the understanding that the traditional action rights of industrial organisations were not touched upon and were sufficient to protect the Swedish labour market from unwanted 'dumping' by workforce from new Member countries. This position was however challenged in the relevant Swedish legal literature on labour relations which pointed out the problems of the so-called 'Swedish social model' within the European Union[28] – a model which relied on self-regulation and collective action by the industrial partners themselves and made the state remain 'neutral' and to abstain from intervening in industrial relations. This understanding of industrial relations also seems to explain the reference of the Swedish Labour court concerning the non-implementing legislation of Directive 96/71 in Sweden with regard to working conditions (details in section 5.2.2).

4.3 Restrictions on the provision of services

As the case shows, the boycott by Byggnads is the strongest form of a restriction; indeed it made the rendering of services by Laval in Sweden impossible and caused great harm both to Laval and to the Latvian workers it had posted while relying on its freedom to provide services. Article 49 TEC is directed both against 'discriminations' and against 'restrictions'.[29] For a preliminary examination of the legality of the boycott under EU law, it is sufficient that there is a restriction which is forbidden unless it can be justified. The question of discrimination will be discussed within the possible justifications (section 5.1.3).

---

25 Case C-113/89, *Rush Portuguesa* v. *Office National d'immigration* [1990] *ECR* I-1417; C-369 and 376/98, *Criminal proceedings* v. *Arblade* [1999] *ECR* I-8454.

26 Case C-445/03, *Commission* v. *Luxembourg* [2004] *ECR* I-10191 para. 38.

27 N. Reich, *Understanding EU Law*, 2nd edn. (Antwerpen, Intersentia 2005) pp. 84-85.

28 See the authors cited in *supra* n. 21.

29 Case C-76/90, *Säger* [1991] *ECR* I-4221 para. 12 and later cases.

Under EU law, this action is the very negation of the freedom to provide services. In its effects, the restriction forced upon Laval by the action of Byggnads is similar to the re-incorporation requirement imposed by German law on foreign companies. In its *Überseering*-judgment,[30] the Court wrote:

> 'The requirement of re-incorporation of the same company is therefore tantamount to outright negation of the freedom of establishment …'

This restriction can lead to a double consequence under the case-law of the Court: an obligation on the part of the (Swedish) state under Article 10 TEC to ensure that the freedom to provide services is guaranteed (section 4.3.1), or against the Swedish labour unions themselves under the 'horizontal direct effect' theory of Article 49 TEC (section 4.3.2).

4.3.1 *Obligations of the Swedish state*

As mentioned above, the Swedish state takes a position of 'neutrality' in industrial relations. It does not interfere in industrial conflicts. However, under Community law such an obligation may exist according to Article 10 TEC as has been pointed out in *Commission* v. *France*,[31] later upheld and qualified in *Schmidberger* v. *Austria*.[32] The social action which was before the Court differed considerably with regard to the present case: *Commission* v. *France* concerned an obviously illegal action including violence against the Spanish transit of fruit and vegetables. *Schmidberger*, on the other hand, was concerned with an ecologically motivated and peaceful demonstration resulting in the closure of the Brenner Autobahn for 30 hours. The first action was certainly not justified under any principle, and therefore the French state had a duty to intervene to protect the Spanish exporters' right of free movement; the omission of such an intervention amounted to a breach of Community law and could eventually lead to state liability under the so-called '*Francovich*' principle.[33] In the second case, the demonstration was justified under fundamental rights principles, namely freedom of association and freedom of expression under Articles 11 resp.10 ECHR, and it was in itself proportionate; therefore, there was no duty on the part of the Austrian state to intervene and stop the demonstration in order to avoid an impediment to the free movement of goods by lorries which could not use the Brenner Autobahn during the time of the demonstration.

Industrial action by labour unions, their influence on free movement, and obligations of Member States arising therefrom have not yet been subject to scrutiny by the ECJ. It is submitted that similar principles will apply to industrial action.

However, these questions need not be discussed in detail. The Swedish state is not a partner in this litigation. The referring court is obviously only concerned with

---

30 Case C-208/00, *Überseering* [2002] *ECR* I-9919 para. 81.

31 Case C-265/95, *Commission* v. *France* [1997] *ECR* I-6959.

32 Case C-112/00, *supra* n. 16.

33 Cases C-6 and 9/90, *Francovich et al.* v. *Italy* [1991] *ECR* I-5357.

the action by Byggnads, not directly with the position of the Swedish state. This may only become important in the context of the legality of the 'Lex Britannia' under EC law, which will be dealt with under the justifications (section 5.1)

4.3.2 *Effects of Article 49 TEC against Byggnads, et al.?*

The main legal question in the case concerns, however, the effects of Article 49 TEC against the action of Swedish labour unions. The case-law of the ECJ is evolving and is not yet clear with regard to the position of labour unions in industrial action infringing free movement.

The traditional approach to the freedoms enshrined in the EC Treaty has been concerned exclusively with *state action*. This seems to be suggested by their very place within the EC Treaty, namely Article 3(1)(c) and 14(2) concerning the establishment of an internal market without frontiers among the Member States. Restrictions on market access by private persons are usually caught by the provisions on competition under Article 81/82 TEC. This seems to exclude the applicability of Article 49 and the other Community freedoms to privately imposed restrictions.

Such a narrow interpretation is however not required from the very wording and system of the Treaty.[34] Article 49(1) TEC itself takes a somewhat broader view as it aims at the abolition of restrictions on the freedom to provide services, wherever they come from. The Court, in a series of cases, had therefore extended the applicability of Article 49 (and other freedoms, namely Art. 39 and 43 TEC) to privately imposed restrictions.

This case-law already started with *Walrave*[35] in 1974 concerning restrictions on free movement imposed by by-laws of sporting associations. This case-law, which takes a functional, not a formal approach to interpreting fundamental freedoms, was continued in the well-known *Bosman* case.[36] This case was concerned with the free movement of workers, even though the Court also referred to services. This case-law was confirmed and justified in *Angonese*.[37] The restriction on the free movement of workers in this case resulted from a collective agreement between the defendant (the savings bank) and a labour union in the province of Bolzano whereby language proficiency certificates had to be confirmed by and an examination held in the province, while other certificates were not accepted. The effect of a state-imposed restriction and one imposed by social actions is obviously the same – a fact to be remembered in the *Laval* case.

In the later *Wouters* case[38] the Court held, summarising its case-law as follows:

---

[34] P.-C. Müller-Graff in R. Streinz (ed.), *EUV/EGV, Kommentar* (München, Verlag C.H. Beck 2003), Art. 49 paras. 65-69.

[35] Case 36/74, *Walrave* v. *Union Cycliste internationale* [1974] *ECR* 1405.

[36] Case C-415/93, *ASBL* v. *Bosman* [1995] *ECR* I-4921 paras. 83-85.

[37] Case C-281/98, *R. Angonese* v. *Casa di Risparmio de Bolzano* [2000] *ECR* I-4139.

[38] Case C-309/99, *J.C.J. Wouters et al./Algemene Raad van de Nederlandse Orde van Advocaten* [2002] *ECR* I-1577; for a discussion see N. Reich, *Understanding EU law*, 2nd edn. (Antwerpen, Intersentia 2005), pp.18-19.

> 'It should be observed at the outset that compliance with Articles 52 and 59 (now Art. 43 and 49 EC/NR) of the Treaty is also required in the case of rules which are not public in nature but which are designed to regulate, collectively, self-employment and the provision of services. The abolition, as between Member States, of obstacles to freedom of movement for persons would be compromised if the abolition of State barriers could be neutralised by obstacles resulting from the exercise of their legal autonomy by associations or organisations not governed by public law ...' (para. 120).

The case concerned a regulation by a professional organisation which restricted free movement rights. Again the Court was willing to directly apply Articles 43 and 49 TEC, possibly in parallel to the competition rules. The main reason for extending the provisions of free movement also to collectively-imposed restrictions seems to be the *effet utile* theory: From the point of view of the person whose 'fundamental freedom' as a subjective right under Community law is impaired, thus violating the provisions of Community law, it does not make any difference whether this restriction originates from a regulation of the state or from collective action.

In the case at hand, the boycott by Byggnads against Laval was intended to achieve a 'regulation', namely the conclusion of a collective bargaining agreement or a supplement according to Swedish law. This would have resulted in Laval having to pay Swedish wages and benefits, thereby losing its competitive advantage which allowed it in the first instance to win the Vaxholm contract. At the same time, it would have set aside the agreement which Laval had concluded with LCWA in the summer of 2004.

4.4 Preliminary results of the discussion

As a preliminary result of this discussion, it can be clearly stated that the boycott by Byggnads violated Laval's right to freely provide services. Labour union actions are not exempted from a *prima facie* application of the free movement rules. Since Article 49 TEC is applicable in this context, other EC provisions need not be discussed in detail. Byggnads may be liable for a breach of Community law if its action cannot be justified. This will be discussed in section 5.

5. Justifications

The main problems in the case are concerned with the question of justification, as the Swedish Labour Court itself seems to imply. The examination will have to undergo certain steps which are suggested by the questions of the referring court, namely

- the Swedish *Lex Britannia* (5.1)
- the importance of Directive 96/71 (5.2)
- general principles of Community law (5.3).

5.1 The Lex Britannia

The Swedish *Lex Britannia* amended the Medbestämmandelagen (MBL – law on workers' participation in decisions) in 1991[39] and allows Swedish labour unions to start industrial action against an undertaking which has not (yet) concluded a bargaining agreement with a representative labour union of its employees. Vice versa, there is a 'Friedenspflicht', that is a duty to abstain form industrial action only in those cases where a binding collective agreement already exists. The 1991 amendment limited this 'Friedenspflicht' to those agreements to which Swedish law '*directly*' applies, thus excluding collective bargaining agreements concluded with non-Swedish labour unions. Industrial action is therefore not prohibited when a foreign employer carries out temporary activities in Sweden and an overall assessment of the situation leads to the conclusion that the connection to Sweden is so weak that the MBL cannot directly apply to industrial relations. The 1991 amendment wanted to combat so-called 'wage dumping' by foreign service providers made possible by the prior case-law of the Arbetsdomstolen, whereby Swedish labour unions had to recognise foreign collective bargaining agreements in the sense of the 'Friedenspflicht' even if the wages negotiated were below Swedish standards. According to the *travaux préparatoires*, the Lex Britannia is intended to allow trade unions to act in order to ensure that all employers active in the Swedish market pay salaries and grant other conditions of employment in line with those which are usual in Sweden and to create conditions of fair competition on an equal basis between Swedish undertakings and entrepreneurs from other countries.

As the *Laval* case clearly shows, today's importance of the Lex Britannia in Swedish industrial relations is twofold:

- with regard to the Swedish state, it allows it to remain 'neutral' in industrial conflicts, thus confirming the practice of the Swedish social model of the state not interfering in industrial relations,[40] including the setting of wages;
- with regard to Swedish labour unions, it gives them a tool for industrial actions against so-called 'wage dumping' by non-Swedish undertakings and will exempt them from civil liability in case of a boycott or other industrial action to impose a collective agreement against non-complying foreign undertakings.

When discussing the compatibility of the Lex Britannia with EU law, it is not necessary to enter into the entire complexity of industrial relations in Sweden. This would certainly not be the task of the ECJ. The questions to be answered are much more limited. They can be limited to three clearly defined problem areas:

---

[39] For a detailed description see the reference order of the Arbetsdomstolen of 15.9.2005, p. 4 of the provisional English translation.

[40] This argument was used in not condemning the Swedish state in the *Gustafsson* case, paras. 49, 54, even though it caused strong dissent, e.g., by Judge Martens, joined by Judge Matscher on pp. 668-673, particularly criticising the disproportionate nature of the action of the Swedish labour unions against Mr Gustafsson.

- The applicability of the Lex Britannia only arises *vis-à-vis* undertakings established in the European Union, not in non-Member countries.
- The application of the Lex Britannia seems to be unproblematic in those cases where the foreign undertaking providing services in Sweden has not concluded any collective agreement with a labour union from its home country.
- Since the Lex Britannia is an enabling law by exempting labour unions from civil liability for industrial action where a 'Friedenspflicht' is said not to exist, its compatibility with Community law will only arise in cases where it has been used to initiate and eventually to justify industrial action against an undertaking established in a (new) Member country.

The case before the Court qualifies under all three conditions which will be examined consecutively.

5.1.1 *Industrial action against an undertaking established in the European Union*

The Lex Britannia does not contain a specific exemption concerning industrial action against undertakings established in an EU Member State. This 'omission' by the Swedish legislator had been criticised by several Swedish experts when Sweden acceded to the European Union, but it was not taken up by the Swedish legislator during the ratification proceedings of the Treaties with the new Member States. There is no exclusion in Swedish law concerning the continued application of the Lex Britannia *vis-à-vis* undertakings from new Member countries. Swedish law wants to apply the Lex Britannia also against service providers established in the European Union. Vice versa, the general provisions of the freedom to provide services apply in full as has been demonstrated above against industrial action (section 3). Only when there is a specific justification for a restriction on providing services can the enabling provisions of the Lex Britannia continue to be applicable and may be invoked to justify industrial action by Byggnads.

The case-law of the ECJ with regard to the restrictions allowed under Article 49 TEC is relatively well developed and quite clear in its main principles:

- Restrictions may be justified to protect posted workers.
- Even if allowed, these restrictions must be proportionate and non-discriminatory.
- Restrictions are not allowed to close the national labour market and to shield national businesses from competition by service providers established in the European Union.

Already in the case of *Rush Portuguesa*[41] the Court said:

> '.... Community law does not preclude Member States from extending their legislation, or collective labour agreements entered into by both ides of industry, to any per-

[41] See n. 25.

> son who is employed, even temporarily, within their territory, no matter in which country the employer is established; nor does Community law prohibit Member States from enforcing those rules by appropriate means' (para. 18).

Obviously, this exemption does not apply in the *Laval* case. The Lex Britannia is, as we have argued, an enabling legislation, not a protective one as in the *Rush Portuguesa* case.

Later cases impose certain limits on protective legislation for workers. In *Finalarte et al.* V. *Urlaubs- und Lohnausgleichskasse der Bauwirtschaft, et al.*[42] the Court insisted that it may serve the protection of workers, but 'cannot be justified by economic aims, such as the protection of national businesses …'. Obviously, the State cannot, by enacting enabling legislation, try to achieve a similar objective, that is to protect national businesses and labour. The yardstick for legitimate restrictions on the freedom to provide services is always the protection of posted workers, not the prevention of competition on the labour market.[43]

The case *Commission* v. *Luxembourg*[44] concerned a Luxembourg regulation requiring a prior authorisation for the posting of (non-EU) workers. The Court recognised that the protection of workers must be regarded as an overriding reason relating to the public interest which may justify a restriction on the freedom the provide services; the *Laval* case, however, is not concerned with protecting Latvian but Swedish workers (and businesses) and therefore does not fall into this category. The Court also accepted as an 'overriding reason of general interest' the desire to 'avoid disturbances on the labour market…', e.g., by bringing in (non-EU) workers for the purpose of placing workers. This argument, however, cannot be used in the *Laval* case because its posted workers were of Latvian origin and therefore they themselves may make use of the freedom of movement under Article 39 TEC which had not been restricted by Sweden via transitory arrangements. Different to Luxembourg legislation, the Swedish Lex Britannia is not directed as such against foreign service provides, respectively workers, but it may be used for the same purpose because the state delegates its responsibility for free movement to the social partners without making sure that abuses as in the *Laval* case can be prevented.

The 'neutrality' of the Swedish state is in reality a delegation of power to labour unions to restrict the EU freedoms, if the undertaking providing services from another EU country has not complied with Swedish labour standards. Labour unions are, of course, not forced to take such action, they are only enabled to do so by the privilege of being exempted from civil liability. But as practice shows, they will usually take action if a home business (like in the *Gustafsson* case) or an EU undertaking (like in *Laval)* do not comply with Swedish labour standards. Since the Swedish state had given them the power to restrict fundamental freedoms, they can therefore be held liable for violations of Community law and cannot escape their

---

[42] Joined cases C-49/98, *Finalarte et al.* [2001] *ECR* I-7831 para. 39.

[43] Case C-164/99, *Portugaia Construções* [2002] *ECR* I-787.

[44] Case C-445/03, *Commission* v. *Luxembourg* [2004] *ECR* I-10191 paras. 38-39.

responsibility by relying on the Lex Britannia which by its very wording allows them to impose such restrictions (section 5.3).

5.1.2 *Equivalence of Swedish and Latvian collective bargaining agreements?*

The action of the Swedish labour unions under the Lex Britannia could still be justified to protect foreign posted workers. Such an action of 'solidarity' would probably not violate Community law if the Latvian posted workers were not enjoying any protection which EU and Swedish law requires as a minimum standard. Such a standard could be implemented by the conclusion of a collective bargaining agreement between the undertaking which was posting workers, namely Laval, and a trade union representing Latvian posted workers, that is one under *Latvian jurisdiction* under the conflict rules applicable to the cross-border provision of services.

Indeed, such an agreement had been concluded on 4 September 2004 between Laval and the Latvian Construction Workers Association (LCWA), after Byggnads had threatened industrial action against Laval. It did not exist at the time when Laval won the tender, nor when it started work in Sweden. There has been criticism that such an agreement is a 'circumvention' of Swedish social legislation and that it still allowed 'wage dumping'.

This criticism is not justified for a number of reasons. First of all, the Latvian posted workers were, because they only temporarily took up work in Sweden, still subject to Latvian labour legislation. As the Court already held in *Rush Portuguesa*, 'such workers return to their country of origin after the completion of their work without at any time gaining access to the labour market of the host country' (para. 15). Therefore, Latvian law determines the conditions for the conclusion and validity of a collective bargaining agreement. The Swedish labour unions have no mandate to impose their conditions on undertakings which are not under their jurisdiction. They cannot argue that they acted to protect Latvian workers – quite to the contrary: they forced them out of work. In reality, they wanted to protect their members from unwanted competition by social action which was formally allowed to them under the Lex Britannia but which contradicted the very essence of EU fundamental freedoms. Finally, there is nothing in the judgment of the Arbetsdomstolen suggesting that the collective agreement between Laval and LCWA was invalid or concluded in bath faith; anyhow, this must be determined by Latvian law and courts, and not by Swedish law.

The mere fact that the wages agreed between Laval and LCWA are below Swedish standards does not in any way allow the validity of the collective bargaining agreement to be challenged. Such a challenge would amount to a denial of the freedom of association under Article 11 ECHR which must be recognised on equal terms to Latvian and Swedish labour unions, even if the outcome of bargaining is different.

The only means available to the Swedish state, respectively Byggnads, is to rely on the options included in Directive 97/61 concerning minimum wages and work conditions to which we will turn later (section 5.2). They cannot be simply set aside by not recognising the collective bargaining agreement under Latvian law.

5.1.3 *The discriminatory element of action inherent in the Lex Britannia*

Since the Lex Britannia is an enabling law, its discriminatory elements can only be seen once it is put into action. The *Laval* case provides striking evidence in this direction. Byggnads used the exemption from 'Friedenspflicht' as allowed by the Lex Britannia to start industrial action against Laval which in the end made impossible the rendering of cross-border services in Sweden. Laval sought an injunction against this action in order to be able to continue providing its services as agreed under the construction contract with the city of Vaxholm which was refused by the first judgment of the Arbetsdomstolen. The combined working of the Lex Britannia as an enabling law for Byggnads and as an exemption from liability prevented the provision of services. The Lex Britannia is therefore the relevant and decisive reason for an unjustified restriction of Article 49 TEC.

Compared to the situation of a Swedish undertaking, Laval was clearly treated in a discriminatory way. Under the existing practice of the Lex Britannia, it could not invoke its collective bargaining agreement with LCWA as an element of the 'Friedenspflicht' which would make industrial action by Byggnads illegal and could therefore be prevented by an injunction before the Swedish labour court.

It cannot be argued that Byggnads merely wanted Laval to offer its services on the same terms as Swedish construction companies, and that they were therefore treated on equal terms. Such an argument disregards the difference between Swedish and Latvian undertakings in providing services. By forcing 'equal conditions' upon them, in reality existing differences are levelled down. This is the opposite of non-discriminatory treatment: Laval was deprived of its competitive advantage and discriminated against. Byggnads was using the instruments of the Lex Britannia to impose restrictions on the freedom to provide services for merely economic grounds which cannot be justified. Since the Lex Britannia does not prohibit such an abuse of industrial action, this omission by the Swedish legislator clearly violated Community law; such violations cannot justify action by Byggnads.

5.2 **Directive 96/71**

5.2.1 *Objectives of the directive*

Directive 96/71 was adopted under the internal market jurisdiction concerning the provision of (cross-border) services. It therefore wants to implement the basic principle of Article 49 TEC as it had been developed by the case-law of the ECJ, in particular since *Rush Portuguesa*. This starting point must be kept in mind when interpreting it. Therefore, the Directive should not be applied in such a way as to make cross-border provision of services via posted workers impossible or unreasonably risky or costly. The host Member State must guarantee that posting remains possible within the framework of the Directive. It should not be used for merely economic grounds in order to protect national businesses or to close markets from competition.

At the same time, the Directive, according to recital 5, wants to promote a 'climate of fair competition and measures guaranteeing respect for the rights of workers.'[45] Therefore, a '"hard core" of clearly defined protective rules should be observed by the provider of services notwithstanding the duration of the worker's posting', recital 14. The second objective of the Directive is the protection of posted workers, not of workers of the host country.[46] These rules are contained in Article 3. They also imply a conflict rule, namely that not only the law of the home country of the service provider, but also in certain aspects the law of the host country is applicable, that is the law of the country where the posted workers perform the work according to the service contract which the provider has concluded in the host country. It therefore amends the rules of the applicable law under Article 6 of the Rome Convention to protect posted workers and to make possible their equal protection under the law of the host Member State.[47]

5.2.2 *Article 3(1) of the Directive 96/71*

As far as the *Laval* case is concerned, it seems to us that only the question of 'minimum rates of pay' in the sense of paragraph 1, second indent under (c) is controversial.[48]

The Directive sets out a number of requirements that must be observed in order to 'overrule' the rates of pay which have been agreed upon by the provider with 'his' workers, or which are applicable according to a collective agreement concluded in the home country, as in the *Laval* case. The conditions which are listed in the two indents of paragraph 1 of Article 3, namely minimum wages imposed either by law (or regulation), or by collective agreements or arbitration awards declared universally applicable, are not relevant here. Sweden does not have a system of state minimum pay (as in France), nor one of declaring collective agreements universally applicable within the meaning of paragraph 8 (as in Germany). Sweden deliberately refrained from implementing (c) because of its 'social model' which means that the state takes a neutral position with regard to industrial relations and leaves it to the social partners to find adequate pay rates in collective bargaining

---

[45] G. Langenfeld in E. Grabitz/M. Hilf (eds.), *Das Recht der EU* – Kommentar, Art. 137 EGV Rdnr. 52: 'Vermeidung von sog. "Sozialdumping" – avoidance of social dumping'; P. Davies, 'Posted Workers: Single Market or Protection of National Labour Law Systems?', 34 *CML Rev.* (1997) p. 571 at pp. 572-575, referring to the ambiguities of the directive; somewhat broader W. Däubler, 'Die Entsenderichtlinie und ihre Umsetzung ins deutsche Recht', *EuZW* (1997), p. 613 at p. 615: 'zwingende Gründe lägen in der Vermeidung der Arbeitslosigkeit, in der Erhaltung der Tarifautonomie in den betroffenen Branchen sowie in deren Schutz gegen Wettbewerbsverfälschung'.

[46] There had been some criticism, in particular in German legal literature, whether the Directive could be based on the internal market jurisdiction of the EC, a criticism not taken up by the ECJ, however; W. Däubler, *supra* n. 45 at pp. 614-615.

[47] C. Barnard, *EC Employment Law*, 2nd edn. (Oxford, Oxford University Press 2000) at pp. 177-178; M. Franzen, 'Die EG-Entsende-Richtlinie', *ZEuP* (1997), p. 1095 at pp. 1064-1070.

[48] For a recent clarification see case C-341/02 *Commission* v. *Germany* [2005] *ECR* I-2733 para. 24.

proceedings which are enforced by the mechanisms available under the Medbestämmandslagen, as amended by the 'Lex Britannia'.

5.2.3 *The option for collective agreements under Article 3(8)*

Paragraph 8 of Article 3 extends the effects of collective agreements with regard to pay rates which may also be imposed on posted workers under certain conditions which have so far not yet been interpreted by the ECJ. They therefore need careful scrutiny.

(1) The first condition requires a *decision* of the host Member States, namely

> 'In the absence of a system for declaring collective agreements or arbitration awards to be of universal application … , Member States, may, *if they so decide* (emphasis added, NR), base themselves on …'

As has been correctly observed by Davies[49]

> '… in determining whether collectively agreed standards apply for the purposes of the Directive, Member States may substitute for the test of obligation the test of applicability in fact …'

The Arbetsdomstolen, in its order for reference, explains that 'the responsibility for deciding what is an acceptable standard for terms and conditions of employment has thus been transferred to the organisations in the Swedish employment market.'[50] It is not clear how this has been accomplished, particularly *vis-à-vis* foreign service providers who may not know the specifics of the Swedish labour market. The Directive is silent as to the form and requirements of such a decision. By an *argumentum e contrario*, it need not be a legally binding instrument. On the other hand, from the very purpose of the Directive, namely not to serve as a basis for preventing competition and at the same time to protect posted workers, it must be required that such a decision be expressly taken and be rendered transparent for the industries listed in the Annex, which is applicable to the *Laval* case concerned with construction work. Both the foreign service provider and the posted workers must know under what conditions they perform work in the host state, as expressly spelled out in Article 4(3) of Directive 96/71. It should be remembered that a similar *requirement of transparency* has been developed by the ECJ in public procurement, respectively state aid matters, if Member States want to enforce certain justified protective objectives.[51]

---

[49] See *supra* n. 45 at p. 580.

[50] See *supra* n. 39 at p. 10.

[51] Cf., case C-513/99, *Concordia Bus Finland Oy AB* v. *Helsingin jaupunki* [2002] *ECR* I-7213 paras. 62, 67 for environmental standards; C-280/00, *Altmark Trans et al.* v. *Nahverkehrsgesellschaft Altmark* [2003] *ECR* I-7747 para. 90 for public transport.

It is not known whether Sweden has taken such an express decision, and whether is was transparent to Laval when tendering for the construction contract in Vaxholm. The referring court mentions that there is 'no express provision concerning the application of terms and conditions of employment in collective agreements' in Swedish legislation. In any case, there are anyhow serious doubts that this was the case because the originally proposed wage of 80 Kroner was accepted in the tendering procedure, the pay rate was raised to 109 Kr. only after industrial action was threatened by Bynaggds, while the wage level demanded was 145 Kr. It seems that Laval did not know under what conditions it could participate in the tendering for construction work, and in its concrete provisions. Such legal and economic insecurity violates the very essence of the freedom to provide services: the provider must know his *quid pro quo* – otherwise competition cannot work effectively, and markets cannot be opened.

(2) Even if there is no doubt concerning the (express and transparent) 'decision' of the Swedish state, as a second requirement the collective agreement must either 'be applicable to all similar undertakings in the geographical area and in the profession or industry concerned', or has been 'concluded by the most representative employer's and labour organisations at national level and which apply throughout the national territory.' According to the Commission, this means that the Member States can include agreements or awards which are complied with by the great majority of 'national-level undertakings'. The key factor is the extent to which the national-level undertakings are real or potential competitors to the service provider.[52] Obviously this is a question of fact which cannot be answered by the ECJ. There are, however, serious doubts that these requirements have been fulfilled in the *Laval* case:

- it is not sure that the wage level agreed in a collective agreement in the construction business in the Vaxholm (Stockholm) area amounts to the originally required 145 Kr.;
- even if Byggnads had concluded a collective agreement with the relevant Swedish employer's association as the most representative organisation, it is not evident that this agreement is applied 'throughout national territory' and not only regionally.

Byggnads seems to take the view that Article 3(8) must be understood in such a way that it also allows it to take industrial action to *extend* the application of a collective agreement to foreign service providers. It refers to recital 12 of the Directive which reads:

> 'Whereas Community law does not preclude Member States from applying their legislation or collective agreements entered into by employers and labour, to any person

[52] Cited by Barnard, *supra* n. 47 at p. 175 note 399.

who is employed, even temporarily, within their territory, although his employer is established in another Member State; whereas Community law does not forbid Member States to guarantee the observance of those rules by the appropriate means.'

As can be seen from the very wording of the recital, it only reiterates what has already been said in paragraphs 1 and 8 of Article 3 of Directive 96/71. It says nothing about corresponding rights of trade unions, but only of Member States. The argument that in the case of Sweden the state, by virtue of the Lex Britannia, has delegated this power to trade unions is irrelevant because the Lex Britannia itself violates Community law and therefore cannot serve to justify the action of Byggnads to extend its collective agreements to EU service providers.

The same is true of recital 22 of the Directive to which the order for reference by the Arbetsdomstolen refers. It reads that the Directive is without prejudice to Member States' legislation governing the right to take industrial action. It does not say anything – and cannot do so – about the limits of industrial action under *primary Community law*, as has been set out above.

(3) It should be remembered that paragraph 8 of Article 3 refers to paragraph 1, including (c) which only talks of 'minimum rates of pay', not of 'normal pay' as agreed in collective bargaining. There is some doubt that the Swedish system allows such a distinction to be made between 'minimum' and 'normal' rates of pay. Such a distinction is however necessary in order not to take away from foreign service providers their competitive advantage which they may have by paying lower wages to their workforce under the jurisdiction of their home country, but may still incur higher costs because of offering work in a different country where they need to provide the costs for transportation, shelter and living of the posted workers. The application of the normal wage rates in the host country may be disproportionate in special circumstances, as the Court spelt out in *Portugaia Construções.*[53]

(4) Finally, a fourth and decisive requirement, namely 'equality of treatment' must be guaranteed. This 'equality' principle is violated when the collective agreement allows or at least tolerates an undercutting of the agreed pay rates, while such practice is not tolerated *vis-à-vis* foreign service providers. This principle had been developed by the ECJ in *Portugaia Construções* with regard to collective agreements which have been declared universally applicable, as in Germany.[54] *A fortiori* it must also be applied to collective agreements which are *de facto* universally applicable.[55]

5.2.4 *Enforcement of eventual minimum pay obligations?*

Even if we take the view (which we do not share) that the requirements of Article 3 paragraph 8 are met in the *Laval* case, and that therefore the posted Latvian workers

[53] Case C-164/99, *Portugaia Construções* [2002] *ECR* I-787 para. 30; see V. Hatzopoulos and T.U. Do, 'The case law of the ECJ concerning free provision of services', 43 *CML Rev.* (2006), p. 923 at pp. 974-975.

[54] At para. 34.

[55] Davies *supra* n. 45 at p. 581.

should have been paid at hourly wage rates of around 145 Kroner, a refusal to do so by Laval does not automatically mean that industrial action by Byggnads would be justified by imposing a collective bargaining agreement upon Laval. Article 5(2) of the Directive requires that Member States 'shall in particular ensure that adequate procedures are available to workers and/or their representatives for the enforcement of obligations under the Directive'. Article 6 makes it possible to institute proceedings in the courts of the host Member States, even if this would not have been possible under the then applicable rules of Article 5(1) of the Brussels Convention.[56]

In the *Laval* case, the protective ambit of Article 5/6 is turned upside down by the boycott by Byggnads. The posted Latvian workers were not allowed to enter the building site and perform the contract. They were sent home and laid off. A claim against their employer is theoretically possible but *de facto* frustrated by the industrial action by Byggnads. Instead of protecting posted workers, is does exactly the opposite: it deprives them of their opportunity to work and eventually to claim Swedish wages (should they be applicable under Article 3(8) of Directive 96/71) by using the mechanisms of Article 5/6. This is in clear violation of the *Wolff* judgment of the ECJ[57] where the Court insisted that

> '… Member States must ensure, in particular, that workers have available to them adequate procedures in order actually to obtain minimum rates of pay.'

The boycott is made possible by the Lex Britannia which, as we have said, in itself violates EU law insofar as it allows discriminatory and selective action against service providers from EU countries, and deprives posted workers of their rights to which they are entitled under Directive 96/71. In reality, the boycott aimed at closing the Swedish labour market to EU service providers and their posted workers. This is not a legitimate aim under Community law.

5.3 Public policy exceptions under Article 3(10) in conjunction with constitutional law

Article 3(10) of Direction 96/71 finally allows the host Member State to apply to posted workers provisions of its laws, regulations and administrative provisions governing matters additional to those set out in Article 3(1), provided that these additional rules fall within the category of 'public policy provisions'.[58] Byggnads and the Swedish government argue that the *Medbestämmandelagen* with the special rules of the *Lex Britannia* must be characterised as such 'public policy provisions' because they enshrine the Swedish 'social model' in order to avoid 'social dumping'

---

[56] Davies *supra* n. 45 at p. 578; Barnard *supra* n. 47 at pp. 176-177; *Franzen supra* n. 47 at p. 1071.

[57] Case C-60/03, *Wolff & Müller GmbH* v. *Jose Filipe Pereira Félix* [2004] *ECR* I-9553 at 29.

[58] Davies *supra* n. 45 at p. 582.

Such an interpretation could possibly be also based on constitutional considerations which had been discussed *supra* (section 3.4). In *Omega*,[59] the Court linked the 'public policy' concept to fundamental rights protection, in this case the right to human dignity. The same should be true with the relevance for public policy of the defence of social rights by collective action by trade unions which are, as we have shown, guaranteed under Article 28 of the Charter of Fundamental Rights and indirectly in Article 136(1) TEC and Article 11 ECHR.

But even under such an interpretation of the public policy provisions it must be in conformity with the requirements of equal treatment and in compliance with the Treaty.[60] This is not the case with the Lex Britannia because of its discriminatory effect towards EU-based enterprises by discarding the collective bargaining agreements concluded with their home trade unions (section 5.1.3). Second, public policy provisions must be construed strictly as an exception from the freedom to provide services under primary Community law to which, as is shown by the legal basis of the Directive, namely the internal market provisions, it should contribute to improving competitive conditions and not create new obstacles; therefore, national provisions invoking public policy reasons may not serve merely to protect economic goals, namely the national labour market against alleged 'social dumping'.

Third, in our opinion paragraph 10 of Directive 96/71 only concerns provisions beyond the list of Article 3(1), that is other matters than minimum rates of pay. Insofar as the *Lex Britannia* enables Swedish labour unions to impose their national standards of wage bargaining on EU-based service providers, this is possible only under the criteria of Article 3(1)(c), respectively paragraph 8 which have already been discarded. The 'public policy proviso' is not meant to give additional rights to Member States or their trade unions concerning pay rates beyond paragraphs 1 and 8 of Article 3.

6. Effects of an eventual non-justification of industrial action

As we have argued, the boycott by Byggnads against Laval is a clear infringement of the Community rules on the freedom to provide services. It cannot be justified neither by primary nor by secondary law, in particular Directive 96/71.

On the other hand, one might argue that this violation is due exclusively to the action, respectively the omission of the Swedish state and cannot simply be imputed to Byggnads. The action by Byggnads seemingly conformed to the then effective Lex Britannia and was upheld in the first proceedings where Laval sought an injunction before the Swedish Arbetsdomstolen. The Swedish government, in public statements, defended the action of Byggnads as being compatible with Community and Swedish law. Must Byggnads answer for a manifest breach of Community law by the Swedish state?

---

[59] Case C-3602, *Omega Spielhallen und Automatenaufstellungs-GmbH* v. *Oberbürgermeisterin der Stadt Bonn* [2004] *ECR* I-9609 para. 35.

[60] See *supra* n. 59 at para. 36.

Obviously this is a new and delicate question, and it is not necessary to give a general answer.[61] If the action by Byggnads would have been limited to a solidarity action, similar to the *Brenner-Autobahn* case cited above,[62] trying to convince the Swedish legislator to act in order to guarantee minimum pay, as provided under Directive 96/71, or to assist Latvian workers in their possible demand for higher wages, to protest in general against a policy of wage dumping seemingly allowed under Community law, one could probably not have objected to the legality of such action under Article 11 ECHR.

The *Laval* case, however, is different in its intensity and extent: the boycott which is challenged here completely prevented the access of Laval to the Swedish construction market. It made impossible for Laval the performance of its contracts which it had concluded on the one hand with the city of Vaxholm, and on the other with its Latvian workers. It is a particularly grave and manifest violation of a Community freedom which is rendered impossible through industrial action.

There is no clear precedent, as far as we know, which clarifies the conflict between Community and national law in cases where a private association – in our case: a trade union – has relied on a national exemption or enabling regulation to seemingly justify its action. The principle of the primacy of Community law will apply here, but it is usually confined to a conflict between the Community and Member States, according to Article 10 TEC, and not to the triangular relationship between the Community, Member States, and private associations.

If, however, as we have argued above referring to the case-law of the Court, the fundamental freedoms of Articles 39 and 49 TEC are also applicable to collective regulations restricting their exercise as in the *Laval* case (section 4.3.2), the same rule must apply with regard to justifications. Member States and collective entities are treated on the same footing. They cannot hide behind a Member State law seemingly justifying their action, if this very justification – the Lex Britannia – itself violates Community law because of its discriminatory character against a collective bargaining agreement from other EU jurisdictions.

A similar line of argument can be found in the application of the EU competition rules. Community competition law has clearly established that a private party (in the cases at hand: an undertaking) cannot rely on Member State rules to justify its actions if these rules in themselves violate the primacy of EU law. The two leading cases are the *German insurers*[63] for the relation between exempting or regulating

[61] See now N. Reich, 'Horizontal liability under EC law – "Hybridisation" of remedies for compensation in case of breaches of EC rights', 44 *CML Rev.* (2007) to be published with detailed references.

[62] See *supra* n. 16.

[63] Case C-45/85, *Verband der Sachversicherer* v. *Commission* [1987] *ECR* 405 para. 22; see also case C-198/01, *Consorzio Industrie Fiammiferi* (CIF) [2003] *ECR* I-8055 para. 46, with regard to sanctions this depends on the freedom which undertakings enjoy; paras. 56-57: no justification for practices which are likely further to exacerbate the adverse effects on competition, but this may be a mitigating factor concerning penalties; comment C. de la Torre, 'State Action Defence in EC Competition Law', *World Competition* (2005), p. 407; there is no case-law yet with regard to civil liability.

national provisions and Article 81 TEC, and *Alcan*[64] for the recovery of illegally paid out state aid, if recovery was barred by state procedural rules.

In the German insurance case the Court stated:

> '… Community law does not, however, make the implementation of the provisions of Articles 85 and 86 (*now Arts 81 and 82 EC, NR*)… dependent upon the manner in which the supervision of certain areas of economic activity is organised by national legislation'

In *Alcan*, it was said that there is no 'legitimate expectations' defence in receiving the aid against the provisions of EC law, even if national procedural rules have been followed or are opposed to the recovery of the aid. The reason behind such a strict rule enforcing the recovery of state aid against national law is that 'a diligent businessman should normally be able to determine whether that procedure (*under the Community state aid rules, NR*) has been followed.'

Goyder[65] has analysed the existing case-law of the Court by postulating a 'second rule':

> 'Undertakings do not escape Articles 81 or 82 merely because of state action affecting their markets.'

Admittedly, similar case-law has not yet been developed regarding breaches of Community freedoms by private parties because in most cases the Member State was liable for the breach. It is not suggested here that a private party like a trade union should be responsible for each and every breach, and that it can never rely on a state-imposed or authorised justification. This is particularly true with regard to the rights of labour unions to collective action which is respected not only by Swedish, but also by Latvian and Community law.

It is submitted, however, that there are certain limits to such action, namely when they make impossible the exercise of Community freedoms and cannot reasonably be justified. Byggnads could not expect that its action was completely justified, even if in the first proceedings by Laval before the Swedish labour court no injunction was granted which inhibited its actions.

The goal of the action by Byggnads was obviously the protection of Swedish labour standards and indirectly Swedish businesses, even though the Swedish state had opened the labour and service markets to providers from the new Member States. The means of its action, namely the total and prolonged boycott of the construction site, was excessive and non-proportional.

Should Byggnads be condemned to pay compensation to Laval, it may be possible for it to have recourse against the Swedish state for creating and making possible such a situation. But this is not part of the litigation before the Court. It is

---

[64] Case C-24/95, *Land Rheinland-Pfalz* v. *Alcan* [1997] *ECR* I-1591 para. 25.

[65] D.G. Goyder, *EC Competition Law*, 4th edn. (Oxford, Oxford University Press 2003), at p. 478; similar to case C-67/96, *Albany supra* n. 14 at para. 65.

certainly not a defence which can be used by Byggnads against Laval. Byggnads decided to take the risk to violate Community law by starting a total boycott against Laval, thus impairing its freedom to provide services.

If such clearly *disproportionate industrial action* would be allowed, the Community freedoms would become a hollow symbol in the future. They would only be protected against Member State regulation or omission, but could not be enforced against private action. Such a grant to unlimited, uncontrolled and disproportionate action against fundamental freedoms by private associations would set aside the developments of Community law since *Walrave* and *Bosman* and only encourage other collective entities to do the same, with the Member State hiding behind such a misunderstood concept of autonomy.

Another important point should be made in the litigation before the Court: the boycott against Laval by Byggnads concerns an enterprise from a new Member State which had been promised in the Accession Agreements with Latvia the right to full market access in the European Union. Sweden did not avail itself of the possibilities of invoking temporarily 'national measures', as had been the case with Germany and Austria, until 2011 at the latest. The action by Byggnads, made possible and supported by the Lex Britannia, ran counter to this very promise given by the Swedish government to service providers from the new Member countries. If such actions were to be allowed in the future, they could be commenced at any time even after the lapsing of the transitory arrangements with the new Member States by threatening to boycott any EU enterprise entering the Swedish market so as to 'defend' Swedish labour standards. The Swedish 'social model' would result in closing its market for construction services and would make free movement impossible for times to come. This is obviously a serious violation of that which lies at the very heart of Community law and which cannot be justified by the freedom of industrial action.

7. Annex: Opinion of AG Mengozzi of 23 May 2007

The opinion of AG Mengozzi covers 42 pages and gives a very detailed overview of Swedish and Community legislation and social practice with regard to the conflict which arose in *Laval*. The AG takes as a starting point – just as this author – the direct effect of Article 49 TEC to social action by labour unions (paras. 155-161) and rejects the argument of the Swedish and Danish governments that the – admittedly – fundamental right to strike is 'beyond the reach' of EC Law (paras. 233-236). A strike or boycott as in the *Laval* case must therefore be regarded as a 'restriction on the freedom to provide services' (para. 233), which can however be justified by action to protect (which?) workers and to combat 'social dumping' (para. 249), provided that it adheres to the proportionality criteria (discussed in great detail in paras. 245 et seq.). AG Poiares Maduro took a similar view with regard to the freedom of establishment of Article 43 in his opinion (paras. 23, 33, 40) in the *Viking* case on the same day.

The methodological starting point of the AG, however, is different from the one of this author insofar as he interprets in great detail Article 3(1) and (8) of Directive 96/71 and their *de facto* implementation via the Swedish system of collective bargaining. The *Lex Britannia* is therefore for him without problems as it ensures the effectiveness of the Swedish system (para. 185), without being measured under Article 49 and the mutual recognition principle, on which we had insisted (*supra* section 5.1). The core of the analysis is therefore on Article 3(8) of Directive 96/71 which enables Swedish trade unions not only to set minimum rates of pay as prescribed in paragraph 1 but to insist on full compliance with Swedish wage levels, perhaps under the somewhat lighter regime of so-called tie-in conditions, without becoming a member of a trade association. In his opinion this is also justified under the minimum protection clause of Article 3(7) (paras. 172/197). A conflict with Directive 96/71 and later Article 49 TEC only arises where the wage rates as enforced by the Swedish trade unions also include certain contribution fees, supervision charges, insurance premiums and the like which cannot be subsumed under the concept of 'pay' or which are already covered by the home country jurisdiction (para. 281).

In my opinion, such an argument – which is presented in a shortened version here – is not in compliance with the Directive itself nor with Article 49 TEC. A complete levelling up of 'minimum rates of pay' to the 'normal rates' paid in Sweden even if the provider is already bound by a collective agreement in his home country – as justified without argument in paragraphs 194/202 of the opinion – means *de facto* that the competitive advantage of the Latvian service provider is completely eliminated, and therefore the very basis of the directive – which is, according to its preamble, to remove obstacles to the freedom to provide services, while guaranteeing the posted workers certain social standards and by avoiding 'social dumping' – is circumvented and effectively frustrated. This seems to be implicitly recognised by the AG himself in paragraph 206, without however drawing the necessary legal consequences from this statement:

> 'By imposing strict equality of treatment between foreign service providers and those domestic undertakings, the Swedish system appears in fact to disregard the very characteristics of the freedom to provide services by fully assimilating the temporary posting of workers by a service provider of a Member State to Sweden to a permanent activity carried on by undertakings that are established in Swedish territory.'

The Swedish system, in imposing *equal rates of pay to unequal economic conditions* – namely permanent work on the one hand performed in Sweden on a regular basis vs. temporary work done by posted workers from a service provider established in another EU country on the other – amount to indirect discrimination which should not be allowed under Article 49 or under Directive 96/71 which is a mere concretisation. The minimum protection clause should, as is usual in EC law, be interpreted strictly in the light of the fundamental freedoms of *Laval* to offer its services EC-wide, and not serve as a basis to effectively seal off the Swedish labour market.

The opinion further does not evoke the transparency argument written into Article 4 which is important for the foreign service provider on whether or not to take the considerable costs of going onto a foreign market. Finally, the AG leaves outside his opinion the position of Latvian workers – those seemingly to be protected – which is expressly foreseen in Article 5/6 (for a differing view see para. 176 relating it to Swedish conditions, not to the protection of posted workers!).

The analysis of Article 49 and especially the proportionality argument is somewhat more critical to the practice of the Swedish labour unions and shows more 'sympathy' with the situation of Laval.

> 'In that connection, it seems to me that the fact of making the very possibility of applying a given rate of pay conditional upon prior signing up to all the conditions of a collective agreement that apply in practice to undertakings established in Sweden in the same sector and in a similar situation goes beyond what is necessary to ensure the protection of workers and to prevent social dumping' (para. 280).

As a result, the opinion gives a somewhat blurred picture: by generously interpreting Article 3(1), (7) and (8) of Directive 96/71 in the sense of Swedish wage conditions, the competitive effect of the wage advantage of Laval by posting its workers who are under Latvian jurisdiction and bargaining agreements is neutralised. However, the way collective bargaining was imposed on Laval, on the one hand, and the excessive charges put onto the wage package, on the other as allowed by Swedish practice, seem to contradict the proportionality principle enshrined in Article 49 and therefore make the boycott illegal. One will have to wait and see how the Court finally decides.

Chapter 4
CONSOLIDATING THE ENLARGEMENT AGENDA FOR SOUTH EASTERN EUROPE

Steven Blockmans

1. Introduction

With the creation of the European Coal and Steel Community (ECSC) in 1951 and the European Economic Community (EEC) in 1957, memories of Charlemagne were never far off. Geographically speaking, the common territory of the six founding states of the ECSC, the EEC and Euratom overlapped to a large extent with the Frankish Empire that Charlemagne united with fire and sword in the 8th century. While his empire was large, it was also weak. The European Communities of the 1950s, however, have gradually and peacefully expanded to cover almost the entire continent and have been granted the powers to potentially form the strongest union of free and prosperous states that Europe has ever seen. Over a period of fifty years, the progressive and peaceful spread of the rule of law and democracy has seen authoritarian regimes transform into secure, stable and dynamic democracies. Successive enlargements of the European Union are making a reality of Robert Schuman's vision of a united and peaceful continent.

After six rounds of enlargement, the European Union currently has 27 members and provides a common roof not only for a Catholic, Protestant, Orthodox and Islamic Europe, but also for a Latin, Germanic, Slavic and Celtic Europe. But the EU's expansion has a price. In the wake of the 'big bang' enlargement of 2004 and 2007, the populations (and political elites) of some Member States seem to suffer from both 'enlargement blues', i.e., the impact of the last round of accession, and 'enlargement fears', i.e., the prospect of the further expansion of the Union, in particular with Turkey. Since the 'No' votes in France and the Netherlands on the ratification of the Treaty establishing a Constitution for Europe, the EU's enlargement plans became snarled up in a much bigger argument between rival groups of Member States that disagree about the long-term objectives of the Union, its shape and final borders.

This paper argues that, despite the apparent *malaise* of the European project and the difficulties in finding a political compromise on institutional reform and agreement about the geometry of participation in the 'deepening' of the project, this is not and should not be the end of the road for European Union enlargement. The rationale for this is simple. The European Union has already started accession

S. Blockmans and S. Prechal, eds., Reconciling the Deepening and Widening of the EU

negotiations with Turkey and Croatia, and it has granted candidate country status to the Former Yugoslav Republic of Macedonia. Moreover, the rest of the Western Balkans (Albania, Bosnia-Herzegovina, Montenegro and Serbia, including Kosovo) have also been promised a membership perspective and have been granted a 'potential' candidate country status. It would be politically unwise for the European Union to retreat from its commitments under the enlargement agenda for South Eastern Europe for it would undermine the EU's authority as a negotiating partner, not only *vis-à-vis* the candidate and the potential candidate countries, but indeed internationally. Moreover, it could be risky to renege on those commitments because it would rid the governing coalitions in (potential) candidate countries of their claim that speedy economic, administrative and legal reforms are needed to join the European Union. This, in turn, could lead to a polarisation of the political landscape of these countries and potentially disrupt a valuable process that is helping to build stable and effective states in some of the poorest and most volatile parts of the Western Balkans (Kosovo and Bosnia-Herzegovina). For these and other reasons, the European Union cannot step down from its role as the promoter of 'peace, security and progress in Europe and in the world' (preamble to the TEU). In a similar vain, the European Union and its Member States cannot hold the (potential) candidate countries hostage to a discussion on Europe's future status. Of course, further enlargements cannot be self-defeating, in the sense that they would weaken the fabric of the Union to such an extent that they would threaten the very aims of peace, security and progress on the European continent which they seek to achieve. The best way forward for the European Union is to reconcile its 'widening' and 'deepening' agendas.

On the 'widening' side of the spectrum, efforts should be made to consolidate the enlargement agenda so as to prevent the European Union from importing problems that it cannot solve or that it can address more powerfully in the pre-accession phase (e.g., ending the division of Cyprus and fighting corruption in Bulgaria and Romania). Membership conditionality is the key instrument geared towards reform and integration of European Union candidate countries. Over the years, the content of European Union membership conditionality has developed in parallel with (i) the evolution of the European Union *acquis*, (ii) a decreasing level of preparedness on the part of candidate countries and (iii) growing opposition in European Union Member States to further enlargement. This paper touches upon all three phenomena by paying attention to new and specific membership conditions (section 3) and the revised framework for accession negotiations as applied to the current candidate countries (section 4). Before venturing into the possible answers to the question how the enlargement agenda for South Eastern Europe can be further consolidated, the state of affairs will be given of the pre-accession processes of the countries of South Eastern Europe (section 2). Some concluding remarks will wrap up this paper (section 5).

2. The state of affairs

2.1 Turkey

In 1959, the Turkish Government asked the EEC to enter into negotiations on an association agreement.[1] The Council responded positively. After four years of negotiations, the Association Agreement between the EEC and Turkey was signed on 12 September 1963 in Ankara and entered into force on 1 December 1964.[2] The primary objective of the so-called 'Ankara Agreement' was 'to promote the continuous and balanced strengthening of trade and economic relations' (Art. 2(1)) between Turkey and the Community by establishing a customs union (Art. 2(2)). Yet, the preamble to and Article 28 of the Agreement stated another objective, namely to facilitate the accession of Turkey to the EEC 'at a later date'. At the time of its conclusion, however, political and security motives prevailed over economic rationale and stood in the way even of normal association.[3] The Turkish occupation of Northern Cyprus (since 1974), condemned by the UN Security Council in Resolution 353 (1974), brought EEC-Turkey relations to a historical low.[4] As a result, the schedule for the transition of the association to the establishment of a customs union was not adhered to and the free movement of workers was not introduced.

It was only in 1986, after improvements in the Turkish political system, that the association was revived. On 14 April 1987, Turkey applied for membership of the Community.[5] In its so-called *avis*, the European Commission advised the Council not to enter into negotiations with Turkey for reasons of the EEC's own unsettled constitutional system and economic, democratic and human rights concerns.[6] Instead, the Commission proposed to enter into negotiations on a customs union. The Council adopted this recommendation and thereby rejected the Turkish application for the time being.[7] In spite of this setback, Turkey's will to accede to the EC/EU remained unaltered. Virtually all Turkish governments have put European

[1] Initially, Turkey even wanted to start accession negotiations with the EEC. See E. Lenski, 'Turkey (including Northern Cyprus)', in S. Blockmans and A. Łazowski (eds.), *The European Union and Its Neighbours: A Legal Appraisal of the EU's Policies of Stabilisation, Partnership and Integration* (The Hague, T.M.C. Asser Press 2006), pp. 283-313; and K. Ertekin, *Der türkische Beitritt zur Europäischen Gemeinschaft* (Frankfurt, Peter Lang 1989).

[2] Agreement of 12 September 1963 establishing an Association between the European Economic Community and Turkey, by way of Council Decision 64/732, *JO* 3687/64 (English version: *OJ* 1977 L 361/29). An Additional Protocol was signed on 23 November 1970 and entered into force on 1 January 1973; original version published in *JO* 1972 L 293/68 (English version: *OJ* 1977 L 361/60).

[3] E. Esen, *Die Beziehungen zwischen der Türkei und der EG unter besonderer Berücksichtigung der innertürkischen Auseinandersetzungen um die Assoziation 1973-1980* (Bonn, Centaurus 1990) p. 223 et seq.

[4] See M. Bozkurt, *Die Beziehungen der Türkei zur Europäischen Union* (Frankfurt, Peter Lang 1995).

[5] *Bull. EC* 4-1987, points 1.3.1 and 1.3.2.

[6] SEC (89) 2290 final of 20 December 1989.

[7] *Bull. EC* 1/2-1990, p. 77 et seq.

Union membership on their political agenda. The Community and Turkey continued to negotiate with a view to entering into the final stage of the association. By way of Decision 1/95 of the EC-Turkey Association Council, the customs union was gradually established.[8]

Relations again turned sour in 1996 when Turkey threatened to veto the envisaged accession of the Czech Republic, Hungary and Poland to NATO if it was not accepted as an official candidate for European Union membership. This attempt at blackmailing the European Union was sharply criticised.[9] In 1997, the Luxembourg European Council decided not to invite Turkey to the enlargement negotiations with the associated Central and Eastern European Countries (CEECs) and Cyprus.[10] In retaliation, the Turkish Government suspended political dialogue with the European Union and blocked all European Union attempts towards reconciliation.[11] Only after the Commission proposed strategies to involve Turkey in the enlargement process and after the first steps to that end were taken by the Cardiff European Council of 15 and 16 June 1998,[12] did Turkey end its self-imposed isolation and re-engage in a dialogue with the European Union.

The European Council, at its historic Helsinki summit of 10-11 December 1999, finally granted candidate country status to Turkey and decided to apply the criteria established by the 1993 Copenhagen European Council in the pre-accession process.[13] With this decision, the European Council confirmed the qualification of Turkey as a 'European' state in the 1963 Ankara Agreement. However, public opinion on the issue remains split.[14] This led the 2002 Copenhagen European Council to envisage accession negotiations in 2005 if Turkey would fulfil the Copenhagen political criteria.[15] Since 2002, Turkey has adopted an impressive amount of internal legal reforms.[16] On the basis of the Commission's positive recommenda-

---

[8] Decision No. 1/95 of the EC-Turkey Association Council of 22 December 1995 on implementing the final phase of the Customs Union, *OJ* 1996 L 35/1.

[9] See T. Buerkle, 'EU Confirms Turkey's Right to Join, but Not Now', *International Herald Tribune* (17 March 1997) p. 5.

[10] Conclusions of the Presidency, Luxembourg European Council, 12 and 13 December 1997, *Bull. EU* 12-1997, point I.6.31.

[11] See E. Lenski, *supra* n. 1, at p. 287, with references to 'Türkei kündigt aus Enttäuschung Ende des Dialogs mit der EU an', *Der Tagesspiegel* (15 December 1997) p. 1; and P. de Graaf, 'EU wil relatie met Turkije verbeteren' [EU wants to improve relationship with Turkey], *De Volkskrant* (5 March 1998) p. 4.

[12] European Commission, Communication of 4 November 1998, COM (98) 124 final; and Conclusions of the Presidency, Cardiff European Council, 15 and 16 June 1998, *Bull. EU* 6-1998, point I.21.68.

[13] Conclusions of the Presidency, Helsinki European Council, 10 and 11 December 1999, *Bull. EU* 12-1999, point I.3.12.

[14] See, e.g., F. Mayer and J. Palmowski, 'European Identities and the EU', 42 *JCMS* (2004) p. 573 at p. 579; and S. Blockmans and A. Łazowski, 'The European Union and Its Neighbours: Questioning Identity and Relationships', in S. Blockmans and A. Łazowski (eds.), *supra* n. 1, pp. 3-18.

[15] Conclusions of the Presidency, Copenhagen European Council, 11 and 12 December 2002, *Bull. EU* 12-2002, point I.6.19.

[16] See the (revised) Turkish National Programme for the Adoption of the Acquis, available at: <http://europa.eu.int/comm/enlargement/turkey/pdf/npaa_full.pdf>. On recent amendments to the Turk-

tion,[17] the European Council of December 2004 decided to start negotiations on 3 October 2005.[18] The European Council made the opening of negotiations subject to the political condition that Turkey enacts amendments to six statutes relating mainly to the judiciary and judicial rights. Moreover, Turkey committed itself to recognise the Republic of Cyprus by signing the Adaptation Protocol to the Ankara Agreement.[19] Respect for human rights, the principle of democracy and the rule of law (especially the role of the Turkish army) will continue to be contentious issues in the time to come. [20]

Turkey's path towards accession will be a long and winding road. So far, the accession negotiations have been the slowest ever between the European Union and a candidate country.[21] Eighteen months into the process, only one negotiating chapter (research and education) has been opened and provisionally closed. On 11 December 2006, the European Union General Affairs and External Relations Council concluded that

> 'the Member States within the Intergovernmental Conference will not decide on opening chapters covering policy areas relevant to Turkey's restrictions as regards the Republic of Cyprus until the Commission verifies that Turkey has fulfilled its commitments related to the Additional Protocol,'[22]

---

ish legal system, see P. Tanlak, 'Turkey EU Relations in the Post Helsinki Phase and the EU Harmonisation Laws Adopted by the Turkish Grand National Assembly in August 2002', *SEI Working Paper* No. 55 (Brighton 2002); M. Sen, 'Turkey', in A. Ott and K. Inglis (eds.), *Handbook on European Enlargement – A Commentary on the Enlargement Process* (The Hague, T.M.C. Asser Press 2002), pp. 341-346; and K. Başlar and E. İshakoğlu, 'National Report on Turkey', in A.E. Kellermann, J. Czuczai, S. Blockmans, A. Albi and W.Th. Douma (eds.), *Impact of EU Accession on the Legal Orders of New Member States and (Pre-)Candidate Countries* (The Hague, T.M.C. Asser Press 2005), pp. 195-239.

[17] European Commission, Recommendation on Turkey's progress towards accession, COM (2004) 656 final, p. 9 et seq.

[18] Conclusions of the Presidency, Brussels European Council, 16 and 17 December 2004, *Bull. EU* 12-2004, point I.7.22. For backgrounds, see *infra* n. 47.

[19] For additional conditions and action points, see Council Decision 2003/398/EC of 19 May 2003 on the principles, priorities, intermediate objectives and conditions contained in the Accession Partnership with Turkey, *OJ* 2003 L 145/40 (Revised Accession Partnership). From a legal point of view, the northern part of Cyprus acceded to the Union as part of the Republic of Cyprus. Application of the *acquis*, however, is suspended for those areas in which the Government of the Republic of Cyprus does not have effective control, that is to say, Northern Cyprus. See Art. 1 of Protocol No. 10 to the Act of Accession of 16 April 2003, *OJ* 2003 L 236/955. While the EU continues to support efforts towards the reunification of Cyprus, no substantive rules on direct trade between the Member States and the northern part of the island have so far been adopted. See N. Skoutaris, 'The Application of the *Acquis Communautaire* in the Areas not Under the Effective Control of the Republic of Cyprus: The Green Line Regulation', paper presented at the Jean Monnet Module on Advanced Issues of European Law, Dubrovnik, 2 May 2007.

[20] See, e.g., S. Kardas, 'Human Rights and Democracy Promotion: the Case of Turkey-EU Relations', 1 *Alternatives: Turkish Journal of International Relations* (2002) p. 144. See also K. Hughes, 'Turkey and the European Union: Just Another Enlargement?', *Friends of Europe Working Paper* (June 2004).

[21] By way of comparison: negotiations with the CEECs took four and a half years.

[22] Council conclusions of 11 December 2006, doc. 16289/06 (Presse 352), at 9.

i.e., opening its ports and airports to Greek Cypriot ships and aircraft. In an unprecedented move in the history of European Union enlargement policy, eight chapters were suspended: free movement of goods (Chapter 1), the right of establishment and the freedom to provide services (Chapter 3), financial services (Chapter 9), agriculture and rural development (Chapter 11), fisheries (Chapter 13), transport (Chapter 14), customs union (Chapter 29) and external relations (Chapter 30).[23] The European Council some days later endorsed the conclusions: 'Turkey has not fulfilled its obligation of full non-discriminatory implementation of the Additional Protocol to the Association Agreement.'[24]

The EU's decision to partially suspend Turkey's membership talks has triggered widespread disillusionment in Turkey. Conscious of the fact that it was crucial to show Turkish citizens that the European Union remained committed to stick to its end of the deal and to move the accession process forward, a second chapter (enterprise and industrial policy) was opened on 29 March 2007. Taking into account Turkey's state of preparations, in line with the Council conclusions of 11 December 2006 and on the understanding that Turkey would continue to make progress in the alignment with and implementation of the *acquis*,[25] the European Union noted that in order for the chapter to be provisionally closed, two benchmarks would have to be met: Turkey's full and non-discriminatory implementation of the Additional Protocol to the Association Agreement and providing the Commission with a revised comprehensive industrial policy strategy aiming at strengthening Turkey's industrial competitiveness.[26] At the same time, the European Union hinted that three more chapters (economic and monetary affairs, the compilation of statistics, and financial control) might be opened.

While the accession process is more or less back on track, talks with Turkey might last at least ten to fifteen years. Moreover, some problems are not likely to be solved during the accession negotiations. This has led the Commission to propose long transition periods or even – in the case of the free movement of workers – permanent safeguard clauses (see section 4). At the end of the accession process, the Member States' parliaments each still have a veto on every Act of Accession.

---

[23] For reactions in the press, see 'EU "partly suspends" Turkey talks', *BBC News*, 11 December 2006; and M. Buenderman, 'EU clinches deal on Turkey talks', *EUObserver.com*, 11 December 2007.

[24] *Bull. EU* 12-2006, point I.5.10.

[25] On 17 April 2007, Turkey's Minister for Foreign Affairs, Abdullah Gul, unveiled his country's 400-page roadmap towards EU membership, with details on forthcoming legislative proposals aiming to put Turkey's laws into line with the *acquis* by 2013. Commenting on the plan, Turkey's Chief Negotiator Ali Babacan said that '[t]his will be a programme for continuing our reforms, covering all 35 chapters, including those suspended because of the link to Cyprus. We have decided to separate the formal process of negotiations from the domestic efforts of Turkey (…).Turkey needs reforms in a short time.' On the Cyprus issue, Babacan said that his country was waiting for the EU's embargo on the Turkish part of the island to be lifted. He underlined: 'This is our position at any cost'. See also L. Kubosova, 'Brussels declines to endorse 2013 date for Turkey's EU entry', *EUObserver.com*, 17 April 2007.

[26] On the insistence of Spain, special reference was made to the sector of shipbuilding. See 'Turkey: Spain blocks second chapter, progress likely Tuesday', *seeurope.com*, 26 March 2007.

In some Member States, most prominently in France, referenda will be held on the possible accession of Turkey. Considering the current unenthusiastic attitude of the majority of the populations of some Member States towards European Union accession of Turkey, these ratification procedures may prove problematic.

2.2 Stabilisation and Association Process

2.2.1 *Raising the threshold*

Initiated by the Commission in 1999,[27] the Stabilisation and Association Process (SAP) specifically aims to assist each of the countries of the Western Balkans in meeting the relevant European Union criteria and to be ultimately accepted as official candidates for membership. The one incentive which the SAP shrank from providing, however, was an explicit promise of European Union membership. At the 2000 Santa Maria da Feira Council, the European Union stated that the SAP countries are 'potential candidates', which undisputedly represented a promotion but not a breakthrough that went all the way.[28] The 24 November 2000 Zagreb Summit of heads of state and government of European Union Member States and SAP countries set the seal on the Process by gaining the region's agreement to the applicable set of objectives and conditions.[29] The EU's commitment under the SAP was to offer the states of the Western Balkans enhanced trade liberalisation, improved financial and economic assistance, a regular political dialogue, cooperation in Justice and Home Affairs and, in particular, a new tailor-made category of contractual relations based on Article 310 TEC: Stabilisation and Association Agreements (SAAs).[30]

At the 21 June 2003 EU-Western Balkans Summit in Thessaloniki, it was acknowledged that the SAP would remain the framework for the European course of the Western Balkan countries, 'all the way to their future accession'.[31] Crucially, it was agreed that the SAP (and the prospects it offers) would serve as the anchor for reform in the Western Balkans, in the same way as the pre-accession process had done in Central and Eastern Europe. To that end, the SAP needed to be strengthened and enriched with elements from the enlargement process, so that it could better meet the new challenges as the countries move from stabilisation and reconstruction to sustainable development, association and integration into European

[27] See COM (99) 235 final, Brussels, 26 May 1999.

[28] *Bull. EU* 6-2000, point I.49.67. For a critical view on this promise of a perspective of membership, see O. Anastasakis and D. Bechev, *EU Conditionality in South East Europe: Bringing Commitment to the Process* (Oxford, SEESP 2003). On the use of the concept 'potential' candidate countries, see *infra* section 2.2.5.

[29] *Bull. EU* 11-2000, point I.6.57.

[30] Analysis of the SAAs shows considerable similarities with the earlier EAs. See D. Phinnemore, 'Stabilisation and Association Agreements: Europe Agreements for the Western Balkans?', 8 *EFA Rev.* (2003), pp. 77-103, at pp. 79-81.

[31] For the full text of the declaration of the EU-Western Balkans Summit at Thessaloniki, see *Bull. EU* 6-2003, point 1.6.70.

structures. In the light of the latter, the European Council endorsed 'The Thessaloniki Agenda for the Western Balkans: Moving Towards European Integration.'[32] Very much like Agenda 2000 set the tune for the pre-accession process of the CEECs, the Thessaloniki Agenda served both to confirm the conditionality developed under the SAP and to list the domains in which progress was expected to be made:

- consolidation of peace and the promotion of stability, democracy, the rule of law, and respect for human and minority rights;
- respect for the inviolability of international borders, peaceful resolution of conflicts and regional cooperation;
- the fight against terrorism, violence and extremism, be it ethnically, politically or criminally motivated;
- the full implementation of Resolution 1244 (1999) of the UN Security Council on Kosovo and of the 'standards before status' policy;
- the full compliance with the Dayton/Paris agreements and subsequent Peace Implementation Council decisions, the Ohrid and Belgrade agreements;
- the full support of the International Criminal Court, its work and the integrity of its statute; and
- the full cooperation with the International Criminal Tribunal for the former Yugoslavia, in particular with regard to the transfer to The Hague of all indictees and full access to documents and witnesses.

The Thessaloniki Agenda was also meant to strengthen the political visibility of the SAP by launching the high-level multilateral EU-Western Balkans Forum and 'European Partnerships' (reminiscent of the Accession Partnerships for the CEECs), as well as promoting the decisions for enhanced cooperation in the areas of political dialogue and the Common Foreign and Security Policy, parliamentary cooperation, support for institution-building, the opening of Community programmes and regional economic development.

The instruments covered by the SAP were declared open to all countries of the region on equal terms. Their actual availability, however, is conditional upon each country's compliance with the general and country-specific conditions set out by the European Union. Although anchored in a common set of political and economic conditions, the approach of the SAP is thus flexible enough to allow each country to move ahead at its own pace. An annual review mechanism assesses each country's performance in meeting the conditions. The recommendations contained in the Commission's progress reports, as well as the Council's annual assessment are intended to help the SAP countries focus their attention for the year ahead on specific priority areas. Hence, the emphasis of the SAP is placed on differentiation according to the specific needs and situations of each country, as

[32] For the text of the Thessaloniki Agenda, see Annex A to Council Conclusions of 16 June 2003, Press Release No. 10369/03 (Presse 166), para. 1.

well as on improvements in the relations within the entire region. An enhanced form of conditionality is thus the glue of the SAP.

The reasons for 'upgrading' pre-accession conditionality were essentially two-fold. Firstly, the challenges in the Western Balkans went beyond those concerning economic and political transition which had been posed by the CEECs over the preceding decade. Therefore, a new type of relationship responding to the particular needs of the Western Balkans was deemed necessary. Secondly, by the spring of 1999, the European Union was making headway towards realising its most ambitious enlargement to date. The prospect of up to 12 new entrants over the next few years was unprecedented. Added to this was the question of admitting Turkey into the accession process. Faced with such an overwhelming enlargement agenda, there was little enthusiasm for widening it further by offering Europe Agreements to the countries of the Western Balkans, thereby raising expectations of pre-accession aid and encouraging membership applications. Mindful of this and anxious to cause concern among the candidate countries about their position in the enlargement process, the European Union had to avoid any formulations which might raise objections and potentially undermine reform efforts in those countries. This was recognised in, *inter alia*, the title of the SAAs. Their purpose was not just association but first and foremost, in the short-term at least, stabilisation.

2.2.2 *A graduated process*

The application of conditionality in the SAP has to be seen as a graduated process. For instance, the start of SAA negotiations requires a lower level of compliance than the conclusion of the agreements (which, in turn, requires a lower level of compliance than the opening of the accession treaty). Before negotiations for the conclusion of an SAA can start, a certain level of progress must be made. The Commission observes and evaluates the situation in the country, in particular the fulfilment of the relevant conditions such as the presence of functioning democratic structures, respect for human rights, fundamental freedoms and the rule of law, as well as the cooperation with neighbouring countries.[33] In doing so, the Commission is guided by reports of other international organisations, committees or institutions which are active in the region, such as NATO, OSCE and the Council of Europe. The results are published in annual country reports, in which the Commission reviews compliance with the EU's political and economic criteria by each of the countries concerned. Once the Commission judges that a country has made sufficient progress in its domestic reform process, it begins, with the approval of the Council, to carry out a study on the feasibility of the opening of negotiations for an SAA. Following the completion of this so-called 'feasibility

[33] See the Council's adoption, on 29 April 1997, of specific guidelines in the form of 'Conclusions on the principle of conditionality governing the development of the European Union's relations with certain countries of south-east Europe'. See *Bull. EU* 4-1997, point 2.2.1.

study' and a positive assessment by the Council that a Western Balkan country has indeed made sufficient progress in meeting the SAP conditions and that it has the capacity to negotiate and implement the far-reaching political and economic obligations under an SAA, the Commission submits a formal proposal on the negotiating directives for an SAA. If adopted by the Council, the negotiations are conducted by the Commission in consultation with a special committee created by the Council for that purpose. SAAs, like EAs, are mixed agreements. Hence, to enter into force they require the approval of the Council (by way of a decision),[34] the assent of the European Parliament (Articles 300(3) and 310 TEC), as well as ratification by all European Union Member States and the non-Member State concerned. In anticipation of the full ratification of an SAA, the trade provisions may enter into force via interim agreements. Political dialogue can already be established as well.

2.2.3 *Croatia*[35]

The SAA with Croatia was signed on 29 October 2001.[36] Ratification in Croatia followed shortly thereafter, on 5 December 2001. The EP gave its assent on 12 December 2001. In anticipation of the full ratification of the SAA, the trade provisions already entered into force via an interim agreement.[37] While a majority of the Member States also ratified the SAA Croatia within the usual timeframes, the Netherlands, the United Kingdom and Italy for a long time withheld (notification of) ratification of the agreement because of their negative perception of Croatia's willingness to cooperate with the ICTY.[38] In the meantime, Croatia applied for European Union membership.[39] When it became clear that cooperation with the ICTY would become a strict condition for Croatia to open accession negotiations with the European Union, the obstructive trio dropped its opposition towards ratifica-

---

[34] Since the transfer of responsibility for relations with the Western Balkans from DG RELEX to DG ELARG in November 2004, SAAs are signed by a ministerial representative of the country holding the Presidency of the Council, the EU Commissioner for Enlargement and a ministerial representative of the Western Balkan country concerned.

[35] On the rise, fall and rebirth of Croatia, see M. Tanner, *Croatia: A Nation Forged in War* (New Haven, Yale University Press 1997).

[36] See COM (2001) 371 final, Brussels, 9 July 2001.

[37] Interim Agreement on trade and trade-related matters between the European Community, of the one part, and the Republic of Croatia, of the other part, *OJ* 2001 L 330/3. The interim agreement entered into force on 1 March 2002.

[38] See S. Rodin, 'Croatia', in S. Blockmans and A. Łazowski (eds.), *supra* n. 1, 357-389. These countries referred to Croatia's apparent inability to arrest the indicted General Ante Gotovina and hand him over to the ICTY in The Hague. Gotovina, the UN tribunal's third most wanted fugitive, disappeared the day before the ICTY made his indictment public, in July 2001, and was finally arrested on 7 December 2005 and subsequently transferred to The Hague. He is indicted for ordering the killing of more than 100 ethnic Serbs and expelling 150,000 more during and after Zagreb's final offensive in August 1995 to recapture Croatian lands seized by Serb forces (Operation Storm). The pressure on Croatia to find and arrest Gotovina has provoked negative feelings towards the European Union, as many Croatians perceive him as a war hero rather than a war criminal.

[39] See doc. 6991/03 ELARG 19 COWEB 28, 20 February 2003.

tion of the SAA.[40] Thanks to this, an Enlargement Protocol to the SAA Croatia could also be negotiated and concluded in order to take account of the accession of ten new Member States to the European Union on 1 May 2004.[41] On 17-18 June 2004, the European Council decided to follow up on the Commission's positive *avis* on Croatia's application for membership and grant candidate status to the country, thereby opening it up to increased financial and technical assistance.[42] At its Brussels summit in December 2004, the European Council requested the Council of Ministers to agree on a negotiating framework with a view to opening accession negotiations with Croatia on 17 March 2005, thereby rewarding Croatia's ongoing preparations for membership with a firm date for starting accession talks.[43] The opportunity, however, was subject to an equally firm condition: full and unequivocal cooperation with the ICTY. Croatia was given exactly three months to arrest Gotovina and hand him over to the ICTY. Despite strong eleventh-hour lobbying by Croatia to prevent the consequences of its failure to arrest and extradite Gotovina, 'the absence of a common agreement' among the 25 European Union Member States on the issue of full cooperation with the ICTY led the Council to take the unprecedented decision to postpone the start of membership talks.[44] The Council was careful, however, to underline that accession negotiations with Croatia could open as soon as there was proof that Croatia was fully cooperating with the Tribunal. To prove its point, but without offering an early resolution of the standoff, the Council adopted the negotiating mandate for the Commission[45] and created a special task force to monitor Zagreb's cooperation with the ICTY.[46] Just

---

40 Stabilisation and Association Agreement between the European Communities and their Member States, of the one part, and the Republic of Croatia, of the other part, *OJ* 2005 L 26/3. The SAA entered into force on 1 February 2005.

41 See Council and Commission Decision 2005/205/EC of 21 February 2005, *OJ* 2005 L 68/30 and Protocol to the Stabilisation and Association Agreement between the European Communities and their Member States, of the one part, and the Republic of Croatia, of the other part, to take account of the accession of the Czech Republic, the Republic of Estonia, the Republic of Cyprus, the Republic of Hungary, the Republic of Latvia, the Republic of Lithuania, the Republic of Malta, the Republic of Poland, the Republic of Slovenia and the Slovak Republic to the European Union, *OJ* 2005 L 26/222.

42 For the *avis*, see COM (2004) 257 final, Brussels, 20 April 2004; for the decision by the European Council, see *Bull. EU* 6-2004, point I.7.31.

43 See *Bull. EU* 12-2004, point I.6.16. For a description and analysis of the road travelled by Croatia to get to that point, and a little further, see D. Jović, 'Croatia and the European Union: A Long Delayed Journey', 8 *Journal of Southern Europe and the Balkans* (2006), pp. 85-103.

44 Council Conclusions of 16 March 2005, Press Release No. 6969/05 (Presse 44); reproduced in *Bull. EU* 3-2005, point 1.5.1.

45 Ibid.

46 See L. Kubosova, 'EU to send monitoring team to Croatia', *EUObserver.com*, 23 March 2005. Chaired by the Minister for Foreign Affairs of Luxembourg, the task force brought together representatives of the Commission, the SG/HR and the next two EU presidencies – the UK and Austria. These two countries held diametrically opposed views during the Council debate of 16 March 2005. The UK was against the opening of negotiations because it was convinced that Croatia was not fully cooperating with the ICTY. Austria, on the other hand, wanted to open membership talks with Croatia on 17 March 2005, because such a decision would enhance Austria's economic and political position in the region.

hours ahead of the crucial meeting of the Council of Ministers on 3 October 2005 in Luxembourg, the task force gave its positive opinion after it was informed by the Chief Prosecutor of the ICTY that, despite the fact that Gotovina remained at large, Croatia was 'fully cooperating' with the Tribunal.[47] Noting the clear commitment by the Croatian Prime Minister that full cooperation would be maintained until the last remaining indictee was in The Hague and as long as required by the ICTY, the Council of Ministers concluded that Croatia had fulfilled the remaining condition for the start of accession negotiations.[48] The accession negotiations were officially launched immediately after the Council meeting, i.e., in the early hours of 4 October 2005.[49]

The formal start of the accession negotiations was followed by the opening of the so-called 'screening process' by the Commission on 20 October 2005. In the course of this process, an examination takes place of the degree of harmonisation of national legislation with the *acquis*. The examination is conducted for each chapter individually. After the screening process with Croatia was completed on 23 October 2006,[50] the decision on the opening of negotiations for individual chapters, depending on the evaluated readiness of Croatia, is made by the Member States within the Council.[51] During this phase, the subject of negotiations are the condi-

---

[47] Carla del Ponte was heavily criticised by her own staff for the sudden U-turn in the approach taken towards Croatia. See 'Carla del Ponte bescheinigt Zagreb überraschend "uneingeschränkte Zusammenarbeit" bei der Kriegsverbrecher-Suche', *Süddeutsche Zeitung*, 4 October 2005. Del Ponte was reported as having said at a press conference in Luxembourg, that '[f]or a few weeks now, Croatia has been cooperating fully with us and is doing everything it can to locate and arrest Ante Gotovina.' This statement stood in sharp contrast to what the Chief Prosecutor said after a meeting with Prime Minister Sanader and President Mesić in Zagreb on 30 September 2005: 'You cannot imagine how disappointed I am. [The] prime minister has promised me full cooperation but we still have the same problem. Gotovina is still at large.' It is thought that del Ponte succumbed to heavy political pressure. The Chief Prosecutor herself denied such allegations. Whatever there may be of this, del Ponte's announcement on 3 October greatly facilitated an agreement by Austria – a strong ally of Croatia – on the opening of accession talks with Turkey, which Vienna had blocked until the last minute. Incidental or not, Gotovina was arrested on 7 December 2005. See *supra* n. 38.

[48] See Council Conclusions of 3 October 2005 in Press Release No. 12514/1/05 REV 1 (Presse 241). The Council confirmed that sustaining full cooperation with the ICTY would remain a requirement for progress throughout the accession process. It invited the Commission to continue to monitor this closely, on the basis of regular reports from the ICTY, and report back to the Council if full cooperation were not to be maintained. The Council noted that an assessment of cooperation with the ICTY would form part of the Commission's reports to the Council on Croatia's fulfilment of the political criteria. The Council agreed that less than full cooperation with the ICTY at any stage would affect the overall progress of the negotiations and could be grounds for triggering the mechanism in para. 12 of the negotiating framework. See section 4 of this chapter.

[49] The UK Presidency insisted that negotiations had been opened on 3 October 2005, i.e., before 24:00 hrs GMT.

[50] By 15 September 2006, the explanatory stage of screening had been completed on 31 chapters and bilateral screening on the first 26. The Commission had sent fifteen screening reports to the Council. For two Croatia had submitted its negotiation positions: one chapter has been subsequently opened and provisionally closed (Science and Research).

[51] According to the European Council, the difficult policy dossiers such as administrative and judicial reforms and the fight against corruption will be opened early. See European Council conclu-

tions under which Croatia will have to adopt and implement the *acquis* in the respective chapter, including the transitional periods which Croatia may have requested in the screening phase. Chapters that might raise difficulties in Croatia's accession negotiations are free movement of capital (in view of the currently very tolerant Croatian laws which allow European Union citizens to purchase real estate), competition policy (in view of the fact that Croatia spends a greater percentage of its national wealth on state aid to companies than any European Union Member State) and judiciary and human rights (rights of minorities, refugee return, impartial prosecution of war crimes trials, judicial and public administration reform, fighting corruption).[52] It was, however, in a different dossier that Croatia had the dubious honour of being the first candidate country ever to experience the discomfort of the revised accession negotiations procedure. Slovenia briefly blocked the opening of EU-Croatia negotiations on a next chapter of European Union legislation by not giving its approval for a European Commission screening report on the extent to which Croatia's fisheries legislation conforms to the *acquis*. Slovenia argued that Croatia had failed to implement a bilateral border agreement on the basis of which Slovenian fishermen (operating from the Bay of Piran, Slovenia's sole outlet to the sea and the object of a dispute between the two countries since their secession from the SFRY in 1991) should be able to enjoy their rights of passage through Croatian waters.[53] The blockage by Slovenia served as a brief beating of the drums to raise awareness among European Union members of the country's remaining land and sea border disputes with Croatia and to warn the latter to solve the matter or risk a real interruption of the accession negotiation process.

From here onwards, until the conclusion of the Accession Treaty, the revised procedure as described below (see section 4) will be applied.[54] Croatia is hoping to conclude its European Union membership talks by 2009, so that it can take part in the European Parliament elections of that year.[55]

---

sions of 14-15 December 2006 in Press Release No. 16879/06 CONCL 3, Brussels, 15 December 2006, para. 7. This way, the EU avoids giving the impression that the negotiations will be easy.

52 These items were highlighted by the President of the Commission in his speech to the Croatian Sabor. See J. Barroso, 'Leading by example: Croatia's road to EU membership', Zagreb, 16 February 2006, SPEECH/06/96. More generally, see T. Ćapeta, D. Mihelin and S. Rodin, 'Croatia', in A. Kellermann, J. Czuczai, S. Blockmans, A. Albi and W. Douma (eds.), *supra* n. 16, pp. 69-112.

53 See H. Mahony, 'Slovenia blocks EU-Croatia talks over fishing dispute', *EUObserver.com*, 19 October 2006; and N. MacDonald, 'Rocky road from independence to EU accession', *Financial Times*, 30 October 2006. See also the warning in the conclusions of the Council of Ministers (GAERC), Press Release No. 16289/06 (Presse 352), 11 December 2006, at 10.

54 For more details on the negotiations on the accession of Croatia to the EU, see the website specifically designed by the Ministry of Foreign Affairs and European Integration for the Negotiating Team for the Accession of the Republic of Croatia to the European Union, available at <http://www.eu-pregovori.hr/default.asp?ru=447&sid=&akcija=&jezik=2>.

55 As reported in 'Croatia screening: new chapters opened', *Euractiv.com*, 15 November 2005.

2.2.4 *Macedonia (FYROM)*[56]

The SAA with FYROM was signed on 9 April 2001.[57] Ratification in Macedonia followed shortly thereafter, on 12 April 2001. The European Parliament was also quick to give its assent to the agreement (on 3 May 2001). In anticipation of the full ratification of the SAA, the trade provisions already entered into force via an interim agreement.[58] After ratification by the then still fifteen Member States of the European Union, the SAA FYROM entered into force on 1 April 2004.[59] Eight days earlier, Macedonia had applied for accession to the European Union.[60] When the Council requested the Commission to give its opinion on Macedonia's application for membership on 1 October 2004, the Commission submitted to the Macedonian authorities a *questionnaire* with over 2,500 questions on the political, economic and administrative situation in the country. The answers, which were transferred to the Commission on 14 February 2005, formed the basis for the *avis* on the starting of accession negotiations. In the preparation of its opinion, the Commission also used feedback from its delegation in Skopje, from the international organisations active in the country, as well as statistical and economic information from sources such as the OECD and the IMF. On 9 November 2005, the Commission published its *avis*.[61] Despite the Commission's positive stance towards the opening of accession negotiations with Macedonia, the granting of candidate country status was thrown into doubt when France threatened the other Member States to put all enlargement issues aside if the Council could not agree on its financial perspective for 2007-2013, the first budget to include the ten new Member States.[62] After two days of nervous negotiations, the European Council of

---

[56] On the historical trajectory of Macedonia, see R. Detrez, *Macedonië: land in de wachtkamer* (Antwerp, Houtekiet 2002); and J. Phillips, *Macedonia: Warlords & Rebels in the Balkans* (London, I.B. Tauris 2004). The term 'Macedonia' is used here as an informal name. Greece believes that the name Macedonia should properly be applied to its own Northern region with origins dating from the time of Alexander the Great. On the name issue, see M. Craven, 'What's in a Name? The Former Yugoslav Republic of Macedonia and Issues of Statehood', 16 *Australian YIL* (1995), pp. 199-239.

[57] See COM (2001) 90 final, Brussels, 19 February 2001.

[58] Interim Agreement on trade and trade-related matters between the European Community, of the one part, and the former Yugoslav Republic of Macedonia, of the other part, *OJ* 2001 L 124/2. The interim agreement entered into force on 1 June 2001.

[59] Stabilisation and Association Agreement between the European Communities and their Member States, of the one part, and the former Yugoslav Republic of Macedonia, of the other part, *OJ* 2004 L 84/13. The SAA FYROM thereby replaced the Cooperation Agreement between the European Community and the former Yugoslav Republic of Macedonia, *OJ* 1997 L 348/2, which had been in force since 1 January 1998. On 21 February 2005, the Council and the Commission adopted Decision 2005/192/EC, *OJ* 2005 L 63/21, on the conclusion of the Protocol to the SAA FYROM to take account of the accession to the European Union of the ten new Member States. For the text of the Protocol, see *OJ* 2004 L 388/3.

[60] See Council Conclusions of 17 May 2004, Press Release No. 9210/04 (Presse 149).

[61] COM (2005) 562, Brussels, 9 November 2005.

[62] See A. Rettman, 'Macedonia should not be held hostage, Denmark says', *EUObserver.com*, 15 December 2005.

December 2005 reached an agreement on the financial perspective,[63] thereby averting the threat of deep political rifts within the Union as well as delays over further enlargement. Macedonia was granted European Union candidate country status in the early morning hours of 17 December 2005.[64] The European Council spoke highly of Macedonia's 'significant progress' in implementing the Ohrid Framework Agreement,[65] securing minority rights, implementing the SAA and fulfilling the political criteria for European Union membership, but made it clear that Skopje's new status did *not* automatically mean the opening of accession negotiations. For that, Macedonia would first have to show 'further significant progress' in each of the above-mentioned domains.[66] Crucially, the European Council also referred to the debate on the 2005 enlargement strategy paper,[67] as first provided for by the Council on 12 December 2005,[68] and the Union's own absorption capacity as two of the specific benchmarks for taking 'further steps'.[69] Thus, the start of Macedonia's entry talks has been tied to the much broader debate among the European Union Member States on the Union's future and its ability to absorb more newcomers.[70] Bilateral issues may also feature. The Greek government, for example, has announced that it will veto Macedonia's accession to the European Union if the country seeks to accede as 'Macedonia', as opposed to its internationally recognised name, currently the Former Yugoslav Republic of Macedonia.[71] Accordingly, it may take months, possibly years, before membership talks with Skopje actually open. This casts a gloomy spell over the rest of the region's membership prospects.

2.2.5 *The 'potential' candidate countries*

For reasons already explained, the inclusion of a membership perspective for the countries of the Western Balkans came against a background of reticence towards any firm commitment to admit the SAP countries into the European Union at a future date.[72] The current commitment towards Albania, Bosnia-Herzegovina,

---

[63] *Bull. EU* 12-2005, point I.4.6.

[64] *Bull. EU* 12-2005, point I.12.24.

[65] The Agreement signed in August 2001under the auspices of the EU's High Representative for the CFSP had prevented the escalation of low-intensity fighting into a full-scale civil war. See C. Piana, 'The EU's Decision-making Process in the Common Foreign and Security Policy: The Case of the Former Yugoslav Republic of Macedonia', 7 *EFA Rev* (2002), pp. 209-226.

[66] *Bull. EU* 12-2005, point I.12.25.

[67] COM (2005) 561 final, SEC (2005) 1421-1424, 1426, 1428 and 1433, Brussels, 9 November 2005.

[68] *Bull. EU* 12-2005, point 1.5.4. The Council concluded that the 2005 enlargement strategy paper prepared by the Commission was a good basis for discussion on enlargement in 2006, but it also noted that 'care should be taken to anchor and develop support for the enlargement process across the EU, to ensure effective conditionality at all stages of the process in a fair and rigorous way, and to reiterate encouragement to reform and stability to all candidate countries, particularly the Western Balkans.'

[69] *Bull. EU* 12-2005, point I.12.25.

[70] See the contribution of Fabian Amtenbrink to this volume.

[71] See 'Greece to say "No" to FYROM', *Euractiv.com*, 2 September 2005.

[72] See *supra* section 2.2.1. See also R. Biermann, 'Die Europäische Perspektive für den westlichen Balkan', 51 *Osteuropa* (2001), pp. 922-937, at pp. 926-927.

Montenegro and Serbia (including Kosovo) follows declarations that were made at the June 2000 European Council in Santa Maria da Feira and at the Zagreb summit of November 2000, to the effect that the Western Balkan countries are 'potential candidates' for European Union membership.[73] Although this notion has no official definition and does not confer on the holder a legally enforceable right to membership, politically speaking, the term 'potential candidate' recognises the Union's willingness to see membership ambitions of the status holder realised in the future. However half-hearted the Member States' commitment to enlarge 'their' Union with the Western Balkans may at first have seemed, the repeated confirmation thereof[74] has provided the 'able and willing' governments of the countries in the region with a justification for difficult political and economic reforms and a means to rally support for tough decisions at home.[75]

Albania's drive to conclude a SAA,[76] the eagerness of political leaders to guide Bosnia-Herzegovina into the European Union,[77] and the successful efforts of Montenegro on a peaceful withdrawal from the state union with Serbia to speed up the process of European integration, all attest to the fact that the only worthwhile 'carrot' the European Union can offer the Western Balkan countries in exchange for concerted efforts to create lasting peace and stability in the region is the prospect of full membership. The case of Serbia and Montenegro (SaM) is special. On 3 October 2005, the Council gave the Commission the mandate to conduct nego-

---

[73] *Bull. EU* 6-2000, point I.49.67; and *Bull. EU* 11-2000, point I.6.57.

[74] Most vocally at Thessaloniki in 2003, *Bull. EU* 6-2003, point I.17.

[75] Others have criticised the EU's unwillingness to make a full commitment to integrate the countries concerned and have pointed out that an integration strategy which revolves around the promise of the perspective of membership does not necessarily trigger the reforms most needed in unstable societies. See, e.g., D. Triantaphyllou, 'The Balkans between Stabilisation and Integration', in J. Blatt, et al., 'Partners and Neighbours: A CFSP for a Wider Europe', 64 *Chaillot Papers* (2003), pp. 60-76.

[76] The SAA was signed on 12 June 2006. For the text of the SAA, see COM (2006) 138 final, Brussels, 21 March 2006. Pending the ratification of the SAA, the trade and trade-related provisions of the agreement entered into force on 1 December 2006 (see *OJ* 2006 L 318/26) by way of an Interim Agreement (published in *OJ* 2006 L 239/2) that replaces the 1992 Trade, Commercial and Economic Cooperation Agreement. See also Council Regulation (EC) No. 1616/2006 of 23 October 2006 on certain procedures for applying the Stabilisation and Association Agreement between the European Communities and their Member States, of the one part, and the Republic of Albania, of the other part, and for applying the Interim Agreement between the European Community and the Republic of Albania, *OJ* 2006 L 300/1. For an analysis of the political, economic and social transformations needed to make Albanian membership possible, see M. Bogdani and J. Loughlin, *Albania and the European Union – the tumultuous journey towards integration and accession* (London, I.B. Tauris & Co Ltd 2007).

[77] Despite the fact that the two most wanted Bosnian Serb indictees, Radovan Karadžić and Ratko Mladić, were still at large, the Commission on 21 October 2005 recommended the opening of negotiations on an SAA with BiH and presented draft negotiating directives for adoption by the Council. The move was widely seen as a reward for the difficult agreements reached between the Federation of BiH and the Republika Srpska on military reforms. SAA negotiations were officially opened on 25 November 2005, the same week as the tenth anniversary of the Dayton Peace Agreement. It took BiH one year to conclude SAA negotiations with the EU. Due to continuing problems surrounding the reform of the police, however, the European Commission has postponed the signing of the SAA until final agreement is reached.

tiations on a SAA with the state union of Serbia and Montenegro.[78] The opening of negotiations by European Commissioner Olli Rehn in Belgrade on 10 October 2005 marked the fifth anniversary of the democratic uprising that removed Slobodan Milošević from the Presidential peluche. On that occasion, Rehn warned that the conclusion of SAA negotiations would only be possible if Karadžić and Mladić were handed over to The Hague in the meantime. However, after the ICTY's Chief Prosecutor in February 2006 told the BBC that General Mladić was within 'immediate reach' of the Belgrade authorities, a statement which provoked a flurry of media reports which first claimed, later denied that Mladić had been captured, the European Union hardened its tone. Although not laid down in black and white in the Council Conclusions of 27 February 2006, the European Union was reported as having given SaM a one-month deadline to send Mladić to The Hague or face the disruption of SAA talks. The controversies over the circumstances of the death and the burial of Milošević in March complicated Belgrade's efforts to transfer the war-time general. This was recognised by the ICTY's Chief Prosecutor, when she positively reported in Brussels on SaM's cooperation with the Tribunal. Accordingly, the European Union opened the political round of SAA talks with SaM on 5 April 2006, while at the same time keeping up the pressure by extending the deadline for the transfer of the fugitive with one extra month. As SaM was unable to meet the new deadline, the Council on 3 May supported the Commission's decision to call off further SAA negotiations.[79] On 21 May 2006, 55.5% of the Montenegrin voters opted for independence in the nation-wide referendum which was considered to be free and fair. In a special session on 3 June, the parliament in Podgorica passed a declaration on the independence of the Republic of Montenegro. On 5 June, the parliament in Belgrade declared the Republic of Serbia the legal successor to the state union and gave all state institutions 45 days to complete the separation. On 12 June, the Council of the European Union decided to develop bilateral relations with the new sovereign and independent Republic of Montenegro.[80] On 24 July, the Council adopted the decisions authorising the Commission to negotiate an SAA with Montenegro.[81] At the same time the Council amended the negotiating directives for the SAA with Serbia. The latter had no implication for the Commission's decision to freeze SAA negotiations as long as Serbia fails to arrest and extradite Ratko Mladić.[82]

---

[78] See Council Conclusions of 3 October 2005, in Press Release No. 12515/1/05 REV 1 (Presse 242).

[79] See Council Conclusions of 15 May 2006, in Press Release No. 9001/06 (Presse 126).

[80] See Council Conclusions of 12 June 2006, in Press Release No. 9947/06 (Presse 162).

[81] See Council Conclusions of 24 July 2006, in Press Release No. 11556/06 (Presse 216).

[82] See further *infra* section 3.3.

3. Novelties in pre-accession conditionality

3.1 Multi-dimensional nature

Membership conditionality is primarily defined by the requirements of Articles 49 and 6(1) TEU. According to Article 49 TEU, 'any European state' which respects the principles set out in Article 6(1) TEU (liberty, democracy, respect for human rights and fundamental freedoms and the rule of law) may apply to become a member of the Union. The application of these articles (in their previous forms and numbers – Art. 237 EEC, Art. 98 ECSC, Art. 205 EAEC, Art. O TEU) proved to be enough to allow the EC/EU to expand to 15 members without undermining its functioning.[83] But the prospect of the 'reunification of Europe' after the fall of the iron curtain and the entry of 12 or more mostly poor post-communist members, triggered the June 1993 European Council Summit at Copenhagen to develop more stringent criteria to measure the level of preparedness of both these candidates and the European Union.[84] Since 1993, membership requires:

(a) that the candidate country has achieved stability of institutions guaranteeing democracy, the rule of law, human rights and respect for and protection of minorities;
(b) the existence of a functioning market economy, as well as the capacity to cope with competitive pressures and market forces within the Union;
(c) the ability to take on the obligations of membership, including adhering to the aims of political, economic and monetary union;
(d) the Union's capacity to absorb new Members, while maintaining the momentum of European integration, is also an important consideration in the general interest of both the Union and the candidate countries.[85]

As has been noted in section 2.2, European Union conditionality has been further upgraded into a multi-dimensional instrument geared towards reform and integration of the failed and weak states of the Western Balkans.[86] Special requirements reflect the distinct historical trajectory and peculiar problems of the countries in the region. In addition to the membership conditions of Articles 49 and 6(1) TEU and the 1993 Copenhagen criteria, pre-accession conditionality for the Western Balkans is established by:

[83] See F. Hoffmeister, 'Changing Requirements for Membership', in A. Ott and K. Inglis (eds.), *supra* n. 16, pp.90-102; and K. Smith, 'The Evolution and Application of EU Membership Conditionality', in M. Cremona (ed.), *The Enlargement of the European Union* (Oxford, OUP 2003), pp. 105-139.

[84] See C. Hillion, 'The Copenhagen Criteria and their Progeny', in C. Hillion (ed.), *EU Enlargement: A Legal Approach* (Oxford, Hart Publishing 2004), pp. 1-22; and M. Cremona, 'EU Enlargement: Solidarity and Conditionality', 30 *EL Rev.* (2005), pp. 3-22.

[85] *Bull. EU* 6-1993, point 13.

[86] For an elaborated analysis, see S. Blockmans, *Tough Love: The European Union's Relations with the Western Balkans* (The Hague, T.M.C. Asser Press 2007), pp. 241-307.

(e) the conditions flowing from the 1999 Stability Pact for South Eastern Europe and the Stabilisation and Association Process, which reiterate the Copenhagen criteria and add the condition of regional cooperation through political dialogue and the conclusion of (free trade) agreements with countries in South Eastern Europe (see section 3.2); and
(f) the country-specific conditions for the opening and conclusion of SAA talks, i.e., the conditions that arise out of the peace agreements and political deals (the Dayton, Erdut, Ohrid and Belgrade Agreements, UNSC Res. 1244), e.g., the full and unequivocal cooperation with the International Criminal Tribunal for the former Yugoslavia (see section 3.3).

The European Commission in its annual reports closely monitors progress in fulfilling the seemingly ever-increasing body of membership conditions. Through the screening process and the accession negotiations, the Commission identifies the main weaknesses and technical adaptations needed by the (potential) candidate countries and accordingly sets out priorities and benchmarks, and directs European Union funds towards relevant projects. Similarly, the SAP is monitored and reviewed annually in order to highlight the key priorities and channel funds in the Western Balkans. On top of all this, the Union is applying, for the first time in its history, the fourth Copenhagen, i.e., the Union's capacity to absorb new members, while maintaining the momentum of European integration.[87]

3.2 The requirement of regional cooperation

3.2.1 *Conundrum*

Whereas regional cooperation was encouraged among the countries that signed Europe Agreements with the Union, it was never made a distinct feature of their associations. In the case of the SAAs, regional cooperation is viewed as a key element in the stabilisation of the Western Balkans and is made an explicit condition before the countries of the region can join the European Union (see Art. 3 of the existing SAAs). However difficult it is to enforce this additional conditionality, the importance attached to it has been underlined by the Commission, which noted in its first annual report on the SAP: '[i]ntegration with the European Union is only possible if future members can demonstrate that they are willing and able to interact with their neighbours as European Union Member States do.'[88] In Article 4, SAA signatories commit themselves to 'continue and foster cooperation and good neighbourly relations with the other countries of the region.' The SAAs explicitly refer to such relations covering the movement of persons, goods, capital, and services, as well as the development of projects of common interest. In the SAA with Croatia, specific examples are given: 'refugee return and combating

[87] See the contribution by Fabian Amtenbrink in this volume.
[88] See COM (2002) 163 final, Brussels, 4 April 2002, at 11.

organised crime, corruption, money laundering, illegal migration, and trafficking.' To achieve regional cooperation on these issues, the SAA countries are expected to conclude conventions between each other. SAA signatories are also obliged to engage in regional cooperation with the other countries covered by the SAP (Art. 13). The political dialogue, held within a multilateral framework (Arts. 7 and 8), shall also contribute to the development of regional cooperation and good neighbourly relations. In fact, these provisions codify a proliferation process which was already underway in South Eastern Europe. Apart from a matrix of bilateral free trade agreements,[89] a whole range of regional initiatives for political dialogue has been developed. Notable examples are the Central European Initiative, the Black Sea Economic Cooperation, the South East Europe Cooperation Process and the Southeast Europe Cooperation Initiative.[90]

In spite of these commendable developments, the heterogeneity of the Western Balkans contradicts those elements of SAP conditionality which promote a greater degree of regional cooperation. The differences in the Western Balkans are the consequence of centuries of recompositioning the region. This *a priori* differentiation is at the root of the varying progress in bilateral relations with the European Union, which in turn exacerbates local disparities. For their part, most Western Balkan states tend to regard regional schemes with a certain suspicion, sceptical of the benefits they can generate or concerned that they might impede closer bilateral relations with the European Union.[91] In such a context, it is difficult to see how the differentiating effect of conditionality could generate healthy competition among Western Balkan states when the stronger feel that they are delayed by the weaker, while the weaker do not benefit from the progress of the stronger. Hence, the European Union is confronted with a conundrum: how to effectively reconcile the regional approach that is essential for the stabilisation of the Western Balkans with the requirement of evaluating countries on the basis of their individual performances, a concept which lies at the heart of the European Union pre-accession process?

---

[89] A matrix of the free trade agreements in South Eastern Europe is available at <http://en.wikipedia.org/wiki/Stability_Pact_for_South_Eastern_Europe#FTA_Progress>. See also European Commission, 'Trade in South Eastern Europe', MEMO/06/155, Brussels, 5 April 2006.

[90] For an overview and analysis of these and other initiatives, see D. Lopandić, *Regional Initiatives in South Eastern Europe* (Belgrade, European Movement in Serbia 2001). Many of these regional initiatives have been criticised because of the modesty of their objectives, their partly overlapping memberships and agendas indicating a lack of complementarities, and the limited concrete results they have yielded. See, e.g., O. Anastasakis and V. Bojičić-Dželilović, *Balkan Regional Cooperation and European Integration* (London, Hellinic Observatory LSE 2002); and A. Petričušić, 'Regional Cooperation in the Western Balkans – A Key to Integration into the European Union', 1 *Croatian Yearbook of European Law and Policy* (2005), pp. 213-233.

[91] See O. Anastasakis and V. Bojičić-Dželilović, *Balkan Regional Cooperation and European Integration* (London, LSE 2002); and D. Bechev, 'Carrots, Sticks and Norms: The EU and Regional Cooperation in South-East Europe', 8 *Journal of Southern Europe and the Balkans* (2006), pp. 27-43.

3.2.2 *Reconciling enhanced bilateralism with enhanced multilateralism*

The creation of a free trade area in South Eastern Europe provides the missing incentive for regional cooperation. After all, the economic interdependence of the countries of the Western Balkans is vital for the future of the region. The economic sustainability of their small and unattractive markets depends on the creation of a common economic area that will attract foreign direct investment. Thus, in an economic sense, a regional approach is a necessary precondition for development. In this respect, the entry into force of the Energy Community Treaty creating an Energy Community between the European Community, on the one hand, and Albania, Bulgaria, Bosnia-Herzegovina, Croatia, FYROM, Montenegro, Romania, Serbia and the United Nations Mission in Kosovo (on behalf of the entity pursuant to the UN Security Council Resolution 1244 (1999)), on the other hand, is a unique development which should be welcomed.[92] While this form of 'enhanced multilateralism'[93] is limited to the creation of an integrated market in natural gas and electricity,[94] the Energy Community Treaty does provide a legal framework (i.e., a new international organisation equipped with autonomous decision-making powers and legal instruments) to export and extend the EC's *acquis* on energy, the environment, competition and renewables to the Western Balkans.[95] Article 94 of the Treaty prescribes that the institutions of the Energy Community shall interpret any term or concept used in the Treaty that is derived from EC law in conformity with the case-law of the ECJ or the CFI. Where no interpretation from those courts is available, the Ministerial Council of the Energy Community will give guidance in interpreting the Treaty, not prejudging any interpretation of the *acquis* by the ECJ or the CFI at a later stage. As such, the Energy Community Treaty aims to create a stable regulatory and market framework capable of attracting investment so that all parties have access to the continuous gas and electricity supply that is essential for economic development and social stability. The Energy Community Treaty forms a model for the integration of the small markets of South Eastern Europe in other segments of the EU's single market. An example of the latter is the creation, by 2010, of a European Common Aviation Area.[96] Like the integration

[92] See Council Decision 2006/500/EC of 29 May 2006 on the conclusion by the European Community of the Energy Community Treaty, *OJ* 2006 L 198/16. The Treaty entered into force on 1 July 2006 for a period of 10 years. The Energy Community Treaty is not a mixed agreement. EU Member States may become participants in the Energy Community pursuant to Art. 95 of the Treaty. For an analysis of these and other peculiarities of the Energy Community Treaty, see F. Hoffmeister, 'Die Beziehungen der Europäischen Union zu den Staaten des Westbalkans', in S. Kadelbach (ed.), *Die Außenbeziehungen der Europäischen Union* (Baden-Baden, Nomos 2006), pp. 125-150, at pp. 132-138; and S. Blockmans, *supra* n. 86, pp. 317-318.

[93] See also the contribution of Adam Łazowski to this volume.

[94] The integrated market may involve at a later stage other energy products and carriers, such as liquefied natural gas, petrol, hydrogen, or other essential network infrastructures.

[95] See Title II of the Treaty.

[96] See European Commission, Proposal for a Council Decision on the conclusion of the Multilateral Agreement between the Republic of Albania, Bosnia and Herzegovina, the Republic of Bulgaria,

efforts of the six founding states of the ECSC in the fields of coal and steel were a precursor to the decision to expand their cooperation to other domains of their economies with the creation of the EEC, the Energy Community Treaty heralded the resuscitation of a much broader platform to realise their economic ambitions: the Central European Free Trade Agreement (CEFTA).

Since its enactment in 1992, CEFTA has aimed at ensuring both the free commercial flow of products and services between countries sharing a common European Union perspective and political stability in Central and Eastern Europe.[97] As such, CEFTA has made a valuable contribution in preparing the CEECs for the competitive forces on the single market and – ultimately – accession to the European Union. The founding members of CEFTA (the Czech Republic, Hungary, Poland, and Slovakia) left CEFTA when they acceded to the European Union in 2004. So did Slovenia. In view of the departure of Bulgaria and Romania following their accession to the European Union on 1 January 2007, CEFTA was preserved by extending it to cover the rest of the Western Balkan states. On 19 December 2006, the political leaders of the countries and territories involved (Albania, Bosnia-Herzegovina, Croatia (a party since 2002), FYROM (since 2006), Moldova, Montenegro, Serbia and the United Nations Interim Administration Mission in Kosovo) signed a new CEFTA.[98] The Agreement focuses on the promotion of simpler and less bureaucratic procedures and the introduction of modern trade provisions in areas such as harmonisation, competition, state aid, services and the protection of intellectual property rights. As such, the Agreement assists Montenegro and Serbia (including Kosovo) in their preparation for WTO membership, because the two processes are rooted in the same goals and rules of progressive liberalisation of trade. The European Union, which is not a party to the Agreement, has strongly supported an accord on the enlargement of CEFTA because of the complementary nature of the regional cooperation stemming from CEFTA's principles within the European Union integration process.[99] As such, the cooperation of the Western

---

the Republic of Croatia, the European Community, the Republic of Iceland, the former Yugoslav Republic of Macedonia, the Kingdom of Norway, Serbia and Montenegro, Romania and the United Nations Interim Administration Mission in Kosovo on the Establishment of a European Common Aviation Area (ECAA), COM (2006) 113 final, Brussels, 14 March 2006. Already, bilateral agreements between the EC and countries of the region are concluded in this field. See, e.g., Agreement between the European Community and Bosnia and Herzegovina on certain aspects of air services, *OJ* 2006 L 169/48.

[97] The original 1992 Agreement is reproduced in its entirety in 34 *ILM* (1995), pp. 8-42, with an accompanying note from P. Kornfeld, 'CEFTA', 34 *ILM* (1995), pp. 3-7. See also D. Lopandić, *Regional Initiatives in South Eastern Europe* (Belgrade, European Movement in Serbia 2001), pp. 93-102.

[98] See Memo, 'A New Regional agreement to develop Trade in South Eastern Europe', Brussels, 19 December 2006.

[99] See Council Conclusions of 20 March 2006 in Press Release No. 7035/06 (Presse 69); and European Trade Commissioner Peter Mandelson, 'Remarks at the launch of CEFTA expansion negotiations', SPEECH/06/228, Bucharest, 6 April 2006. Others have made the argument that extending the matrix of bilateral trade agreements into a pan-regional trade association is likely to be inadequate. See D. Kernohan, 'Reverse Balkanisation? Trade Integration in South-East Europe', *CEPS Working Document*, No. 249, August 2006. Kernohan argues that it would be better to extend the present Customs

Balkan states in CEFTA meets two important requirements of European Union (pre-)accession conditionality: regional cooperation and readiness for the competitive impact of participating in the EU's single market.

3.3 ICTY conditionality

The European Union has defined full cooperation with the ICTY as a threshold conditionality when it comes to the process of the integration of the countries of the Western Balkans. The challenge facing the European Union at present is how to translate the post-war conditionality of the ICTY, which is charged with examining concrete crimes in the cases of Gotovina, Mladić and Karadžić, into one that looks towards the future and concentrates on the strengthening of European values across the region. While the unprecedented decision by the Council to postpone the start of membership talks with Croatia was – incidental or not – followed by the arrest of war-time General Gotovina and his transfer to The Hague, a similar decision to suspend negotiations on an SAA with Serbia failed to cajole Belgrade into compliance with ICTY conditionality.

Arguably, full cooperation with the ICTY should remain mandatory for the opening of accession negotiations with the European Union. A failure to transfer a single high-profile fugitive to the Tribunal, however, should not hold entire countries back in their development when it comes to negotiating and signing SAAs. In partial recognition of this, and despite the opposition of the United Kingdom and the Netherlands, the strict requirement of handing over Mladić to the ICTY seems to have been dropped by the Council in an attempt to lessen the blow of an internationally imposed decision to allow Kosovo to secede from Serbia.[100] As was to be expected, the European Union scored the scorn of Carla del Ponte, the ICTY's Chief Prosecutor.[101] But what should be learned from these experiences is that ICTY conditionality, at least in the phase of negotiating and signing SAAs, should be understood more broadly than just the need to transfer one or two suspected war criminals to The Hague.[102] Instead, ICTY conditionality should concentrate on the willingness of Western Balkan societies as a whole to examine the causes and consequences of their troubled past. Hence, the European Union should attach more importance than it does now to the readiness and ability of the domestic judicial, religious and educational authorities to deal with the war-related crimes

---

Union with Turkey to include trade with the entire South East European zone of countries linked to the EU.

[100] The Council in February 2007 assured the EU's readiness to resume SAA negotiations with a new government in Belgrade 'provided it shows clear commitment and takes concrete and effective action *for* full co-operation with the ICTY.' See Council Conclusions of 12 February 2007, in Press Release No. 6037/07 (Presse 18), at 13 (emphasis added).

[101] See 'Del Ponte again urges EU not to resume SAA talks with Serbia', *Southeast European Times*, 16 February 2007.

[102] For the counterarguments, see G. Evans and J. Lyons, 'No Mladic, no talks', *International Herald Tribune*, 21 March 2007; and S. Freizer and A. Stroehlein, 'The EU's inexcusable pardon for Serbia', *European Voice*, 29 March 2007.

of the past and to promote tolerance and reconciliation. In this respect, recent judgments by Bosnian, Croatian and Serbian courts convicting war criminals to long prison sentences should be taken as a positive sign.[103] Hence, the European Union was right to look at the broader picture and no longer outsource the decision-making on compliance with ICTY conditionality to the single-minded Chief Prosecutor of the Tribunal.

4. The revised procedure for accession negotiations

4.1 Protecting the Union

The European Council, at its 16-17 December 2004 summit in Brussels, agreed on a revised framework for every future round of accession negotiations, to be created 'according to own merits and specific situations and characteristics of each candidate state.'[104] It adopted this new approach to soothe worries in some Member States over its decision to open accession talks with Turkey (most vocally Cyprus, France and Austria),[105] and to a lesser extent with Croatia (the Netherlands, the United Kingdom and Italy).[106] The European Council stressed, for instance, that long transition periods, derogations and specific arrangements could in the future be imposed in areas such as freedom of movement of persons, structural policies or agriculture.[107] The proliferation of different sorts of transitional arrangements in previous accession treaties[108] and the safeguard clauses taken up in the sixth Accession Treaty with Bulgaria and Romania are indicative in this respect.[109] With respect to the latter, the proper use of a membership postponement clause, i.e., in the absence of a promised date of entry (which is the new norm), an economic safeguard clause, and internal market and JHA safeguard clauses are temporary measures which could act as a powerful lever for reform. More prob-

---

[103] See, e.g., 'Croatian Court Charges Glavas, Six Others with 1991 Crimes Against Ethnic Serbs', *Southeast European Times*, 11 April 2007; N. Wood, 'Serbian court convicts 4 in Srebrenica murders', *International Herald Tribune*, 10 April 2007; and N. Wood, 'Serbia praised over trials of alleged war criminals', *International Herald Tribune*, 3 January 2006.

[104] See *Bull. EU* 12-2004, point I.8.23.

[105] For background and analysis, see E. Lenski, 'Turkey (including Northern Cyprus)', in S. Blockmans and A. Łazowski (eds.), *supra* n. 1, pp. 283-313.

[106] See *supra* sections 2.2.3 and 3.3.

[107] And all matters relating to freedom of movement of persons would allow 'a maximum role of [those] individual Member States' that are afraid that their labour market will be flooded with Turkish workers. The European Council emphasised that transitional arrangements or safeguards should be reviewed regarding their impact on competition or the functioning of the internal market.

[108] See, e.g., K. Inglis, 'The Union's Fifth Accession Treaty: New Means to Make Enlargement Possible', 41 *CML Rev.* (2004), pp. 937-973; and K. Inglis, 'The Accession Treaty and its Transitional arrangements: A Twilight zone for the New members of the Union', in C. Hillion (ed.), *supra* n. 84, pp. 77-109.

[109] See A. Łazowski, 'And Then They Were Twenty-Seven … A Legal Appraisal of the Sixth Accession Treaty', 44 *CML Rev.* (2007), pp. 401-430, at pp. 410-419.

lematic is the fact that the European Council even went as far as to suggest that *permanent* safeguard clauses, defined as 'clauses which are permanently available as a basis for safeguard measures', could be imposed.[110] Although the introduction of permanent safeguard clauses seems reasonable from the political point of view of some Member States, it is highly questionable for a 'constitutional' order such as that of the European Union, for it would violate one of the most fundamental legal principles upon which the single market is built: the prohibition of discrimination on the ground of nationality.[111]

Like in previous pre-accession rounds, all Member States will take part in chapter-by-chapter negotiations with each candidate. But there will be more chapters to be negotiated by present and future candidate countries. Instead of the 31 chapters that Bulgaria and Romania had to negotiate, Croatia and Turkey are looking at 35 chapters. This is the result of both a technical rearrangement – certain chapters were considered to be too lengthy and were chopped up, smaller ones were merged[112] – and the introduction of a new package on judiciary and human rights. The latter reflects a normative advancement in comparison with previous rounds of accession negotiations, because the political Copenhagen criteria on respect for democracy, human rights and the rule of law have now been incorporated in a so-called '*acquis* chapter.' From now on, candidate countries will have to show that they have the administrative capacity to effectively apply and implement the *acquis* on human rights and – crucially when dealing with the countries of South Eastern Europe – minority rights.

4.2 Benchmarking

Another novelty in the revised procedure agreed to by the December 2004 European Council concerns the right of the Council, acting by unanimity on a proposal by the Commission, to lay down benchmarks for the provisional closure and, where appropriate, for the (re)opening of each chapter. Depending on the chapter concerned, these benchmarks will refer to legislative alignment and a satisfactory track

---

110 See *Bull. EU* 12-2004, point I.8.23.

111 See U. Becker, 'EU-Enlargements and Limits to Amendments of the EC Treaty', 15 *Jean Monnet Working Paper* (2001), available at <http://www.jeanmonnetprogram.org>; A. Bodnar, 'Transitional Periods for Employment – 'Second Class' EU Citizenship?', in O. Zetterquist (ed.), *Law and Modernity* (Cracow, Polpress 2004); pp. 121-138; C. Hillion, 'The European Union is dead. Long live the European Union…', 29 *EL Rev.* (2004), pp. 583-612, at p. 593; and C. Hillion, 'You Cannot Have Your Cake and Eat It! The Limits to Member States' Discretion in EU Enlargement Negotiations', Inaugural lecture, Leiden University, 21 March 2006. For a more optimistic view, see D. Thym, *Ungleichzeitigkeit im Europäischen Verfassungsrecht* (Baden-Baden, Nomos 2002), p. 341.

112 For example, the chapter on the free movement of persons was divided into a chapter on the free movement of workers and the one dealing with the right of establishment and the free movement of services; the chapter on agriculture was separated into a chapter on agriculture and rural development and one on food safety, veterinary and phytosanitary policy. On the other hand, the chapters on industrial policy and small and medium-sized enterprises were merged into one chapter on enterprise and industrial policy.

record of implementation of the *acquis* as well as obligations deriving from contractual relations with the European Union. Thus, after agreement has been reached between the European Union and the candidate country on an individual chapter of the negotiations and once the set benchmarks have been met, the respective chapter is considered temporarily closed. The formal decision is made by the Intergovernmental Conference at ministerial level. If, before the Accession Treaty has been concluded, a new *acquis* falling within the scope of a specific chapter is developed or if the candidate country does not meet the set benchmarks or obligations assumed under the respective chapter, negotiations on that chapter can be reopened. The revised procedure thus provides for an extra 'big stick' to make sure that candidate countries *deliver* on each of the chapters – something about which the Commission had become distrustful after the experiences in the fifth round of enlargement negotiations. In fact, the December 2004 European Council stated that the new frameworks for negotiations would be established by the Council on a proposal by the Commission, 'taking account of the experience of the fifth enlargement process and of the evolving *acquis*.' Under the terms of the frameworks, 'the shared objective of the negotiations is accession', but 'the outcome cannot be guaranteed beforehand'. In one way, the European Council merely stated the obvious, namely that accession negotiations have – and have always had – an open-ended character. But the political signal towards new candidate countries cannot be underestimated: they have to comply with the conditions and stick to the rules or see their pre-accession path (partially) blocked by the European Union. In cases where a candidate seriously and persistently breaches the principles of liberty, democracy, respect for human rights, fundamental freedoms and the rule of law, negotiations can be suspended altogether. In such a case, the Commission will, on its own initiative or at the request of one third of the Member States, recommend the suspension of negotiations and propose the conditions for eventual resumption. The Council will decide by qualified majority on such a recommendation, after having heard the candidate state, whether to suspend the negotiations and on the conditions for their resumption. The procedure further prescribes that Member States will act in the IGC in accordance with the Council decision, without prejudice to the general requirement for unanimity in the IGC, and that the European Parliament will be informed. However, if a candidate is not in a position to assume, in full, all the obligations of membership – diplomatic language for a failure in negotiating accession – the European Union will nevertheless ensure 'that the candidate state concerned is fully anchored in the European structures through the strongest possible bond.' Supposedly, the old-time candidate would then fall back to its associate status.

Negotiating chapters that are expected to raise difficulties in the accession processes with the current candidate countries are agriculture and rural development, food safety, veterinary and phytosanitary policy, environment, free movement of capital (in view of the currently very tolerant laws which allow European Union citizens to purchase real estate), competition policy (in view of the fact that these countries spend a greater percentage of their national wealth on state aid to companies than any European Union Member State), and judiciary and human rights (rights of minorities, refugee return, impartial prosecution of war crimes trials, judicial and public administration reform, fighting corruption).

5. Concluding remarks

In the wake of the 'big bang' enlargement of the European Union and the 'No' votes in France and the Netherlands on the ratification of the Constitutional Treaty, the Union's enlargement plans became snarled up in a much larger debate between groups of Member States that disagree about the long-term objectives of the , its shape and final borders. As a result, the institutional arrangements needed to take in today's (potential) candidate countries are up in the air. At the 'widening' side of the equation, recent developments have prompted the European Union to reinforce the guiding principle of the pre-accession process: the principle of conditionality. With conditionality now firmly and explicitly built into all phases of the pre-accession process, the countries of South Eastern Europe have a clearly marked path to follow, conscientious of the consequences of not abiding by the conditions imposed upon them by the EU: suspension or cancellation of political negotiations, financial and technical assistance and – *in extremis* – contractual relations.

While EU membership conditionality leads, by definition, to bilateralism and competition, South Eastern Europe also requires a region-wide strategy to prevent the emergence of new 'black holes' in the map of Europe (e.g., Kosovo and Bosnia-Herzegovina). For the Western Balkan countries in particular, it is imperative that they be involved in setting a regional cooperation agenda through political dialogue. However, the structural tension between a regional approach and bilateral conditionality may endanger the coherence of international action towards a region still known to many as a powder keg. After all, the best pupils of the class will 'leave' the region by acquiring a different contractual status in their relations with the Union, thereby increasing rather than reducing the disparities within the region. Such disparities can be prevented by locking the countries of the Western Balkans in an economic process from which they cannot escape. The export and extension of the *acquis communautaire* in several domains of the internal market, whether through sectoral agreements such as the Energy Community Treaty or multilateral agreements such as CEFTA, is a good way to marry the (potential) candidate countries' wishes for enhanced bilateralism with the Union's desire for sustained reform efforts and enhanced multilateralism in South Eastern Europe. In a way, European integration history is repeated in the South Eastern corner of the continent.

The European Union could consolidate its enlargement agenda for South Eastern Europe even further by reinforcing the countries' prospect of future EU membership. It is important that the Union does not give the impression that membership is too distant, as this might lead to rapid domestic deterioration. The confirmation of a tangible prospect of EU membership is the most powerful instrument for the transformation of (potential) candidate countries as it gives the governments a strong incentive and clear message to convince their electorates of the advantages of ethnic reconciliation and the tightening of belts to reform their countries' economic, administrative and legislative structures. The experience of the CEECs illustrates best how the institutionalisation of the EU integration perspective is the most efficient way to foster and accelerate the overall political, economic, administrative and legal reforms in aspirant countries. I have argued elsewhere that a so-called 'Helsinki moment' should be created, in reference to the historic decision of the European Council gathered at Helsinki in December 1999 to grant candidate country status to Turkey.[113] In a similar historic spirit, the European Council should use one of its forthcoming summits to review the achievements of the potential candidate countries in satisfying the 'Copenhagen plus' criteria and grant candidate country status to Albania, Bosnia-Herzegovina, Montenegro, Serbia and – if independent – Kosovo, once these countries have submitted their applications for membership. All countries (including FYROM in case accession negotiations would still not have been opened) should then be presented with their accession roadmaps. This does not mean that all Western Balkan countries should join the European Union at the same time; each country's individual pace of reform will define the speed with which it integrates with the European Union. What it means is an end to the growing fears of some countries that they might be left out of the accession process altogether. The summit should be held soon after the last SAA will have entered into force. Working on the assumption that the European Commission will meet its ambition to conclude the remaining SAAs in 2007, a new 'Helsinki moment' could come as early as in 2008. To that end, popular anxiety over any further EU enlargements, now very apparent in the internal politics of some Member States, should be countered, for – indeed – the European Union 'cannot take a sabbatical' from enlargement while it sorts out its internal rules.[114] Convincing the enlargement-wary citizens of the Union will not be an easy task, but it is necessary if the European Union wants to keep a firm grip on its most effective foreign policy tool for stabilising troubled countries or regions on its borders. A consolidated and recalibrated enlargement process based on a tough love approach may well provide a strong argument in favour of further widening the European Union.

---

[113] See *supra* n. 86, pp. 312-313.

[114] Dixit Olli Rehn, quoted in G. Parker and C. Condon, 'Some Balkan states may find EU's door closed', *Financial Times*, 7 April 2006.

Chapter 5
BOX OF CHOCOLATES INTEGRATION: THE EUROPEAN ECONOMIC AREA AND THE SWISS MODEL REVISITED

Adam Łazowski

1. Introduction

The current discourse on the future of the European Union is dominated by a search for a solution to a true conundrum: how to reconcile deepening with widening. What should be the next step for the European Union? Is the further integration of its 27 Member States a good and realistic scenario? If so, which areas shall be considered as a priority? What about future enlargements of the European Union? Shall this successful policy tool be employed to expand the area of prosperity and stability to the newly born democracies in the Western Balkans and, potentially, to some of the ex Soviet Union countries or even Turkey? Maybe there is an alternative way to achieve gradual integration without immediate membership in the European Union, not undermining the Union's absorption and functioning capacity? Is such an alternative able to meet the needs of both sides? In this paper an attempt is made to explore such alternative models to EU membership.

The relations of the European Union with its geographical neighbours take different forms and are characterised by varying intensity.[1] Although certain policies employed in relations with particular countries can be grouped, *inter alia*, under the umbrellas of the European Neighbourhood Policy or the Stabilisation and Association Process, the detailed arrangements are tailor-made, aimed at benefiting the parties concerned. Bearing this in mind, it is hardly surprising that the intensity and the scope of cooperation varies. In very general terms one may argue that the cooperation takes the form of co-existence cooperation and integration cooperation. In the case of countries which fall under the ambit of Article 49 TEU such cooperation may take the form of pre-accession association with the European Communities, potentially leading to membership of the European Union. The experiences of the past two decades prove that enlargement serves as a successful policy tool for the European Union itself and as an incentive for political, eco-

[1] For an overview of the EU's relations with all its geographical neighbours see S. Blockmans and A. Łazowski (eds.), *The European Union and Its Neighbours. A Legal Appraisal of the EU's Policies of Stabilisation, Partnership and Integration* (The Hague, T.M.C. Asser Press 2006).

S. Blockmans and S. Prechal, eds., Reconciling the Deepening and Widening of the EU

nomic and legal reforms in neighbouring countries.[2] While the number of potential entrants, which have directly or indirectly expressed a desire to accede, is quite impressive, there are countries that, so far, have opted for other forms of integration than membership.[3] The element that differentiates the European Economic Area and the Swiss model from the other neighbourhood policies are integration elements underpinning both frameworks. To this end, they may be referred to as enhanced multilateralism and enhanced bilateralism. The first notion covers frameworks allowing for multidimensional or sectoral integration of groups of countries with the European Community/Union and their Member States. The primary example is the European Economic Area, the most recent, albeit of a sectoral character, is the Energy Community.[4] The enhanced bilateralism model is being employed in the EC/EU's relations with the Swiss Confederation. The parties are bound by a jigsaw puzzle of agreements, out of which two packages of bilateral agreements are of the outmost importance.[5] What merits attention is the fact that the concepts of enhanced multilateralism and bilateralism are theoretically not *per se* mutually exclusive. On the contrary, both may serve as frameworks for the relationship with a country or a group of countries. The end-result of the discussed models is partial integration with the European Union that reflects a box of chocolates, with different layers and juicy pieces to choose from.

The purpose of this article is to take a closer look at the European Economic Area and the Swiss model as examples of enhanced multilateralism and bilateralism (respectively). It is argued that neither of them is capable of being directly applied in the relations with those countries; however, certain well-established elements inherent in those models may potentially serve as a source of inspiration or even a blueprint for the future shape of the EU's relations with some of its neighbouring countries. The starting point of this paper is the presentation of basic elements underpinning the relations between the EFTA countries and the European Union on the one hand, and then Switzerland and the European Union on the

[2] For a legal appraisal of the fifth and sixth enlargements see, *inter alia*, A. Ott and K. Inglis (eds.), *Handbook on European Enlargement. A Commentary on the Enlargement Process* (The Hague, T.M.C. Asser Press 2002); M. Cremona (ed.), *The Enlargement of the European Union* (Oxford, Oxford University Press 2003); C. Hillion (ed.), *EU Enlargement. A Legal Approach* (Oxford, Hart Publishing 2004).

[3] At the time of writing the official candidates include Croatia, Turkey, and the Former Yugoslav Republic of Macedonia. The negotiations with the first two are pending albeit subject to political difficulties in the case of Turkey. Besides, there are a number of countries whose foreign policies are oriented towards EU membership, though formal applications have not yet been submitted. This includes the remaining countries of the Western Balkans as well as Ukraine and Georgia.

[4] The Energy Community Treaty, *OJ* 2006 L 198/18.

[5] For a general overview see, *inter alia*, M. Vahl and N. Grolimund, *Integration without Membership. Switzerland's Bilateral Agreements with the European Union* (Brussels, Centre for European Policy Studies 2006); A. Łazowski, 'Switzerland', in S. Blockmans and A. Łazowski (eds.), *supra* n. 1, p. 147; L. Goetschel, 'Switzerland and European Integration: Change Through Distance', 8 *EFA Rev.* (2003), p. 313; S. Breitenmoser, 'Sectoral agreements between the EC and Switzerland: Contents and Context', 40 *CML Rev.* (2003), p. 1137; F. Emmert, 'Switzerland and the EU: Partners, for Better or for Worse', 3 *EFA Rev.* (1998), p. 367.

other. This is followed by the analysis of a conundrum: how to reconcile the prerequisite of the uniform application of EU law with the fact that the EEA Agreement as well as EC-Swiss Agreements have less ambitious aims than the founding treaties of the European Union. Finally, an attempt is made to predict the future scenarios – the perspectives for both frameworks and their potential application to other neighbours of the European Union.

2. The basics: what do the enhanced multilateralism and bilateralism amount to?

2.1 General remarks

One of the aims of the European Economic Area was the creation of a common economic space between the EFTA countries and the EEC (now EC/EU) members.[6] This factor *per se* implied multidimensional cooperation in integration. The bilateral agreements with Switzerland have less ambitious aims; nevertheless, there are plenty of integration flavours therein. Not only do some of the provisions of the EEA Treaty and bilateral treaties with Switzerland mirror provisions of the Treaty establishing the European Community, but also annexes to those treaties contain exhaustive lists of EC secondary legislation applicable to the EEA-EFTA countries and the Swiss Confederation. The principle of homogeneity underpins the enhanced multilateralism and enhanced bilateralism. In technical terms the third countries have the obligation to apply relevant EC legislation and to interpret particular norms in the light of the case-law of the European Court of Justice. This might be difficult in practice, bearing in mind the different aims of the European Community, the European Economic Area and the EC/EU-Swiss Agreements.

The type of obligation inherent in the two discussed models differs considerably from the notion of 'approximation' employed by the European Communities in numerous association agreements with other geographical neighbours. The latter are characterised by the best endeavours clauses implying the obligation to act, not the obligation to achieve the result.[7] Even the reinterpretation of the Europe Agreements and their transformation into the pre-accession vehicles did not bring them any closer to the type of obligation accepted by the EEA-EFTA countries and Switzerland.

This very basic overview would not be complete without a brief analysis of the substance of the EEA Agreement and the EC/EU Swiss Agreements. The first pro-

[6] For more on the history of the European Economic Area see, *inter alia*, S. Norberg, K. Hökborg, M. Johansson, D. Eliasson and L. Dedichen, *EEA Law. A Commentary on the EEA Agreement*, 1st edn. (Stockholm, Fritzes Wolters Kluwer Sweden 1993); M. Robinson, J. Findlater (eds.), *Creating a European Economic Space: Legal Aspects of EC-EFTA Relations* (Dublin, Irish Centre for European Law 1990).

[7] For a comprehensive overview see A. Łazowski, 'Approximation of Laws', in Ott and Inglis (eds.), *supra* n. 2, at p. 633.

vides for a multidimensional expansion of the internal market to the EEA-EFTA countries. The scope of the EEA Agreement spreads from the four freedoms of the internal market, through state aid and competition law to numerous flanking policies. The legal framework is composed of the EEA Agreement itself and numerous pieces of secondary legislation listed in the annexes to the EEA Agreement.[8] The latter are regularly updated in order to follow developments at the EU level. EC-Swiss relations are characterised by a considerable diversification of the legal framework. It is composed of over 100 international treaties, some of which date back to the 1960s. In practical terms the most important are the Free Trade Agreement[9] and a series of agreements falling under the headings of Bilateral I[10] and Bilateral II.[11] The

[8] One should not forget that the cooperation extends beyond the framework of the European Economic Area. For example, the association of Norway and Iceland with the Schengen *acquis* is based on a separate international treaty, concluded irrespective of the EEA ramifications. For a comprehensive early analysis of the issue, see H. Bull, 'The Schengen Cooperation and Norway', in P.-Ch. Müller-Graff and E. Selvig (eds.), *The European Economic Area – Norway's Basic Status in the Legal Construction of Europe* (Berlin, Berlin Verlag 1997) p. 141.

[9] Agreement between the European Economic Community and the Swiss Confederation, *OJ* 1972 L 300/191 (with subsequent amendments).

[10] Agreement between the European Community and its Member States, of the one part, and the Swiss Confederation, of the other, on the free movement of persons, *OJ* 2002 L 114/6 (hereinafter referred to as the 'EC-Swiss Agreement on the Free Movement of Persons'); Agreement between the European Community and the Swiss Confederation on Air Transport, *OJ* 2002 L 114/73 (hereinafter referred to as the 'EC-Swiss Agreement on Air Transport'); Agreement between the European Community and the Swiss Confederation on the Carriage of Goods and Passengers by Rail and Road, *OJ* 2002 L 114/91; Agreement between the European Community and the Swiss Confederation on trade in agricultural products, *OJ* 2002 L 114/132; Agreement between the European Community and the Swiss Confederation on mutual recognition in relation to conformity assessment, *OJ* 2002 L 114/369; Agreement between the European Community and the Swiss Confederation on certain aspects of government procurement, *OJ* 2002 L 114/430; Agreement on Scientific and Technological Cooperation between the European Communities and the Swiss Confederation, *OJ* 2002 L 114/468.

[11] Agreement between the European Union, the European Community and the Swiss Confederation on the Swiss Confederation's association with the implementation, application and development of the Schengen *acquis*, nyp (hereinafter referred to as the 'EC/EU-Swiss Agreement on Schengen'); Agreement between the European Community and the Swiss Confederation concerning the criteria and mechanisms for establishing the state responsible for examining a request for asylum lodged in a Member State or in Switzerland, nyp (hereinafter referred to as the 'EC-Swiss Agreement on Asylum'); Agreement between the European Community and the Swiss Confederation providing for measures equivalent to those laid down in Council Directive 2003/48/EC on taxation of savings income in the form of interest payments, *OJ* 2004 L 385/30; Cooperation Agreement between the European Community and its Member States, of the one part, and the Swiss Confederation, of the other part, to counter fraud and all other illegal activities to the detriment of their financial interests, nyp; Agreement between the European Community and the Swiss Confederation amending the Agreement between the European Economic Community and the Swiss Confederation of 22 July 1972 as regards the provisions applicable to processed agricultural products, *OJ* 2005 L 23/19; Agreement between the European Community and the Swiss Confederation concerning the participation of Switzerland in the European Environment Agency and the European Environment Information and Observation Network, nyp; Agreement between the European Community and the Swiss Confederation on cooperation in the field of statistics, nyp (hereinafter referred to as the 'EC-Swiss Agreement on Statistics'); Agreement between the European Community and the Swiss Confederation in the audiovisual field, establishing the terms and conditions for the participation of the Swiss Confederation in the Community

two packages of bilateral treaties are filled with integration flavours; therefore they meet the criteria of enhanced bilateralism. The substantive scope of those agreements is very broad. It spreads from the free movement of persons, air transport, and conformity assessment to association with the Schengen *acquis* and the participation of Switzerland in the European Environment Agency.

2.2 The institutional set-up

At this stage it is also important to take a look at the institutional set-up of both frameworks. The European Economic Area is characterised by a complex institutional arrangement, which has been referred to by Cremona as the 'Byzantine structure'.[12] The fulfilment of the ambitious European Economic Area aims required the creation of a sophisticated institutional set-up guaranteeing the effectiveness of the European Economic Area without, at the same time, undermining the autonomy of the EC legal order and its decision-making, on the one hand, and the sovereignty of the EFTA states, on the other. In order to evolve into a homogeneous area, the European Economic Area needed broadly empowered institutions encompassing quasi-legislative, executive and judicial powers. Moreover, only the creation of institutions capable of reacting to the natural development of EC law could secure the dynamic legal regime envisaged by the EEA Agreement.[13] Before the negotiations were initiated various concepts had already emerged, and it was clear that tailoring a functional institutional framework, which would be acceptable to all the parties, would pose a major challenge. Indeed, as Reymond rightly notes, during the negotiations it was 'mainly on the legal and institutional side that significant stumbling blocks appeared.'[14] The task was completed successfully, albeit with serious legal hurdles along the way. The original shape of the judicial architecture was challenged by the European Court of Justice in Opinion 1/91.[15] This led to the creation of a separate EFTA Court for the EEA-EFTA countries on the basis of a separate agreement concluded between the EEA-EFTA countries.[16]

---

programmes Media Plus and Media Training, nyp; Agreement between the Swiss Federal Council and the Commission of the European Communities with a view to avoiding the double taxation of retired officials of the institutions and agencies of the European Communities resident in Switzerland, nyp.

[12] See M. Cremona, 'The "Dynamic and Homogeneous" EEA: Byzantine Structures and Variable Geometry', 19 *ELR* (1994), p. 508 at p. 509.

[13] Ibid.

[14] C. Reymond, 'Institutions, Decision-making Procedure and Settlement of Disputes in the European Economic Area', 30 *CML Rev.* (1993), p. 449 at p. 451.

[15] ECJ, Opinion 1/91 of the Court of 14 December 1991. Opinion delivered pursuant to the second subparagraph of Art. 228(1) of the Treaty. Draft agreement between the Community, on the one hand, and the countries of the European Free Trade Association, on the other, relating to the creation of the European Economic Area [1991] *ECR* I-6079. For an academic appraisal see, *inter alia*, B. Brandtner, 'The "Drama" of the EEA. Comments on Opinions 1/91 and 1/92', 3 *EJIL* (1992), p. 300; H.G. Schermers, 'Opinion 1/91 of the Court of Justice, 14 December 1991; Opinion 1/92 of the Court of Justice, 10 April 1992', 29 *CML Rev.* (1992), p. 991.

[16] Agreement between the EFTA States on the establishment of a Surveillance Authority and a Court of Justice, *OJ* 1994 L 344/1 (as amended).

The European Economic Area is equipped with a so-called two-pillar institutional structure. It is composed of two kinds of bodies. The first are joint EFTA-EC institutions composed of representatives of both sides and the Member States. The second group consists of EFTA or EC institutions which were created to accommodate the needs of the European Economic Area or which previously operated within the respective institutional frameworks. The joint institutions include the EEA Council, EEA Joint Committee, EEA Joint Parliamentary Committee and EEA Consultative Committee. Surveillance is conducted by the EFTA Surveillance Authority and the EFTA Court.[17] The EEA-EFTA countries also established a Standing Committee, which was envisaged to serve EFTA countries as a forum for consultation and shaping common positions. On the EU side, the relevant authorities equipped with surveillance powers are the European Commission and the European Court of Justice.

One of the important characteristics of the bilateral relations between the European Communities/European Union and Switzerland is the lack of a uniform and coherent institutional structure. Cooperation can be effected at various levels, mainly in the framework of joint committees established by the bilateral agreements or, in some cases, in the comitology committees.

The political dialogue is conducted at the highest political level, but its intensity and the rank of the meetings depends mainly on the dossiers occupying the bilateral agenda. During the past decade, most (but not all) of the contacts were obviously dominated by the negotiation of both sets of bilateral agreements. It should be noted that the first general EU-Swiss summit took place on 19 May 2004 and that it focused mainly on the completion of Bilateral II. It is difficult to predict at this stage whether this model of governance at the highest political level will be practiced in the future (as it is, for instance, with Russia and Ukraine).

The institutional framework of the bilateral agreements is highly fragmented and does not include a single set of bodies equipped with powers extending horizontally to all agreements. On the contrary, almost every treaty is administered by a separate joint committee[18] that is composed of representatives of both parties.[19] An analysis of these agreements leads to the inevitable conclusion that most of the committees have similar functions and powers. They may differ from one agreement to another, but it is easy to identify some common denominators. In principle, the main tasks of the joint committees include the administration of the relevant agreements. In the case of selected agreements, the competencies of the joint committees also include dispute settlement. Committees are equipped with decision-making powers and may also have the authority to adopt technical amendments to

[17] For a general overview, see Reymond, *supra* n. 14.

[18] In the case of the EC/EU-Swiss Agreement on Schengen and the EC-Swiss Agreement on Asylum the joint body is called the 'Mixed Committee'.

[19] Details of the EC representation in those committees are regulated in Arts. 2-7 of the Decision of the Council and of the Commission as regards the Agreement on Scientific and Technological Cooperation, of 4 April 2002 on the conclusion of seven Agreements with the Swiss Confederation (2002/309/EC, Euratom), *OJ* 2002 L 114/1.

the existing treaty framework.[20] Detailed provisions on their operation and applicable procedures are included in the rules of procedure adopted by each committee. Joint committees may also set-up working groups. Practice indicates that joint bodies play an essential role in the everyday administration of bilateral agreements. This is particularly visible in cases where they are responsible for the technical adaptation of the treaties. Also, one should note the uniqueness of the EC-Swiss Agreement on Air Transport. The provisions on competition included in Articles 8 and 9 were clearly inspired by Articles 81-82 TEC. The enforcement machinery relies heavily on the EC institutional framework, with the European Commission lying at the heart of the enforcement machinery of the antitrust and merger rules.[21]

3. The conundrum: how to reconcile the prerequisite of uniform application and interpretation of EU law with the enhanced multilateralism and bilateralism?

3.1 Introductory remarks

One of the key integration factors inherent in the discussed models is the obligation imposed on the participating countries to apply selected pieces of the *acquis communautaire* and to interpret the latter in accordance with the relevant case-law of the European Court of Justice. Moreover, since the EU legal system is very dynamic and subject to developments on a daily basis, it had been necessary to tailor special procedural tools in order to secure the uniformity of the EEA and EC/EU-Swiss legal frameworks. The various means of achieving the homogeneity can be grouped into two categories – legislative as well as administrative and judicial. Both are analysed in sections 3.3 and 3.4 of this contribution. At this stage one has to acknowledge considerable differences between both models, reflecting the intensity of integration between the parties and the subtle differences of the aims and goals envisaged for their enhanced cooperation. Despite those modalities one element is just the same – the principle of the homogeneity of the legal frameworks that is a central element of enhanced multilateralism and bilateralism.

It is clear from the fifteenth *tiret* of the Preamble to the EEA Agreement that 'the objective of the Contracting Parties is to arrive at, and maintain, a uniform interpretation and application of this Agreement and those provisions of Community legislation which are substantially reproduced in this Agreement…'. To this

[20] See, for example, Art. 14 of the EC-Swiss Agreement on the Free Movement of Persons; Arts. 21-22 of the EC-Swiss Agreement on Air Transport; Art. 51 of the EC-Swiss Agreement on Carriage of Goods and Passengers by Rail and Road; Art. 6 of the EC-Swiss Agreement on Trade in Processed Agricultural Products; Art. 10 of the EC-Swiss Agreement on Conformity Assessment; Art. 11 of the EC-Swiss Agreement on Government Procurement; Arts. 3-10 of the EC/EU-Swiss Agreement on Schengen; Arts. 3-7 of the EC-Swiss Agreement on Asylum; Arts. 39-40 of the EC-Swiss Antifraud Agreement.

[21] Art. 11 of the EC-Swiss Agreement on Air Transport.

end, Article 6 EEA was tailored to secure the uniform interpretation of provisions originating in EC law throughout the whole European Economic Area. It provides that

> 'Without prejudice to future developments of case law, the provisions of this Agreement, in so far as they are identical in substance to corresponding rules of the Treaty establishing the European Economic Community and the Treaty establishing the European Coal and Steel Community and to acts adopted in application of these two Treaties, shall, in their implementation and application, be interpreted in conformity with the relevant rulings of the Court of Justice of the European Communities given prior to the date of signature of this Agreement.'

This obligation is reproduced in Article 3(1) of the Surveillance Agreement, but in the latter case its scope of application is limited to Protocols 1 to 4 and legislation listed in Annexes I and II to the Surveillance Agreement. It is interesting to note, however, that the EFTA Court has given this obligation a broad interpretation by also applying the case-law of the European Court of Justice to procedural provisions to which this obligation does not formally extend.[22]

In both cases, the obligation extends to ECJ case-law predating the signature of the EEA Agreement. For all subsequent case-law developments, both the EFTA Surveillance Authority and the EFTA Court have an obligation to 'pay due account' to ECJ case-law. However, the distinction should not be considered as a major practical challenge. As noted by Baudenbacher, 'the legally and politically important differentiation between old and new case-law disappears to a large extent.'[23]

In the EC/EU-Swiss framework the interpretation requirement does have such horizontal application. On the contrary, it is only relevant for the purposes of those agreements which impose the obligation on Switzerland to apply the *acquis communautaire*. Whenever this is relevant, parties shall take into account judicial developments predating the signature of Bilateral I and II. This is the case, for instance, with regard to the EC-Swiss Agreement on the Free Movement of Persons. Its Article 16(2) reads that 'account shall be taken of the relevant case-law of the Court of Justice of the European Communities prior to the date of signature.'

---

[22] See, *inter alia*, EFTA Court, Case E-2/94, *Scottish Salmon Growers Association Limited* v. *EFTA Surveillance Authority*, EFTA Court Rep. [1994-1995] 59; Case E-1/95, *Ulf Samuelsson* v. *Svenska staten*, EFTA Court Rep. [1994-1995] 145. In the case E-2/02, *Technologies Bau-und Wirtschaftsberatung GmbH and Bellona Foundation* v. *EFTA Surveillance Authority*, EFTA Court Rep. [2003] 52, the EFTA Court held 'Although the Court is not required by Article 3(1) of the Surveillance and Court Agreement to follow the reasoning of the Court of Justice of the European Communities when interpreting the main part of that Agreement, the reasoning which led that Court to its interpretations of expressions in Community law is relevant when those expressions are identical in substance to those which fall to be interpreted by the Court. As stated in *Scottish Salmon Growers* v. *EFTA Surveillance Authority* … this principle must apply equally to the issue of *locus standi* to bring an action for annulment' (Para. 39 of the judgment).

[23] C. Baudenbacher, 'The EFTA Court and the European Court', in Müller-Graff and Selvig (eds.), *EEA-EU Relations* (Berlin, Berlin Verlag Arno Spitz GmbH 1999) p. 70 at p. 73.

Subsequent case-law is brought to the attention of Switzerland, but its impact on the agreements may be determined by the joint committees. A similar provision can be found in the EC-Swiss Agreement on Air Transport and the EC/EU-Swiss Agreement on Schengen.

3.2 The nature of the European Economic Area and EC/EU-Swiss legal frameworks

Before looking at the conundrum outlined in the title of this section a brief look at the nature and characteristics of the EC/EU legal system is pivotal. As a result of this exercise a proper legal background will be set for the analysis of the legal nature of the EEA and EC/EU-Swiss legal frameworks. It is generally accepted that the European Communities have created a new legal order, different to classical public international law. As the European Court of Justice held in Opinion 1/91, 'the Community treaties established a new legal order for the benefit of which the States have limited their sovereign rights, in ever wider fields, and the subjects of which comprise not only Member States but also their nationals.'[24] Following the judicial developments of the past fifty years, the principles of primacy, direct effect, indirect effect and state liability lie at the heart of this unique legal system. None of them are regulated explicitly in the founding treaties; however, Article 10 TEC and the principle of loyal cooperation enshrined therein have served as a general legal basis for the judicial activism of the European Court of Justice. The uniform application of EU law in the 27 Member States is a prerequisite and a central feature of the legal system. In order to achieve this special administrative and judicial mechanism it had been set forth in the founding treaties. They include the infraction procedure based on Articles 226-228 TEC and 141-143 EAEC and the preliminary ruling mechanism, allowing national courts to refer questions concerning the interpretation of EC law to the European Court of Justice. Unlike the European Economic Area, membership of the European Communities (now the European Union) involves the transfer of the right to exercise certain sovereign rights, allowing the European Union to legislate within its attributed powers. The latter are very broad, spreading from the four freedoms of the internal market and competition law to employment, the environmental and consumer protection.

Bearing in mind these factors, one has to turn to the conundrum. The question is how to reconcile the prerequisite of the uniform application of EU law with the enhanced multilateralism and bilateralism? In other words, how to achieve full homogeneity of the legal spaces, while the aims and goals of the European Economic Area and EC/EU-Swiss cooperation are less ambitious than the ones of the European Communities and the European Union? Potential problems in the con-

[24] Para. 21 of the opinion. This conclusion draws upon the Court's earlier case-law, starting from the early landmark cases of the 1960s. See ECJ, Case 26/62, *Van Gend en Loos* v. *Nederlandse Administratie der Belastingen* [1963] *ECR* 1 at 12; Case 6/64, *Flaminio Costa* v. *ENEL* [1964] *ECR* 585 at 593.

text of the European Economic Area had been acknowledged by the European Court of Justice in Opinion 1/91. The Court held that 'divergences which exist between the aims and context of the agreement, on the one hand, and the aims and context of Community law, on the other, stand in the way of the achievement of the objective of homogeneity in the interpretation and application of the law in the EEA'.[25] The real problem lies much deeper than this. The nature of integration within the European Communities has led to the creation of the new supranational legal order. This is not the case with the European Economic Area or the EC/EU-Swiss model. Therefore the real question is whether the homogeneous interpretation of the same set of rules (for instance the *acquis* on the free movement of persons) is possible where the semantic contexts are so different.[26] Also, to what extent do the constitutional paradigms of the EC legal order spread to the enhanced multilateralism and bilateralism models discussed in this paper? One has to acknowledge that clauses similarly or even equally worded to Article 10 TEC can be found in the EEA Agreement as well as in some of the EC/EU-Swiss Agreements.[27] This factor *per se* does not imply that the interpretation similar to the one inherent in the case-law of the European Court of Justice shall be employed in relation to those provisions. On the contrary, in whatever context, it must take into account the *differencia specificae* of those legal frameworks.

This leads to the following pivotal question: what are the *differencia specificae* of the discussed legal regimes? Do the enhanced multilateralism and bilateralism lead to the creation of new legal phenomena, comparable to the supranational legal order of the European Communities? Or maybe this form of integration operates within the limits of public international law? When it comes to the European Economic Area, the answer to this question has already been provided by the EFTA Court. The situation is different with the EC/EU-Swiss framework. The practice so far has been fairly limited; moreover, the lack of a separate judicial authority similar to the EFTA Court reduces the potential for developments comparable to the European Economic Area.

The nature of the legal order created by the European Economic Area was discussed by the EFTA Court in the advisory opinion in case E-9/97 *Sveinbjörnsdóttir* v. *Government of Iceland*.[28] The EFTA Court argued (when justifying the application of the principle of state liability to the EEA Agreement), that

---

[25] Para. 29 of the opinion.

[26] European Parliament and Council Directive 2004/38/EC on the free movement of persons may serve as an excellent example. It has EEA relevance despite the fact that its roots are closely connected to the concept of the citizenship of the European Union, which does not go beyond the borders of the EU. As a result the same piece of legislation is applicable in different semantic contexts.

[27] For instance, Art. 17 of the EC-Swiss Agreement on Air Transport reads: 'The Contracting Parties shall take all appropriate measures, whether general or particular, to ensure fulfilment of the obligations arising out of this Agreement and shall refrain from any measures which would jeopardise attainment of the objectives of this Agreement.'

[28] EFTA Court, Case E-9/97, *Erla Maria Sveinbjörnsdóttir* v. *Government of Iceland*, EFTA Court Rep. [1998] 95.

'the EEA Agreement is an international treaty *sui generis* which contains a distinct legal order of its own. The EEA Agreement does not establish a customs union but an enhanced free trade area... The depth of integration of the EEA Agreement is less far-reaching than under the EC Treaty, but the scope and the objective of the EEA Agreement goes beyond what is usual for an agreement under public international law.'[29]

This line of reasoning was developed even further in the EFTA Court's judgment in *Ákæruvaldið (The Public Prosecutor)* v. *Ásgeir Logi Ásgeirsson, Axel Pétur Ásgeirsson and Helgi Már Reynisson.*[30] The EFTA Court concluded that the EEA legal order 'is characterised by the creation of an internal market ... the protection of the rights of individuals and economic operators and an institutional framework providing for effective surveillance and judicial review.'[31] By this means, the EFTA Court has argued for yet another new legal system, albeit placed about halfway between the European Communities and classical public international law.[32] This allowed the EFTA Court to search for a fair balance between the imperative of homogeneity and the different aims and lack of legislative powers of the European Economic Area.

From the very beginning, the application of fundamental principles of supremacy, direct effect, indirect effect and state liability of EEA-EFTA countries has been a key issue not only in academic discourse but also in legal practice. The debate is centred on the interpretation of Article 6 EEA, its exact meaning and the scope of its application. One should also acknowledge the eighth *tiret* of the Preamble to the EEA Agreement, which confirms the important role that individuals will play through the exercise of their rights envisaged by EEA law. An important role is also played by Protocol 35 to the EEA Agreement which provides that 'for cases of possible conflicts between implemented EEA rules and other statutory provisions, the EFTA States undertake to introduce, if necessary, a statutory provision to the effect that EEA rules prevail in these cases.' This provision is implemented in both Nordic countries.[33]

This legislative jigsaw puzzle led to opinions touching both extremes. In the early 1990s, for example, Van Gerven already argued for a broad and generous interpretation of the provision in question.[34] He based his proposal on three major

[29] Para. 59 of the opinion.

[30] EFTA Court, Case E-2/03, *Ákæruvaldið (The Public Prosecutor)* v. *Ásgeir Logi Ásgeirsson, Axel Pétur Ásgeirsson and Helgi Már Reynisson*, EFTA Court Rep. [2003] 185.

[31] Para. 28 of the judgment.

[32] As Sevon notes 'Although there are differences in other respects between the Community legal order and the EEA Agreement, it is clear from the above that the latter is far from a standard agreement under public international law.' L. Sevon, 'The Protection of the Rights of Individuals under the EEA Agreement', 24 *ELR* (1999), p. 373 at p. 380.

[33] For instance, section 2 of the Implementing Act in Norway reads as follows: Provisions of Acts of Parliament which serve to fulfil Norway's obligations under the Agreement shall in case of conflict prevail over other provisions which regulate the same matter. The same shall apply for a provision of an administrative regulation which serves to fulfil Norway's obligations under the Agreement [when it] conflicts with another such provision, or with a later Act of Parliament. Sevon, *supra* n. 32, p. 377.

[34] W. van Gerven, 'The Genesis of EEA Law and the Principles of Primacy and Direct Effect', 16 *Fordham International Law Journa*l (1992/1993), p. 955.

arguments. Firstly, Article 6 EEA is broad enough to cover both the principle of supremacy and direct effect (unless stated otherwise as in Protocol 35). Secondly, the differences in the aims and purposes of the European Community and the European Economic Area do not contradict the broad meaning of Article 6. Last but not least, the reasoning of the European Court of Justice only supports the broad meaning of the above-mentioned provision.[35] The President of the EFTA Court, Carl Baudenbacher, takes a softer approach and argues on the basis of practical experience that 'the EFTA Court went for what may be called quasi-direct effect, quasi-primacy, and full state liability.'[36] It proves that the EFTA Court did not adopt as generous an approach as suggested by Van Gerven, but that numerous issues connected with the application of the EEA Agreement at the domestic level and with the enforcement of the rights of individuals are inherent in its judicial practice. Starting from its early judgment in *Restmark*, the EFTA Court has tried to accommodate the effectiveness of EEA law with the limitations discussed in this section.[37] In this judgment, the EFTA Court concluded that

> 'Protocol 35 EEA on the Implementation of EEA Rules stipulates that the EFTA States are under an obligation to ensure, if necessary by a separate statutory provision, that in cases of conflict between implemented EEA rules and other statutory provisions the implemented EEA rules prevail. It is inherent in the nature of such provision that individuals and economic operators in cases of conflict between implemented EEA rules and national statutory provisions must be entitled to invoke and to claim at the national level any rights that could be derived from provisions of the EEA Agreement, as being or having been made part of the respective national legal order, if they are unconditional and sufficiently precise.'[38]

The EFTA Court developed its argumentation in the *Hördur Einarsson* v. *Icelandic State*.[39] In this context, it is particularly important to draw attention to the EFTA Court's judgments in *Erla Maria Sveinbjörnsdóttir* v. *Government of Iceland*[40] and *Karl K. Karlsson hf.* v. *Icelandic State*.[41] In both cases, the EFTA Court, drawing heavily on the case-law of the European Court of Justice, took the opportunity to develop the principle of state liability for a breach of EEA law.[42]

---

[35] Id., at p. 971.

[36] C. Baudenbacher, 'The Implementation of Decisions of the ECJ and of the EFTA Court in Member States' Domestic Legal Orders', *Texas International Law Journal* (2005), p. 383 at p. 386.

[37] EFTA Court, Case E-1/94, *Ravintoloitsijain Liiton Kustannus Oy Restmark*, EFTA Court Rep. [1994-1995] 15.

[38] Para. 77 of the judgment.

[39] EFTA Court, Case E-1/01, *Hördur Einarsson* v. *Icelandic State*, EFTA Court Rep. [2002] 1.

[40] EFTA Court, Case E-9/97, *Erla Maria Sveinbjörnsdóttir* v. *Government of Iceland*, EFTA Court Rep. [1998] 95.

[41] EFTA Court, Case E-4/01, *Karl K. Karlsson hf.* v. *Icelandic States*, EFTA Court Rep. [2002] 240.

[42] See, *inter alia*, S.M. Stefánsson, 'State Liability in Community and EEA Law', in C. Baudenbacher, et al., *The EFTA Court. Ten Years On* (Oxford/Portland, Oregon, Hart Publishing 2005) p. 145.

As already noted, it is far more difficult to determine the nature of the legal framework created by the two packages of bilateral treaties with Switzerland. Despite the clearly visible integration flavours it is not sensible to consider the developing framework in supranational terms. The aims and goal of the cooperation are certainly less ambitious than those of the European Communities or the European Economic Area. Moreover, the cooperation is dominated by traditional methods having their roots in public international law. Certainly, the lack of a complex institutional structure with a court equipped with powers similar to the EFTA Court shapes the type of cooperation and limits the potential of the existing framework.

3.3 Legislative methods for securing homogeneity

The legislative methods for securing the homogeneity of the discussed frameworks have one particular purpose – the adjustment of the EEA and EC/EU-Swiss framework to changes in the a*cquis communautaire*. One has to acknowledge the limited participation of Iceland, Liechtenstein, Norway and Switzerland in the EU decision-making procedures. This participation is primarily limited to the early stages of legislative procedures; therefore it is often referred to as decision-shaping. Participation in meetings of the working groups and various committees allows representatives of those countries to influence the shape of legislation; however, they do not have any voting rights when it comes to the final decision-making. At the same time mechanisms had been developed facilitating regular updates to the lists of the *acquis* which were binding on those countries. The main difference between the EEA and EC/EU-Swiss framework is the character of adjustment procedures laid down in those models. While the European Economic Area is often referred to as dynamic, the EC-Swiss Agreements provide for a static mechanism. In the case of the latter, the only exception is the EC/EU-Swiss Agreement on Schengen, clearly full of dynamic elements. Both are discussed in turn.

When it comes to the European Economic Are the EEA Joint Committee plays a central role in securing homogeneity. In this regard, one of its main tasks is to adjust the EEA Agreement and its annexes to developments in EC law.[43] Practice proves that this remains one of its core activities. For example, in 2003 it adopted 179 decisions incorporating 297 EC acts; this was followed by 181 decisions incorporating 309 pieces of EC legislation in 2004.[44] As already noted, the annexes to the EEA Agreement contain lists of EC legislation with EEA relevance and may be amended by decisions of the EEA Joint Committee. The relevant procedure is laid down in Articles 102-104 EEA. Following the adoption of the EC legislation, the relevant EU decision-making bodies have an obligation to transfer the new legislation to the relevant authorities of EFTA states. It is the task of the EEA Joint

---

43 See Arts. 98 and 102 EEA.

44 Annual Report of the Joint Committee for the Year 2003 on the Functioning of the EEA Agreement, Ref. No. 1034120, at pt. 1; Annual Report of the Joint Committee for the Year 2004 on the Functioning of the EEA Agreement, Ref. No. 1051228, at pt. 1.

Committee to secure the homogeneity of the European Economic Area legal space and to amend the annexes as quickly as possible in order to allow simultaneous entry into force of the legislation in the entire European Economic Area. The consent of all EEA-EFTA states is necessary and to this end an important role is played by the Standing Committee of the EFTA states. The decisions of the EEA Joint Committee are binding and require implementation by the EEA-EFTA countries.

If the achievement of consent runs into difficulties, the EEA Joint Committee will take all possible measures in order to secure a compromise. If unsuccessful, it will 'examine all further possibilities to maintain the good functioning of this Agreement and take any decision necessary to this effect.'[45] The time-limit is six months following the referral or the date of entry into force of the relevant legislation (providing the latter date is the later one). If, following the expiry of the deadline, a compromise is still not within reach, the affected part of the EEA Agreement, as determined by the EEA Joint Committee, is suspended. The already acquired rights and obligations of individuals shall remain unaffected. In such cases, the EEA Joint Committee still has an obligation to take all measures possible to secure a compromise and bring the suspension to an end.

It should be recalled that, formally speaking, legislative powers have not been transferred to the EEA Joint Committee. Therefore, under certain circumstances, the implementation of its decisions may require decisions by national parliaments or even referenda. To this end, Article 103 EEA provides for a special procedure, which was tailored to facilitate the fulfilment of constitutional requirements by the EEA-EFTA states without simultaneously undermining the EEA decision-making procedure. The entry into force of EEA Joint Committee decisions may be conditional on the fulfilment of the relevant constitutional requirements. Under certain circumstances, EEA Joint Committee decisions may also apply on a temporary basis.

Once a piece of EC legislation is brought within the ambit of the EEA framework the EEA-EFTA countries have the obligation to transpose the measures to national legal orders. Article 7 EEA provides that legal acts listed in the annexes to the EEA Agreement (as regularly updated by the Joint Committee) are binding on the parties and 'acts corresponding to an EEC regulation shall as such be made part of the internal legal order of the Contracting Parties.' Unlike in the EC legal order, regulations are not directly applicable and may be transposed into domestic legal orders. In case of delays in the transposition or any shortcomings in this respect, the EFTA Surveillance authority has the power to initiate an infraction procedure and to submit infringement actions to the EFTA Court.[46]

The arrangements are different in the bilateral agreements between the EC/EU and Switzerland. Moreover, there is no uniform model for all agreements falling under the umbrellas of Bilateral I and II. The impact of the developments in EC

---

[45] Art. 102 EEA.

[46] On the legal consequences of delays, see EFTA Court, Case E-3/97, *Jan and Kristian Jæger AS* v. *Opel Norge AS*, EFTA Court Rep. [1998] 1.

law was one of the key issues that had to be addressed during the Bilateral I negotiations. The choice was twofold. The parties could have decided to give the agreements a dynamic character, comparable to the European Economic Area, or a static one, by not creating an obligation to automatically adopt every subsequent amendment to the EC legal framework that could potentially be relevant to the agreements. The decision was not only of legal importance, but also carried considerable political weight. Indeed, as Breitenmoser notes, the EEA's dynamic character was one of the reasons for the EEA referendum fiasco in 1992.[47] Eventually, the parties decided to follow a less controversial, static model and placed the joint committees at the heart of the procedural machinery. In principle, the parties are bound by the relevant *acquis* existing at the time of signature, and the impact of every subsequent development in EC law may be determined by the joint committees. One should not forget, however, the different status of the EC-Swiss Agreement on Air Transport in this respect.

Similar to Bilateral I, some of the agreements falling under the umbrella of the second package require the application of the *acquis communautaire* in bilateral relations as well as the incorporation of some of its parts into the Swiss legal order. Relevant lists of legislation are included in the annexes or are mentioned in the core text of the agreements. The following agreements may serve as an example.

Under the EC/EU-Swiss Agreement on Schengen, Switzerland has an obligation to implement and apply the Schengen *acquis* listed in Annex 1 to the Agreement. This includes, *inter alia*, parts of the Schengen Agreement[48] as well as the Implementing Convention.[49] Moreover, it has an obligation to implement the listed decisions of the Executive Committee and directives and regulations listed in Annex B.[50] Unlike the 1999 package, the update machinery provided in the EC/EU-Swiss Agreement on Schengen has a dynamic character. By this means, even more integration elements are brought into the bilateral relationship. Article 7 of the EC/EU-Swiss Agreement on Schengen specifies that '[t]he adoption of new acts or measures related to the matters referred to in Article 2 shall be reserved to the competent institutions of the European Union.' Those measures shall enter into

---

47 Breitenmoser, *supra* n. 5, at p. 1159. In the referendum organized in 1992 Swiss nationals rejected the Agreement on the European Economic Area, thereby closing the door to Swiss participation in this framework.

48 Agreement signed in Schengen on 14 June 1985 between the Governments of the States of the Benelux Economic Union, the Federal Republic of Germany and the French Republic on the gradual abolition of checks at their common borders, *OJ* 2000 L 239/13.

49 Convention signed in Schengen on 19 June 1990 between the Kingdom of Belgium, the Federal Republic of Germany, the French Republic, the Grand Duchy of Luxembourg and the Kingdom of the Netherlands, implementing the Schengen Agreement of 14 June 1985, *OJ* 2000 L 239/19.

50 *Inter alia*, Council Regulation (EC) No. 1683/95 of 29 May 1995 laying down a uniform format for visas, *OJ* 1995 L 164/1 (as amended); Council Regulation (EC) No. 539/2001 of 15 March 2001 listing the third countries whose nationals must be in possession of visas when crossing the external borders and those whose nationals are exempt from that requirement, *OJ* 1991 L 81/1 (as amended); Council Regulation (EC) No. 1091/2001 of 28 May 2001 on freedom of movement with a long-stay visa, *OJ* 2001 L 150/4.

force simultaneously in the European Community, its Member States and Switzerland. This obligation may be compromised by a decision rejecting the legislation or by different transitional periods for the latter. Article 7 provides for a special procedure that will be applied in order to secure the transposition of new legislation in Switzerland. It is worth mentioning that, in certain circumstances specified therein, the agreement may be terminated.

The EC-Swiss Agreement on Asylum places on Switzerland an obligation to implement Council Regulation 343/2003/EC,[51] Commission Regulation 1560/2003/EC,[52] Council Regulation 2725/2000/EC[53] and Council Regulation 407/2002/EC.[54] It creates similar procedures to the EC/EU-Swiss Agreement on Schengen in relation to updates to the existing legislative framework and the determination of the relevance of ECJ case-law.[55]

It is also worth recalling the EC-Swiss Agreement on Statistics. A multiplicity of legal acts listed in Annex A to the agreement shall be binding upon the parties.[56] In the case of new EC legislation covered by the scope of the agreement, a static update procedure is foreseen. The procedure based on Article 4 of the Agreement is similar to the Bilateral I machinery.

3.3 Administrative and judicial methods for securing homogeneity

The EEA Agreement as well as the EC/EU-Swiss Agreements provide for a number of administrative and judicial methods for securing homogeneity. The EEA model is much richer and comprehensive as it is heavily inspired by the surveillance and enforcement mechanisms, which mirror the ones known from the European Union. As a matter of fact, the maintenance of a homogeneous legal space

---

[51] Council Regulation (EC) No. 343/2003 of 18 February 2003 establishing the criteria and mechanism for determining the Member State responsible for examining an asylum application lodged in one of the Member States by a third-country national, *OJ* 2003 L 50/1.

[52] Commission Regulation (EC) No. 1560/2003 of 2 September 2003 laying down detailed rules for the application of Council Regulation (EC) No. 343/2003 establishing the criteria and mechanisms for determining the Member State responsible for examining an asylum application lodged in one of the Member States by a third-country national, *OJ* 2002 L 222/3.

[53] Council Regulation (EC) No. 2725/2000 of 11 December 2000 concerning the establishment of 'Eurodac' for the comparison of fingerprints for the effective application of the Dublin Convention with a view of helping to determine the Contracting Party responsible for examining an asylum application in accordance with the Dublin Convention, *OJ* 2000 L 316/1.

[54] Council Regulation (EC) No. 407/2002 of 28 February 2002 laying down certain rules to implement Regulation (EC) No. 2725/2000 concerning the establishment of 'Eurodac' for the comparison of fingerprints for the effective application of the Dublin Convention, *OJ* 2002 L 62/1.

[55] See Arts. 4-7 of the EC-Swiss Agreement on Asylum.

[56] For example, Council Regulation (EC, Euratom) No. 58/97 of 20 December 1996 concerning structural business statistics, *OJ* 1997 L 14/1 (as amended); Council Regulation (EC) No. 1172/98 of 25 May 1998 on statistical return in respect of the carriage of goods by road, *OJ* 1998 L 163/1 (as amended); Council Regulation (EC) No. 1172/95 of 22 May 1995 on the statistics relating to the trading of goods by the Community and its Member States with non-member countries, *OJ* 1995 L 118/10 (as amended); Council Regulation (EC, Euratom) No. 1287/2003 of 15 July 2003 on the harmonisation of gross national income at market prices (GNI Regulation), *OJ* 2003 L 181/1.

had been one of the reasons for the creation of the sophisticated, yet complex, institutional framework of the European Economic Area. The situation is very different in the EC/EU-Swiss model where multidimensional executive and, sometimes, quasi-judicial powers are vested in the hands of joint committees. Moreover, the status of the subsequent case-law of the European Court of Justice reflects the static model of the cooperation.

The application of EEA provisions in the domestic legal systems of the EEA-EFTA countries is of pivotal importance, and the role of the EFTA Court in this respect must be emphasized. There are two main types of procedures which may be employed for that purpose. The first is the infraction procedure, the second are advisory opinions delivered at the request of national courts from the EEA-EFTA countries. Both are analysed in turn.

The EEA-EFTA surveillance institutions include the EFTA Surveillance Authority and the EFTA Court. As noted earlier, the powers and jurisdiction of both bodies are regulated thoroughly in the Surveillance Agreement. One of the main tasks of the EFTA Surveillance Authority is to ensure that EEA-EFTA countries fulfil all their obligations under the European Economic Area. To this end, Article 31 of the Surveillance Agreement provides the EFTA Surveillance Authority with powers to initiate infraction procedures before the EFTA Court. The concept of this procedure originates in Article 226 TEC, but certain differences are clearly visible. Firstly, the wording in the Surveillance Agreement is less elaborate in comparison to the TEC. Secondly, the Surveillance Agreement does not include an equivalent to Article 228 TEC (inserted by the Treaty of Maastricht), which allows the European Court of Justice to impose financial penalties on states not implementing Article 226 TEC judgments. Similar to its EC original, the infraction procedure is formally initiated and conducted by the EFTA Surveillance Authority only. The non-judicial mechanism of individual complaints has been developed allowing individuals to participate actively in the enforcement of EEA law, on the one hand, and improving the chances of detecting infringements, on the other. Like the European Commission under Article 226 TEC, the Surveillance Authority has a wide degree of discretion when it comes to submitting actions to the EFTA Court. They have to be preceded by a reasoned opinion. Similarly to the EC/Euratom frameworks, the EFTA Court will determine infringements by reference to the situation on the date set forth in the reasoned opinion.[57] Practice shows that infringements of provisions of the main body of the EEA Agreement as well as infringements of secondary law may lead to infraction procedures at the EFTA Court.

In the course of the past decade, the EFTA Surveillance Authority has taken the opportunity to initiate infraction procedures at the EFTA Court on a number of occasions. One high-profile example is *EFTA Surveillance Authority* v. *The Kingdom of Norway*.[58] The EFTA Surveillance Authority submitted that Norwegian

---

[57] EFTA Court, Case E-3/00, *EFTA Surveillance Authority* v. *The Kingdom of Norway*, EFTA Court Rep. [2000-2001] p. 73, at para. 39.

[58] EFTA Court, Case E-1/02, *EFTA Surveillance Authority* v. *The Kingdom of Norway*, EFTA Court Rep. [2003] 1.

legislation allowing explicit restrictions limiting certain posts exclusively to women was contrary to Articles 7 and 70 EEA,[59] as well as selected provisions of Council Directive 76/207/EEC.[60] In its defence, the Norwegian Government argued that although the contested measures openly discriminated against men, they were still justified in the light of the EC *acquis* and the case-law of the European Court of Justice. The EFTA Court did not share this position and declared Norway to be in breach of EEA obligations. The free movement of services and Icelandic law on the taxation of intra-EEA flights was at stake in *EFTA Surveillance Authority* v. *Iceland*.[61] Icelandic legislation allowed for a differentiated tax on internal and external flights, with the latter incurring the higher rate. According to the plaintiff, this was in breach of EEA obligations. The EFTA Court rejected the argumentation of the Icelandic Government based on the specificity of the country's geographical position and distance separating it from the other EEA countries. Another interesting example is the EFTA Court's judgment in *EFTA Surveillance Authority* v. *Liechtenstein*.[62] This time, the EFTA Surveillance Authority submitted that Liechtenstein banking law was contrary to Article 31 EEA and the freedom of establishment enshrined therein. The legislation in question created a requirement that at least one member of the management board and the executive management should reside in Liechtenstein. This, according to the plaintiff, amounted to covert discrimination, not justifiable under Article 33 EEA or on the grounds of overriding public interest. Having analysed its earlier case-law on the conformity of Liechtenstein's legislation with EEA law,[63] as well as the relevant ECJ case-law on freedom of establishment, the EFTA Court declared that Liechtenstein was in breach of EEA law.

Another important aspect of the EEA surveillance system is advisory opinions which may be delivered by the EFTA Court on the initiative of the national courts of EFTA countries.[64] The advisory opinions have their roots in the preliminary

---

59 The first provision declares that the secondary *acquis* listed in the annexes to the EEA Agreement is binding upon the contracting parties, while the latter creates an obligation to promote equality of genders.

60 Council Directive 76/207/EEC of 9 February 1976 on the implementation of the principle of equal treatment for men and women as regards access to employment, vocational training and promotion, and working conditions, *OJ* 1976 L 39/40.

61 EFTA Court, Case E-1/03, *EFTA Surveillance Authority* v. *The Republic of Iceland*, EFTA Court Rep. [2003] 143.

62 EFTA Court, Case E-8/04, *EFTA Surveillance Authority* v. *The Principality of Liechtenstein*, EFTA Court Rep. [2005] nyr.

63 EFTA Court, Case E-3/98, *Herber Rainford-Towning*, EFTA Court Rep. [1998] 205; Case E-2/01, *Dr. Franz Martin Pucher*, EFTA Court Rep. [2002] 44.

64 Domestic courts of EFTA countries may also request preliminary rulings from the European Court of Justice, providing that the state in question accepts the latter's jurisdiction (see Protocol 34 to the EEA Agreement on the possibility for courts and tribunals of EFTA States to request the Court of Justice of the European Communities to decide on the interpretation of EEA rules corresponding to EC rules). This has never taken place in practice, and the ECJ rejected its jurisdiction without such notification in Case C-321/97, *Ulla-Brith Andersson and Susannne Wåkerås-Andersson* v. *Svenska staten (Swedish State)* [1999] *ECR* I-3551 at para. 29.

ruling procedure, which has a firm and well-developed standing in the law of the European Union.[65] However, there are two key features which make them distinct from preliminary rulings. The first is the non-binding character of advisory opinions.[66] The second is that it is a right and not an obligation to make references (as it is in some cases with preliminary rulings).[67]

Article 34 of the Surveillance Agreement reads as follows:

> 'The EFTA Court shall have jurisdiction to give advisory opinions on the interpretation of the EEA Agreement. Where such a question is raised before any court or tribunal in an EFTA State, that court or tribunal may, if it considers it necessary to enable it to give judgment, request the EFTA court to give such an opinion. An EFTA State may limit in its internal legislation the right to request such an advisory opinion to courts and tribunals against whose decisions there is no judicial remedy under national law.'

As practice proves, advisory opinions are a very important part of the EFTA Court's jurisdiction. When it comes to procedural issues, it has followed the relevant case-law of the European Court of Justice. This relates in particular to such issues as the definition of a court or a tribunal and the admissibility of references. As far as the first is concerned, the leading judicial development is the *Restmark* case. The reference had been submitted by the Appeals Committee of the Finnish Board of Customs. The referring authority requested the interpretation of Articles 11 and 16 EEA (the prohibition of quantitative restrictions and measures having equivalent effect, as well as rules on the adjustment of state monopolies, respectively). The Finnish and Norwegian Governments and the EFTA Surveillance Authority submitted that the reference was not admissible since it was submitted by the Appeals Committee, which could not be regarded as a court or a tribunal within the meaning of Article 34 of the EFTA Surveillance Agreement. The EFTA Court followed the reasoning of the European Court of Justice and in a very casuistic way verified the nature of the referring body. This led to the conclusion that the Appeals Committee had fulfilled all the necessary conditions and that the reference was admissible.[68]

---

[65] For the general regime, see Art. 234 TEC and Art. 150 Euratom. For the special regimes, see Art. 68 TEC and Art. 35 TEU. For a detailed account of the preliminary ruling procedure, see, *inter alia*, L.N. Brown and T. Kennedy, *The Court of Justice of the European Communities*, 5th edn. (London, Sweet & Maxwell 2000).

[66] It is noticeable that in the first years of its operation the EFTA Court had a tendency to describe its decisions delivered in response to requests by national courts as 'advisory opinions'. This practice has subsequently changed and they are now described as 'judgments'.

[67] Under the general preliminary ruling regime, the courts from which there is no further remedy have an obligation to make references, albeit under certain limitations arising from *acte clair* and *acte éclairé* principles.

[68] See also EFTA Court, Case E-8/94 and E-9/94, *Forbrukerombudet* v. *Mattel Scandinavia A/S, Lego Norge A/S*, EFTA Court Rep. [1994-1995] 113; Case E-4/04, *Pedicel AS* v. *Sosial-og helsedirektoratet (Directorate for Health and Social Affairs)*, EFTA Court Rep. [2005] nyr.

Similar to the preliminary ruling regime, references will only be admissible when the EFTA Court's opinion is necessary for the referring court to adjudicate in domestic litigation.[69] This point was recently highlighted in the EFTA Court's judgment in *Paolo Piazza* v. *Paul Schurte AG.*[70] The reference from Liechtenstein's Princely Court of Justice dealt with the conformity of domestic legislation with the principles of free movement of services and free movement of capital (Arts. 36 and 40 EEA, respectively). Following the request of the EFTA Court, the referring court clarified procedural and factual issues. However, this did not stop the Government of Liechtenstein from claiming that the reference was not admissible due to the poor description of the facts and legal circumstances, as well as the potentially hypothetical nature of a reference. The EFTA Court emphasized that the advisory opinion procedure 'is a specially established means of judicial cooperation between the Court and national courts, with the aim of providing the national courts with the necessary elements of EEA law to decide the cases before them.' The EFTA Court then repeated the ECJ's reasoning and argued as follows:

> 'It is for the national court to determine, in light of the particular circumstances of the case, both the need for an advisory opinion in order to enable it to deliver judgment, and the relevance of the questions that it submits. Consequently, where the questions referred concern the interpretation of the EEA Agreement, the Court is in principle bound to give a ruling. However, the Court may not rule on a question, where it is quite obvious that the sought interpretation of EEA law bears no relation to the actual facts of the main action or its purpose, or where the issue is hypothetical.'[71]

The scope of advisory rulings is formally limited to the interpretation of the EEA Agreement. However, following its judgment in *CIBA Speciality Chemicals Water Treatment Ltd. and others* v. *Norwegian State*[72] it is clear that the EFTA Court will interpret this clause broadly as also covering the annexes to the EEA Agreement as well as the secondary legislation listed therein. However, this will not include the provisions of the EFTA which are formally not part of the EEA framework.[73]

Although the advisory opinions delivered by the EFTA Court are formally non-binding, they are followed by the referring courts. It should be added that if the

---

[69] Detailed guidelines for making reference have been published in a special note addressed to national courts. See Note for Guidance on Requests by national courts for advisory opinions, available at: <http://www.eftacourt.lu/default.asp?layout=article&id=129>.

[70] EFTA Court, Case E-10/04, *Paolo Pizza* v. *Paul Schurte AG*, EFTA Court Rep. [2005] nyr.

[71] Para. 21 of the judgment. See also EFTA Court, Case E-1/95, *Ulf Samuelsson* v. *Svenska staten*, EFTA Court Rep. [1994-1995] 145; Case E-5/96, *Ullensaker komune and Others* v. *Nille AS*, EFTA Court Rep. [1997] 30; Case E-2/03, *Ákæruvaldið (The Public Prosecutor)* v. *Ásgeir Logi Ásgeirsson and others*, EFTA Court Rep. [2003] 185; Case E-6/96, *Tore Wilhelmsen AS* v. *Oslo commune*, EFTA Court Rep. [1997] 53. In the latter case, the EFTA Court concluded that some of the referred questions were not admissible due to their hypothetical character.

[72] EFTA Court, Case E-6/01, *CIBA Speciality Chemicals Water Treatment Ltd. and others* v. *Norwegian State*, EFTA Court Rep. [2002] 281.

[73] EFTA Court, Case E-2/03, *Ákæruvaldið (The Public Prosecutor) against Ásgeir Logi Ásgeirsson, Axel Pétur Ásgeirsson and Helgi Már Reynisson*, EFTA Court Rep. [2003] 185.

national court is not satisfied with the reference and requires further assistance from the EFTA Court, there are no formal obstacles against submitting further references. This arrangement follows developments relating to the European Court of Justice and was officially confirmed by the EFTA Court in *CIBA Speciality Chemicals Water Treatment Ltd. and others* v. *Norwegian State*.[74] As already noted, advisory opinions have played an important role in the everyday application of EEA law in EFTA countries. They have served as a pivotal tool securing its uniform application and as an instrument for supporting the implementation of the principle of homogeneity (discussed in the following section). In many ways the EFTA Court is following in the footsteps of the European Court of Justice. A great example of its judicial activism, in which advisory opinions have played a significant role, relates to the principle of state liability adopted for the purposes of the European Economic Area from the EU legal order.[75]

The EEA Agreement provides also for the creation of an information exchange mechanism facilitating the transfer of new developments between the EC and EFTA courts. A central role is played by the EEA Joint Committee, which is also equipped with powers to keep under constant review the relevant developments in the EU judicature.[76] The EEA Agreement puts the EEA Joint Committee at the centre of the dispute-settlement mechanism, which can be used when difficulties arise in arriving at a homogeneous interpretation of the EEA Agreement. It is an interesting – albeit purely theoretical for the time being – example of the political procedure *par excellence*, which can be utilised in order to solve a legal dispute.

The right to take part in pending litigation is yet another tool created in order to secure the homogeneity of the European Economic Area. To this end, for example, the European Commission and the EU Member States may present statements and observations to the EFTA Court. On the other side, the EEA-EFTA countries may proceed equally at the European Court of Justice. It is noteworthy that the European Commission has proved to be very active in this respect.[77]

It cannot slip one's attention that the objective of achieving a homogeneous European Economic Area is not only fulfilled by the EFTA Court and the courts in the EEA-EFTA countries, but also by the European Court of Justice (and the Court of First Instance) and the domestic courts in the Member States. There are numerous examples of case-law dealing with this issue, moreover, where reference is made to the case-law of the EFTA Court.[78]

The EC/EU-Swiss model differs considerably in this respect. There are no similar administrative and judicial mechanisms, comparable to the ones envisaged within the European Economic Area. As already noted, the institutional framework is

---

[74] Para. 12 of the judgment.

[75] EFTA Court, Case E-9/97, *Erla Maria Sveinbjörnsdóttir* v. *Government of Iceland*, EFTA Court Rep. [1998] 95; Case E-4/01, *Karl K. Karlsson hf* v. *Icelandic States*, EFTA Court Rep. [2002] 240.

[76] See Arts. 105-106 EEA.

[77] For a detailed account of cases, see EFTA Court, *Legal Framework, Case Law and Composition 1994-2003* (Luxembourg 2004) pp. 26-27.

[78] See, *inter alia*, Baudenbacher, *supra* n. 42, at pp. 81-95.

very fragmented and composed of joint committees with mandates limited to particular agreements. This feature resembles the less ambitious aims of this form of enhanced bilateralism, operating in institutional terms within the limits of traditional models of cooperation with neighbouring countries. Having said this, one should pay particular attention to the EC/EU-Swiss Agreement on Schengen. Undoubtedly the powers of the Mixed Committee acting in the framework this agreement merit attention. In accordance with Article 10, the Mixed Committee has the authority, *inter alia*, to settle disputes arising from substantially divergent interpretations of the Schengen *acquis* by the European Court of Justice and the Swiss courts and administrative authorities. This permits the conclusion that the Mixed Committee has quasi-judicial powers. It must be remembered that in the case of a failure to settle the dispute, the EC/EU-Swiss Agreement on Schengen will be terminated.

So far, the homogeneity of the interpretation of the *acquis* has not proved to be a problem with detrimental consequences for the coherence of the legal framework, however in the long-term one might consider revisions in this respect. With more litigation based on EC/EU law daunting problems with the interpretation of the *acquis communautaire* seem to be inevitable. At this stage Swiss courts have no jurisdiction to submit references for a preliminary ruling to the European Court of Justice or to request advisory opinions from the EFTA Court.

There is no general framework for the exchange of information on new case-law of the European Court of Justice. However, some of the agreements impose an obligation on the parties to keep under constant review the developments in ECJ case-law. For instance, the EC/EU-Swiss Agreement on Schengen provides for the creation of a special mechanism to secure a regular mutual transmission of case-law. Article 9 of the agreement creates an obligation for Switzerland to submit reports to the Mixed Committee on the application and interpretation of the Schengen *acquis*. In the case of serious divergences, the powers of dispute settlement are vested on the Mixed Committee.

4. The conclusions: is there a future for enhanced multilateralism and bilateralism?

This paper explores the two alternative models of integration without membership in the European Union. As indicated in the introduction, both can be compared to a box of chocolates, where third countries are offered a variety of bits and pieces of the internal market. Such a choice is made with the consent of all the parties involved and for their mutual benefit. The question remains whether there is a future for those integration frameworks. Closely related remains the problem whether any of the models are employable in relations with other geographical neighbours of the European Union.

It seems reasonable to argue that the *status quo* will be maintained as long as the EEA-EFTA countries (especially Iceland and Norway) or Switzerland express no desire to arrange their relations with the European Union in other ways. Membership of the European Union shall not be excluded; however, for political reasons it seems to be a rather long-term perspective. In the short-term the further development of the existing frameworks is more probable. Interestingly enough, the steps taken in the past decade make further use of the enhanced bilateralism more probable than a revision of the Agreement on the European Economic Area. As already noted, the enhanced multilateralism and bilateralism are not *per se* mutually exclusive. In other words, there are no legal and political reasons why both models could be applied in relations with the same country/countries. One shall not exclude a revision of the EEA Agreement to bring it into line with changes introduced in the Treaty establishing a European Community. The corresponding provisions of the EEA Agreement are based on the post-Single European Act version of the EC Treaty and have not been revised since in order to take into account the changes introduced by the Treaty of Maastricht, the Treaty of Amsterdam and the Treaty of Nice.

The employment of either of the models to the relations with other neighbours of the European Union is another issue. The academic discourse in this respect is not a new phenomenon as already in the mid-1990s S. Peers argued that accession to the European Economic Area could serve as a short-term alternative to EU membership for the newly emerging democracies of Central and Eastern Europe.[79] At this stage of European integration it is tempting to consider the enhanced multilateralism and bilateralism as an opportunity for reconciling the widening and deepening dilemma. Membership in the European Economic Area could potentially be an option for countries like Turkey (bearing in mind the current stalemate in the EU accession negotiations), Ukraine, Georgia and a few others. Such a move should not be considered as *finalité*, but rather a first substantive step or an antechamber on the way to the European Union. This could have economic and legal benefits for all sides concerned. This would mean opening the internal market to those countries, albeit presumably subject to transitional periods in sensitive areas (i.e., the free movement of workers). It would also foster the reduction of economic disparities and improve the quality of the approximation of national laws with the *acquis communautaire*. To this end, the European Economic Area could replace the existing EU pre-accession instruments and, thanks to the EEA surveillance system, would ensure an appropriate level of compliance with EU membership requirements. Obviously there are a number of political factors making this option a science-fiction scenario. First, the European Economic Area had been tailored to serve as a bridge between the EFTA countries and the members of the European Economic Community. The three EEA-EFTA countries remain outside the European Union only because none of them has made the decision to accede.

[79] Peers argued that 'Although the EAs may serve well as an interim measure while the EA States become familiar with the EU legal system, a comparison of the EEA with EAs will demonstrate that membership of the EEA is the best way of preparing EA States for EU membership.' See S. Peers, 'An Ever Closer Waiting Room? The Case for Eastern European Accession to the European Economic Area', 32 *CML Rev.* (1995), p. 187 at p. 189.

Potential membership of other countries in the European Economic Area would require a multidimensional reformulation of the aims and goals of the European Economic Area. Secondly, it is very likely that, similar to the case of countries of Central and Eastern Europe, such a scenario would be considered as second-class membership, therefore unacceptable on political grounds. The other arguments against this scenario include the lack of a customs union within the European Economic Area (which could be an issue for Turkey, which already has one with the European Union), the lack of an equivalent to the Common Agriculture Policy and the lack of financial aid comparable to structural funds.

In this context the enhanced bilateralism model used in the relations with Switzerland must be treated with a degree of caution. Such a tailor-made net of bilateral agreements has proved to work well in this framework, however this does not mean that similar good performance may be achieved in relations with other third countries. Notwithstanding the risks associated with the guillotine clause it shall not slip one's attention that the benefits of such an arrangement may only be visible in relations with third countries having well developed administrative and judicial systems. The employment of such a model to countries suffering from serious problems in this respect would put the coherence of the EU legal framework at considerable risk and undermine its effectiveness. In more general terms this would lead to a proliferation of legal regimes, making the entire matrix incomprehensible.

Bearing the above in mind it is argued that the existing models will probably not serve as alternatives to EU membership; however, some of the elements inherent therein may be used as a blueprint for shaping the relations between the European Union and some of its neighbouring countries. On a more general level one has to acknowledge that with the existing models of enhanced multilateralism and bilateralism, an Europe of different speeds is not a mere theoretical notion, but rather a well established feature of European integration. This is not within the European Union itself, but in its relations with carefully selected neighbouring countries.

Chapter 6
ON THE EUROPEAN UNION'S INSTITUTIONAL CAPACITY TO COPE WITH FURTHER ENLARGEMENT

Fabian Amtenbrink

1. Introduction

The timing was anything but perfect: on the eve of the accession of Romania and Bulgaria to the European Union (EU) and at a time when yet another setback in the pre-accession negotiations with Turkey was on the horizon, the European Council in June 2006 announced '... a debate on all aspects of further enlargements, including the Union's capacity to absorb new members ...'.[1] Failing to provide any clues as to the meaning of its remarks, the European Council left plenty of room for speculation about the exact scope and impact of the Union's 'absorption capacity' on future enlargement rounds.

Already the Copenhagen European Council of 1993 had referred to '[T]he Union's capacity to absorb new members, while maintaining the momentum of European integration ...' as an important consideration '... in the general interest of both the Union and the candidate countries ...'.[2] Yet, as these observations were subsequently never transformed into a precondition for enlargement, they remained without practical consequences and were soon to be forgotten. Reintroducing this notion at a time when public support for a widening of the European Union is crumbling has made observers suspect that this time around the European Council could take things rather more seriously. After all, as the recent experience with the Treaty establishing a Constitution for Europe (TCE) highlights, a continuous loss of trust and credibility on the part of citizens in the European institutions and in the European Union as a whole may form a serious stumbling-block for the future of European integration.

This paper offers a contribution to bringing the pieces of the 'absorption puzzle'[3] together in examining what the EU's capacity to accommodate additional members may actually translate to in the institutional sphere and what consequences this may

[1] Brussels European Council of 15/16 June 2006, Presidency Conclusions (10633/1/06 REV 1), p. 18

[2] Conclusions of the Presidency, European Council in Copenhagen 21-22 June 1993, SN 1080/1/93 Rev 1, p. 13. Brackets added.

[3] *The Economist*, 'The Absorption Puzzle', Vol. 380, issue 8484, p. 50.

S. Blockmans and S. Prechal, eds., Reconciling the Deepening and Widening of the EU

have both for the European Union itself and for the prospects of any (future) candidate states to join the European Union. To this end, first the use of terminology by the various Community institutions is examined. What will emerge from this is that the terminology is anything but well defined. Moreover, to the extent that concrete proposals are made, it does not always become clear whether and to what extent these are necessary as a result of the negative impact that enlargement has on today's structures. Indeed, an analysis of the actual impact of further enlargement on the institutional framework is lacking.

Thereafter, the current institutional framework of the European Union is assessed. While it has to be emphasized that the impact of enlargement can and should be studied for all institutions and organs, do to the limited space available the present contribution is restricted to the institutional triangle, as formed by the European Parliament, the Council and the Commission, and to observing a number of major effects which enlargement has for the democratic legitimacy and efficiency of the European Union. What will emerge from this is that the current system is ill-fit (and indeed has been so for some time) to provide an institutional framework that is capable of addressing the challenges arising from a continuous widening of membership in the European Union.

In its third and final part, the contribution turns to the question of how at least some of the shortcomings of the present system could be overcome. In this context a critical look is taken at the TCE which, despite the uncertainties surrounding its coming into force, for some offers the solution to the challenges triggered by enlargement. However, an analysis of the TCE reveals that this assumption may be somewhat misplaced. In fact, further widening may call for more than a mere adjustment of the composition and the decision-making procedures within the confinements of the existing institutional framework.

2. Absorption, enlargement and integration capacity

While somewhat pretentiously declaring that '... the pace of enlargement must take the Union's absorption capacity into account ...' the European Council fell short of offering any meaningful definition in its conclusions.[4] Instead it called upon the Commission to provide a special report '... on all relevant aspects pertaining to the Union's absorption capacity ...' and referred the matter to the European Council meeting in December 2006 when a debate was supposed to take place on all aspects of further enlargements, including the Union's capacity to absorb new members.[5]

One may question the wisdom of openly utilizing a terminology which lacks a proper definition. It would have taken little imagination to predict the speculations and uncertainty that resulted from this communication blunder. Not only did it trigger misinterpretations and misunderstandings, but, moreover, also damaged the cred-

[4] Brussels European Council of 15/16 June 2006, *supra* n. 1, p. 18.
[5] Ibid.

ibility of the Union in the perception of (potential) candidate countries and created false expectations and fears. Enlargement critics could overenthusiastically appreciate the remarks as turning away from the Union's previous pro-enlargement approach, whereas advocates of further widening the Union were up in arms.[6] The term 'absorption capacity' has been criticized as being 'misleading' and 'intellectually dishonest'[7] and some have turned to outright sarcasm linking the European Council's seemingly new approach to 'communist-era toilet paper'.[8] The public outcry in some quarters can be easily explained by the suspicion left by the European Council's choice of terminology that the European Union is planning to take a tougher stance towards any future enlargements by introducing a new accession criterion, subjecting present and future candidate states to additional conditions.

In an apparent attempt to minimize any damage, soon after the publication of the European Council's conclusions the Commission President and a number of political leaders from the Member States publicly relativised and reinterpreted these statements. Moreover, in its 'Special report on the EU's capacity to integrate new members' the Commission refers to 'integration capacity' instead.[9] An explanation for this apparent deviation from the European Council's choice of words is missing in the report. The EP's Committee on Foreign Affairs and the Committee on Constitutional Affairs, both of which published reports independently of each other, were more outspoken in this regard. The so-called Stubb Report by the European Parliament standing Committee on Constitutional Affairs points out that the term 'absorption capacity' does not '... suitably convey the idea it aims to express, inasmuch as the EU does not in any way absorb its members, and therefore proposes that this expression be changed to "integration capacity"...'.[10] Apparently the expression struck a sensitive nerve with some MEPs which are concerned about the role of Member States in the EU structure. In the so-called Brok Report by the EP Committee on Foreign Affairs the term 'integration capacity' has been adopted without any further comment.[11] It is rather remarkable that the subsequent Presidency

---

[6] Also critical with regard to the vagueness of the terminology is M. Emerson, et al., 'Just what is this "absorption capacity" of the European Union?', working paper, Centre for European Policy Studies 2006, on-line available at <http://www.ceps.be> (last visited: 7 May 2007).

[7] Cf., e.g., F. Vibert, 'Absorption Capacity': the Wrong European Debate, Discussion Paper, 21 June 2006, on-line available at <http://www.openDemocracy.net> (last visited: 7 May 2007).

[8] *The Economist*, *supra* n. 3: 'The European Union: tougher and less absorbent than ever! It sounds like communist-era toilet paper.'

[9] European Commission, Communication from the Commission to the European Parliament and the Council on the enlargement strategy and main challenges for 2006-2007, Annex 1: Special report on the EU's capacity to integrate new members, COM (2006) 649 final.

[10] European Parliament Committee on Constitutional Affairs, Report on the institutional aspects of the European Union's capacity to integrate new Member States (2006/2226(INI)) A6-0393/2006, consideration No. 4. The report initially adds to the confusion by referring successively to 'institutional capacity', 'integration capacity' and 'absorption capacity'.

[11] European Parliament Committee on Foreign Affairs, Report on the Commission's Communication on the Enlargement Strategy and Main Challenges 2006–2007 (2006/2252(INI)) A6-0436/2006, cf., e.g., p. 3.

Conclusions of the European Council of December 2006 continue to refer to the 'capacity of the Union to absorb new members'.[12]

While a rather fruitless discourse on diction can thus be observed, a clear definition of what absorption, enlargement or integration capacity actually amounts to is notably absent in all of these documents. Those that were hoping for an extensive definition of the European Council's statement in the Commission's special report are let down by a document which, to a considerable extent, amounts to a self-serving plea in favour of further enlargement. What is missing is a detailed analysis of the impact of further enlargement on European integration or even a clear identification of factors that should become the basis for such an assessment.[13] The Commission observes rather broadly that the capacity of the European Union to take on new members should be assessed based on '[E]nsuring the EU's capacity to maintain the momentum of European integration', '[E]nsuring that candidate countries fulfil the rigorous conditions', and '[B]etter communication'.[14]

Of the three elements identified by the Commission arguably only the first – that is the EU's capacity to maintain the momentum of European integration – is actually linked to the structure of the EU system itself and, as such, can form the basis for a substantive review. For the Commission the three main components determining this capacity are institutions, common policies and the budget.[15] With regard to institutions, the Commission does not offer a structured assessment of the sustainability of the current institutional structure of the European Union against the background of future enlargement rounds. Instead it calls for a new institutional settlement to be concluded by the time of the next enlargement, pointing out that no arrangements for adaptations to the composition and functioning of the Community institutions in an European Union of more than the current number of Member States is currently foreseen with the exception of the future composition of the Commission itself.[16] The Commission emphasizes that '[T]he Union needs to ensure that its institutions and decision-making process remains effective and accountable'. The EP's Stubb Report states that '... before any future enlargement a reform of the European Union is essential to enable it to work more effectively, more transparently and more democratically ...', whereas the Brok Report points out '... that the integration capacity of the Union rests fundamentally on ... its institutional capacity to act and take decisions democratically and efficiently under new circumstances ...'.[17]

---

[12] Presidency Conclusions, European Council of 14-15 December 2006, 16879/06, p. 3.

[13] Moreover, the one and a half page section on the history of the EU's integration capacity adds relatively little to the discussion.

[14] European Commission (2006), *supra* n. 9, p. 20 et seq. Brackets added.

[15] As this contribution focuses on institutional aspects, issues related to the other two elements are not discussed.

[16] European Commission (2006), *supra* n. 9, p. 21, pointing out that the allocation of seats in the European Parliament and the weighing of votes in the Council are central to the EU's capacity to take decisions.

[17] European Parliament Committee on Constitutional Affairs, *supra* n. 10, p. 5; European Parliament Committee on Foreign Affairs, *supra* n. 11, p. 6.

To the learned student of European law these statements may sound all too familiar. Already at the time of the drafting of the Treaty on European Union Piris formulated the question 'After Maastricht, are the Community Institutions More Efficacious, More Democratic and More Transparent?'[18] And, indeed, the Commission itself points out that '[T]he EU does not need new institutional arrangements simply for the sake of enlargement; it also needs them so that the current Union can function better.'[19] Thus, masked behind a new terminology also seems to be one of the longest standing issues in European law – that is how the institutional design can ensure the Union's democratic legitimacy, efficiency and transparency. Not including the pending TCE, since the beginning of the 1990s alone, three consecutive Treaties have aimed to address this issue, whereby namely the institutional reforms foreseen in the 2001 Treaty of Nice were aimed at facilitating enlargement.[20] It introduced provisions allowing for an adjustment of the composition and the *modi operandi* of the Council, the European Parliament and the Commission and aimed at keeping the European Union operational when accommodating up to 27 Member States. Yet, before the ink on the documents was dry the discussion on the Nice leftovers commenced, as further enlargement was already on the political agenda.[21] The Declaration of the Laeken European Council of December 2001 referring to the challenges facing an enlarged Union explicitly observed the existence of a 'democratic challenge facing Europe' and referred to an European Union that '... needs to become more democratic, more transparent and more efficient'.[22]

Overall, the reference by the European Council and the Commission to the Union's future capability to widen and deepen is of such a broad nature that if considered in isolation there is hardly any danger of this ever being utilized as a condition for further enlargement. This may have been a politically-motivated deliberate choice in which case the reference to absorption, enlargement or integration capacity hardly amounts to more than window-dressing and a half-hearted attempt to address the concerns in the Member States that further enlargement will endanger the integration process. The Stubb Report clearly stands out in this regard as it includes a list of no less than 17 reform proposals related to the institutional structure of the European Union, ranging from '... the adoption of a new system of qualified majority voting that enhances the ability of the Council to reach decisions ...' to '... a clear definition of the values on which the Union is founded, as well as the objectives of

[18] J.-C. Piris, 'After Maastricht, are the Community Institutions More Efficacious, More Democratic and More Transparent?', *EL Rev.* (1994), p. 449

[19] European Commission (2006), *supra* n. 9, p. 20.

[20] Cf., Protocol on the enlargement of the European Union, annexed to the Treaty on European Union and to the Treaties establishing the European Communities.

[21] In the words of A. Duff, 'From Amsterdam left-overs to Nice Hangovers', *The International Spectator*, Vol. XXXVI, No. 1, January-March 2001, pp. 13-19.

[22] Laeken Declaration on the Future of the European Union of 15 December 2001 (hereafter: Laeken Declaration) section II para. 1.

the Union'.[23] The source of inspiration for these proposals is quite clear as the report points out that '... all these reforms are already contained in the Constitutional Treaty ...'.

This referral to the TCE and the general reference namely to democratic legitimacy and efficiency give rise to the question whether all proposals are actually directly linked to the effects of enlargement on the institutional framework of the European Union and as such must be understood as a *conditio sine qua non* for further enlargement. The rather diverse list of proposals in particular in the Stubb Report suggests that no clear distinction is made between the need for reforms resulting from the impact of enlargement on the institutional structure of the European Union and the shortcomings of the current EU system which stand apart. Put differently, what is missing is a more detailed analysis of the impact of further enlargement on today's institutional structure and an identification of the features of this framework that make today's system vulnerable to further enlargement. Such an analysis is essential not only from the point of view of the above-mentioned intellectual honesty in the EU's relationship with current and future candidate countries, but also in order to be able to identify which features of today's legal framework have to be amended in order to build a more 'enlargement-proof' institutional framework.

3. In search of the limits of the institutional framework

While the extensively documented challenges which the institutional framework of the European Union faces in particular in terms of democratic legitimation and efficiency emerged before the massive expansion of membership since the mid-1990s, the continuous need to incorporate new Member States into the existing legal framework of the European Union has certainly increased the pressure for continuous institutional adjustments. The Commission and EP reports do not identify the underlying reasons for this. It is presently submitted that this vulnerability has its roots in the complex structure of the European Union which its institutional framework has to accommodate. Indeed, the latter is aimed at maintaining multiple and multilevel equilibria between the Member States and between the citizens of the Member States, as well as between the national and supranational level, which includes the institutional balance on the European level. It is this unique feature of the European legal order that makes its institutions and namely the Council, the European Parliament and the Commission in their composition and decision-making procedures vulnerable to enlargement. Given the central role which these institutions play in the Union/Community legal structure, this has direct effects for the democratic legitimacy and efficiency of the European Union as a whole.

[23] European Parliament Committee on Constitutional Affairs, *supra* n. 10, pp. 6-7. The Brok Report supports these proposals.

3.1 Democratic legitimacy

The further widening of EU membership potentially weakens the existing main channels of democratic legitimacy and, linked thereto, the accountability of the European Union as provided by the Council and the European Parliament.[24]

Based on the allocation of voting rights to Member States, the complex qualified majority voting system applied in reaching the overwhelming majority of decisions in the Council proves to be rather vulnerable to an enlargement of the European Union and, consequently, is justifiably mentioned in the Stubb Report as an issue which needs to be addressed. Accommodating the accession of a new Member State to the European Union does not amount to mechanically assigning voting rights to the newcomer, as the balance in the Council between the existing and/or new Member States also becomes an issue. The current system combines elements of a proportionate representation of Member States with elements of a proportionate representation of the population of the Member States. As a result it does not fully qualify as either form of representation. Put differently, the system can be criticized for the lack of both. Different Member States are assigned different voting rights, whereby a cross-country comparison reveals that these voting rights do not accurately reflect the Member States' share in the overall population of the European Union.[25] This issue has been on the agenda literally since the introduction of qualified majority voting and has made the headlines during every enlargement round.[26] While smaller Member States fear being dominated by the larger ones, the larger Member States' joint concern is that the disproportionate increase in the number of smaller Member States will eventually result in a situation where they, and thus the majority of citizens in the European Union, are regularly outvoted by the former. The safeguard clause in the form of a double-majority requirement introduced into the EC Treaty by the Treaty of Nice corrects this imbalance somewhat in favour of the population requirement by providing Member States with a right to request verification that the Member States constituting the qualified majority represent at least 62% of the total population of the Union.[27] However, this arrangement cannot be put on an equal footing with a rule requiring that a qualified majority decision in the Council is *per se* supported by a number of Member States that reflect a majority of the population of the Union. Moreover, the smaller Member States feel that their fears are verified as larger Member States do not only command more votes, but also have a natural overweight when the 62%

[24] Generally with regard to the notion of democratic legitimacy and accountability in the EU cf., F. Amtenbrink, 'Towards a More Democratic Union? Comments on the Treaty establishing a Constitution for Europe', in K. Inglis and A. Ott (eds.), *EU Enlargement and the Future of the European Union: Unity in Diversity?* (Groningen, Europa Law Publishing 2005), pp. 31-55, with further references.

[25] Art. 205(2) TEC.

[26] Informative in this regard is V. Miller, 'The Extension of Qualified Majority Voting from the Treaty of Rome to the European Constitution', *House of Commons Research Paper*, No. 04/05, 7 July 2004.

[27] Art. 205(4) TEC.

rule is applied. This may be one of a number of reasons why some of the smaller Member States are rather sceptical about the prospect of yet another large country such as Turkey joining the European Union.

The democratic back-coupling of the Council and indeed its accountability is channelled through the governments of the Member States and ultimately rests on the shoulders of the national parliaments. In the Netherlands, in the Lower House of Parliament (*Tweede Kamer*) this task is primarily fulfilled by the standing committee on European affairs (*Commissie voor Europese Zaken*). Parliament is informed of each new Commission proposal by the government, whereby particular attention is paid to its legal basis, as well as the observance of the subsidiary and proportionality principle.[28] Moreover, the government informs Parliament in advance of the agenda of Council meetings and the positions it intents to take. Parliament discusses the government position both prior to and after the Council meetings. However, in the case of the Dutch Parliament, just as any other national parliament, there are limits to the extent that they can hold their own government and indeed the Council accountable. A collective responsibility of representatives of individual Member States for all decisions taken in the Council similar to that applicable to the Commission is neither accepted practice, nor would it reflect the (legal) nature of the Council in today's institutional framework. In a system where the government of a Member State can be outvoted in the Council while at the same time being fully bound by the decision that has been taken, the role of the national parliament in legitimizing decision-making is diminished.[29] So is the extent to which the Council, with the exception of a judicial review of its decisions by the European Court of Justice, can be held accountable. National parliaments can only hold their executives accountable for decisions which they have supported in the Council. While it may be argued that in the end the qualified majority requirement ensures the democratic legitimacy of all decisions taken in the Council, the contribution of individual Member States to the democratic legitimation of the EU's activities varies. With the increase in EU membership also the number of Member States against whose vote decisions can be taken increases.

Discussions on the institutional reforms of the European Union regularly also include calls to enhance the powers of the European Parliament. The Stubb Report is no exception in this regard as it proposes to put the European Parliament on an equal footing with the Council in budgetary and legislative matters. This has much to do with the perception of the European Parliament as the democratic figurehead of the European Union, as its members are directly elected by the citizens of the European Union in the Member States. Yet what is easily pushed aside is the fact that, despite direct elections, the European Parliament does not stand for the proportionate representation of either the citizens of the European Union or the Member States. Simply calling for more power for the European Parliament will not

---

[28] The so-called '*ficheprocedure*'.

[29] Cf., P. Kiiver, *The National Parliaments in the European Union – A Critical review on EU Constitution-Building* (The Hague/London/New York, Kluwer Law International 2006), p. 66.

remedy this insufficiency. Indeed, if the current system is maintained further enlargement will only worsen the situation.

This is due to the fact that under the current legal regime seats are assigned to each Member State individually, whereby a quick comparison between the size of the population per Member State and the number of seats reveals that the system is biased in favour of the citizens of smaller Member States.[30] Similar to what has been observed for the Council, by aiming not only at the equality of citizens, but, indirectly, also of the Member States, the current legal framework applicable to the European Parliament achieves neither. This shortcoming, which has existed since the introduction in 1979 of elections to the European Parliament by direct universal suffrage, is bound to increase as a result of a further enlargement. Generally, enlargement has resulted in an increase in the size of the European Parliament from an already impressive 626 MEPs after the 1999 elections based on 15 Member States to currently 785 MEPs after the fifth and sixth enlargement, thereby temporarily exceeding the maximum number of MEPs of previously 732 as laid down in the EC Treaty.[31] According to the Act of Accession in 2005 with effect from the start of the 2009-2014 term of the European Parliament, the number of MEPs will be capped at 736.[32] This limitation to the membership is understandable from the point of view of preventing the emergence of a voluminous assembly potentially at the expense of efficiency. Yet the downside of placing a ceiling on the maximum number of MEPs is that as new Member States join the European Union the gap in terms of representation between small and large Member States according to the size of population will increase further unless the number of seats allocated to Member States is adjusted yet again. The eventual accession of Turkey, a country with an estimated population of just above 70 million, will have a considerable impact in this regard.

Weiler righly observers that 'a diminution in the specific gravity, in the political weight, in the level of control of each individual within the redrawn political boundaries ...' inevitably results '... from enlarging the membership of the functional polity (when a company issues new voting shares, the value of each share is reduced) and from adding a tier of government thereby distancing it further from its ultimate subjects in whose name and for whom democratic government is supposed to operate.'[33] This does not only hold true for the initial decision to transfer competencies to a new supranational organization, but also for the subsequent expansion

[30] Despite the fact that Art. 190(2) TEC demands unmistakably that the number of representatives elected must ensure the appropriate representation of the people of the states.

[31] Cf., Protocol concerning the conditions and arrangements for admission of the Republic of Bulgaria and Romania to the European Union, *OJ* 2005, L 157/29.

[32] Cf., Act concerning the conditions of accession of the Republic of Bulgaria and Romania and the adjustments to the treaties on which the European Union is founded, *OJ* 2005, L 157/203. According to its Art. 9(1), Art. 189 TEC is amended to now refer to 736 MEPs.

[33] J.H.H. Weiler, 'The State "über alles" Demos, Telos and the German Maastricht Decision', NYU Jean Monnet Online Papers 1995, on-line available at <http://www.jeanmonnetprogram.org/papers/ 95/9506ind.html> (last visited: 7 May 2007), section 3.

of the membership of that organization. The fact that the number of MEPs according to the population ratio increases with each enlargement and that the constituency of the individual MEP grows highlights this point. Already at the next elections to the European Parliament in 2009 all but six Member States will lose seats in the European Parliament ranging from one seat in the case of less populated Member States like Finland and Sweden to six seats in the case of France, Italy and the United Kingdom.[34] These developments will hardly bring Europe's political elite closer to its citizens (electorate).

3.2 Efficiency

The qualified majority system in the Council may also create problems for the efficiency of an increasingly widening European Union. Firstly, observing the amendments to the qualified majority voting in the Council in accommodating for the fifth and sixth enlargement round highlights the gradual raising of the threshold for a qualified majority in the Council, thereby lowering the required votes for a blocking minority. For some the current system '… clearly favours hindering decisions, rather than creating shaping majorities …'.[35] Moreover, each enlargement comes with a further diversification in geographic, cultural and economic terms. New divides may emerge, such as rich versus poor or even old Member States versus new (post-communist) Member States. The accession of Turkey could certainly have a profound impact in this regard. At the same time as the voting power of individual Member States decreases in relative terms as a result of further enlargement, building coalitions with other states will become increasingly important. As Baykal points out: 'The bargaining and compromises, the consensus and disagreement, the balancing of interests and positions will require a new outlook and new considerations.'[36]

The loss of efficiency resulting from this will not only and arguably not even in the first place be felt in the formal voting of the representatives of the Member States at ministerial level in the Council, but mainly in the consultations in COREPER[37] II and I, as well as in the numerous working parties and committees, in which a substantial part of the decision formation takes place. The challenge will be to manage the Council deliberations and preparatory works in an enlarged European Union with an ever growing number of national delegations being added to

[34] The Netherlands will lose two seats, reducing the number of MEPs from currently 27 to 25, whereas Germany as the Member State with the largest population will remain with 99 seats.

[35] T. Fischer and A. Metz, 'The Treaty of Nice – A deadlock for Europe?', *Reform Spotlight* 2004/01, published by the Centre for Applied Policy Research at the University of Munich.

[36] Cf., S. Baykal, 'Unity in Diversity? The Challenge of Diversity for the European Political Identity, Legitimacy and Democratic Governance: Turkey's EU Membership as the Ultimate Test Case', NYU Jean Monnet Working Paper 09/05, p. 24.

[37] *Comité des Représentants Permanents* (Committee of Permanent Representatives). COREPER II includes the Permanent Representatives of the Member States to the EU and COREPER I their deputies.

the different forums.[38] Acknowledging this challenge, the Council already amended its Rules of Procedure in 2004. According to Annex IV, which is dedicated to the working methods for an enlarged Council, national delegations are instructed, among other things, where appropriate to set out the positions they are likely to take in a forthcoming Council meeting in written form before that meeting.[39] Moreover, delegations maintaining identical positions are prompted to make joint submissions. Council meetings are also supposed to be run under a strict regime implemented by the Presidency, among other things ensuring that deliberations are kept within an expectable time frame.

With each enlargement the bottleneck of Article 48 TEU that subjects any amendments of primary Community law to a common accord and, thereafter, ratification by all Member States is crimped tighter. Meaningful institutional reforms, including a further streamlining of the decision-making procedure, but also further integration in existing or new policy areas become increasingly difficult to realize. Ironically this extends to the decision on the accession of new countries to the European Union, as the accession treaties require agreement among all existing Member States. There is thus a real danger that the European Union is gradually crippled, whereby adjustments to internal or external developments become virtually impossible. It is in this regard that the negative correlation between enlargement and the Union's ability to maintain the momentum of integration or, to put it differently, between widening and deepening the integration process, becomes most apparent.

It is questionable whether the instrument of enhanced cooperation can offer an effective solution in this regard. Enhanced cooperation was, as Chalmers, et al., point out, born out of the '... deep-seated differences between the Member States about the pace and extent of integration.'[40] In the light of this purpose it seems rather remarkable that to date no use has been made of this possibility. This may have much to do with the rather elaborate procedural and substantive conditions under which this instrument can be applied in the context of the first, second or third pillar of the European Union. In particular Article 43 TEU restricts the application of enhanced cooperation by stating that any enhanced cooperation has to remain within the limits of the powers of the Community/Union, may not concern areas which fall within the exclusive competence of the Community, and has to respect the *acquis communautaire* and the single institutional framework of the Union. Moreover, at least eight Member States must agree on enhanced coopera-

[38] Generally with regard to managing the Council, COREPER and working group meetings in an enlarged EU cf., N. Bayer, 'EU 25 – Creating a New Design for the Council', *Eipascope* (2004/3), pp. 8-13.

[39] Council Decision of 22 March 2004 (2004/38/EC, Euratom) adopting the Council's Rules of Procedure, *OJ* 2004, L 106/22, as amended by Council Decision (2004/701/EC, Euratom), *OJ* 2004, L 319/15.

[40] D. Chalmers, C. Hadjiemmanuil, G. Monti and A. Tomkins, *European Union Law* (Cambridge, Cambridge University Press 2006), p. 155.

tion and must in principle be supported by a qualified majority in the Council.[41] In the case of enhanced cooperation in the Community pillar any Council decision requires a Commission proposal and, in areas in which the co-decision procedure applies, moreover the assent of the European Parliament.[42] Thus, not only is the procedure for applying enhanced cooperation cumbersome, but the extent to which it can actually be utilized by Member States to substantially deepen the integration process economically and/or politically is arguably limited.

The fear of a loss of efficiency as a result of increasing membership has been the reason behind more recent developments to modify the composition of the Commission. Until now, the number of Commissioners corresponds to the number of Member States. Paradoxically, despite the fact that the Commission and namely its individual members are legally bound to act as independent and impartial promoters of the Community interest, Member States have in the past defended this status quo.[43] In particular in some smaller Member States the perception of the Commission as an indispensable counterweight to a Council which is allegedly dominated by the large Member States has prevailed for a long time and has stood in the way of meaningful reforms. With its function as one of the main policymakers, backed by its near exclusive right of legislative initiatives, as well as its key role in the execution of Community law, the Commission is at the forefront of the interest of Member States which consider a meaningful 'portfolio' for 'their Commissioner' as a question of national prestige. Yet, with continuing enlargement of the European Union, upholding the present system could threaten the future efficiency of the Commission in more than one regard.[44]

Firstly, the decision-making process in the Commission is primarily geared towards achieving consensus, whereas formal voting functions only as a fall-back procedure.[45] However, reaching consensus in a Commission of up to 30 members would be difficult and would in many cases result in agreement on the lowest common denominator. While the problem may be overcome by applying formal voting, this would put the principle of collective responsibility which currently underlies the Commission's actions into question.[46] Moreover, an analysis of the allocation of tasks in the Barroso Commission highlights that a distribution of meaningful portfolios based on the equality of Member States and candidates will be difficult to realize in an European Union of more than 27 Member States.

According to the Protocol on Enlargement, as from the date on which the first Commission following the date of accession of the 27th Member State of the Union

---

[41] Additional conditions apply for the second pillar, cf., Art. 27a(2) TEU.

[42] D. Chalmers, C. Hadjiemmanuil, G. Monti and A. Tomkins, *supra* n. 40, p. 157, wonder what the practical significance of these requirements is.

[43] Critical are F. Amtenbrink and H.H.B. Vedder, *Recht van de Europese Unie*, 2nd edn. (The Hague, Boom Juridische uitgevers 2006), pp. 66-67.

[44] Cf., already J.W. de Zwaan, 'Het Verdrag van Amsterdam, een overzicht', *NTER* (1998), pp. 30-40.

[45] According to Art. 8(2) Rules of Procedure European Commission (*OJ* 2000, L 308/26, as amended), a vote is taken only if any Member so requests.

[46] Cf., Art. 1 Rules of Procedure European Commission.

takes up its duties, the Commission will have to consist of fewer members than the number of Member States in the European Union.[47] Member States will only be allowed to nominate Commissioners based on a rotation system and thus not on each occasion of the instalment of a new Commission. The rotation system which has yet to be established has to ensure that Member States are treated on a strictly equal footing, whereby each successive college is composed in a way that reflects satisfactorily the demographic and geographical range of all Member States of the Union.[48] This may amount to an exercise in squaring the circle and it requires little imagination to foresee that the details of this system will be controversially discussed in the run-up to the unanimous Council decision on the future number of Commissioners and the details of the rotation system. What is more, it becomes clear from the reference to the equality of Member States that Commissioners are essentially still viewed as representatives of the Member States rather than the Community interest as a whole.[49] In any event, doubts may be in place as to whether the compromise that has been found in Treaty of Nice offers a sustainable solution. With each future accession, the position of the individual Member States in the rotation system is bound to become subject to new debates.[50]

4. In search of sustainable solutions

What has become clear from the brief analysis of the institutional triangle is that further enlargement will have a considerable impact on the functioning of these institutions namely in terms of ensuring a sufficient degree of democratic legitimacy for EU activities and in making certain that the institutions are still capable of acting efficiently. The impact of a further deterioration of the already fragile system for the future of European integration should not be underestimated. The recent rejection of the TCE in France and the Netherlands highlight that citizens are increasingly detached from European policies and decision-making.[51] From the analysis of today's institutional structure it becomes clear that further enlargement has the potential to further deteriorate the current situation. Not addressing these challenges adequately may restrain the European Union in its future ambitions to widen and deepen further.

4.1 Treaty establishing a Constitution for Europe – an adequate response?

For some, the solution to at least a majority of the issues raised in the previous section lies in the entering into force of the TCE. Thus, for example, the EP's Brok

[47] Art. 4 Protocol on the enlargement of the European Union, *supra* n. 20.

[48] The equal treatment of Member States relates to the determination of the sequence of and the time spent by their nationals as Commissioner.

[49] Contrary to Art. 213(1) TEC on the independence of the members of the European Commission.

[50] F. Amtenbrink and H.H.B. Vedder, *supra* n. 43, p. 55.

[51] F. Amtenbrink, 'Continuation or Reorientation – What Future for European Integration', Erasmus Law Lectures No. 9 (The Hague, Boom Juridische uitgevers 2007).

Report argues that all necessary reforms in the institutional sphere '… are already included in the Constitutional Treaty, and that their entering into force would allow for the proper functioning of an enlarged Union and ensure its ability to take decisions efficiently and democratically …'.[52] It is presently submitted that this is regrettably not the case as far as enlargement is concerned. Indeed, 'the multi-centred and heterogeneous nature of European governance'[53] is largely preserved despite the grand label which this Treaty has been given.

This becomes first of all clear from studying the qualified majority voting arrangements in the Council as foreseen in the TCE. A system which is at least as equally complex as the current one is introduced, which still aims at reconciling the equality of Member States with the equality of citizens. A qualified majority is defined in the case of an act based on a proposal from the Commission or the Union Minister as being at least 55% of the Member States, comprising at least fifteen of them and representing Member States comprising at least 65% of the population of the Union.[54] In the European Union of 27 Member States a qualified majority would thus have to comprise at least 15 Member States and roughly 314.5 million inhabitants. However, this is not an absolute requirement. By providing that a blocking minority in the Council must include at least four Member States, as the qualified majority will otherwise be deemed to have been attained, the state element outweighs the population element to some degree.[55] Indeed, the size of the Member States in terms of population is irrelevant. Even though Germany, France and the United Kingdom combine approximately 41.5% of the total EU population they could not block a qualified majority decision from being taken. While still comprising a majority of the European Union population, the 65% requirement no longer applies. Therefore, 24 Member States can decide irrespective of the share of the population.[56] What is more, even if this rather complex provision should come into force, it would not provide a sustainable solution, as further enlargement will require yet another readjustment of the balance of power in the Council.

The future efficiency of decision-making is rather doubtful when realizing that the TCE does not abolish unanimity decisions completely.[57] Interesting from the point of view of future enlargement is the wider application of so-called *passerelle* clauses which provide the European Council with the right in certain policy fields to decide unanimously to allow the Council to switch from unanimity to qualified

---

[52] European Parliament Committee on Constitutional Affairs, *supra* n. 10, p. 7.

[53] A description used by J. Zielonka, 'Plurilateral Governance in the Enlarged European Union', 45 *JCMS* (2005), pp. 187-209, at p. 199.

[54] Art. I-25 TCE. In all other cases the qualified majority is defined as at least 72% of the members of the Council, representing Member States comprising at least 65% of the population of the Union.

[55] Art. I-44 (3) TCE redefines the blocking minority requirement in areas where not all Member States are allowed to vote.

[56] For an overview of the majority requirements before and after the Treaty of Nice and in the TCE see D.S. Felsenthal and M. Machover, 'Qualified Majority Voting Explained', 21 *Homeo Oeconomicus* (2004), pp. 573-576 (published by the University of Hamburg Institute of Socio Economics).

[57] Cf., e.g., Art. I-40(6) and III-300(1) TCE in the area of the common foreign and security policy and III-271(1) TCE in the area of judicial cooperation in criminal matters.

majority voting.[58] Despite the fact that this clause effectively provides for a simplified revision procedure, it should not be qualified too quickly as a much needed element of flexibility. Firstly, its application would require a unanimous decision by the Heads of State or Government and the President of the Commission meeting in the European Council and require the consent of the European Parliament.[59] The clause is thus not designed to provide a means to bypass one or a number of Member States which refuse to support a particular legislative proposal. Moreover, as any national parliament can make its opposition known to such a decision so that the European Council can block its application, the possibility that the *passerelle* clause can actually be applied seems rather narrow. A simplified revision procedure is also foreseen for amendments relating to the internal Union policies and action, including namely the provisions on the internal market and economic and monetary union. Compared to the ordinary revision procedure, this could considerably speed up the Treaty amendment procedure. However, this would not result in a substantial widening of the bottleneck of today's Article 48 TEU, as any amendments would still require unanimous decisions by the European Council and approval by the Member States in accordance with their respective constitutional requirements.[60]

As has been observed above, with enlargement the number of Member States that can in certain constellations be effectively outvoted increases and so does the number of national parliaments effectively excluded from participating in the legitimation and accountability of the Council. It could be argued that the TCE is addressing this issue by providing national parliaments with direct access to the legislative process on the Union level. However, rather than participating directly in the policy formation or decision-making process as such, according to Article I-11(3) TCE and the Protocol on the application of the principles of subsidiarity and proportionality national parliaments would monitor compliance primarily of the Commission with the principle of subsidiary.[61] Whether the TCE actually introduces a workable procedure, thereby effectively enhancing the democratic legitimation of the Union activities through the accountability of the Council, the Commission and the European Parliament is questionable.[62] From the point of view of a further enlargement the biggest problem may lie in the high potential of this procedure to politicize and indeed polemise the procedure in ways which are coun-

---

58 Art. IV-444 TCE. Cf., e.g., Art. I-40(7) and 300(3) TCE in the area of the common foreign and security policy. This instrument is not unknown in today's EC Treaty, cf., Art. 42 TEU and Art. 67 TEC.

59 Art. IV-444(3) TCE.

60 Art. IV-445 TCE.

61 Interestingly, in the Netherlands both chambers of Parliament in March 2006 jointly introduced a temporary committee with the task of checking whether Commission proposals observe the subsidiarity and, moreover, also the proportionality principle (*Tijdelijke Commissie Subsidiariteitstoets*). The evaluation period of one year has recently ended. The committee continues its work while its track-record is still being analysed internally at the time of writing this contribution.

62 Critical is G. Davies, 'Subsidiariteit en Bevoegdheden in de Europese Grondwet', in F. Amtenbrink and S.B. van Baalen (eds.), *Europa: eenheid in verscheidenheid?: Groningse beschouwingen over de Europese Grondwet* (Den Haag, Boom Juridische uitgevers 2005), pp. 69-81. Cf., also F. Amtenbrink, 'Europa; Democratischer, Transparanter en Efficiënter?', pp. 121-146, at p. 129.

terproductive for the European legislative process. It is far from certain that the opinion formation in the national parliaments will be in all instances based on the merits of the respective European drafts rather than domestic political considerations. Moreover, it is at least questionable whether national parliaments will actually restrict themselves to the question whether the subsidiarity principle has been observed. Some national parliaments may eventually have to be reminded of the limits of their competence which will cause conflicts. With the number of Member States in the European Union growing, so does the potential for opposition to European legislative activities not necessarily based on its merits.

The TCE does not provide an adequate answer to the challenges facing the European Parliament in an enlarging European Union either, as today's system of disproportionate representation would be granted a quasi-constitutional status. In holding on to today's allocation of seats to Member States, the Treaty restricts the total number of MEPs to 750 and establishes a minimum threshold of 6 members per Member State and a maximum number of members per Member State of 96. Thus, the ratio between the number of seats assigned to a Member State and the share in the population size of the Union would still be progressively more favourable towards less populated Member States.[63] The Treaty veils this issue by more or less elegantly referring to a 'degressively proportional' representation of European citizens. What is more, by taking over the current legal arrangements under the EC Treaty to fix the maximum number of MEPs independent from the number of countries participating in the European Union, with each enlargement the number of citizens an MEP represents will continue to increase. This would hardly bring a continuously widening Europe closer to its citizens and is only likely to play into the hands of those critics that consider a continuation of European integration as the slow death of representative democracy. In the case of further enlargement the European Union would be under pressure to readjust the number of MEPs once again in due course.

With regard to the composition of the Commission, the TCE to a large extent preserves the arrangements agreed upon as part of the Treaty of Nice. However, rather than the Council, it is the European Council which would have to adopt the detailed rules unanimously.[64] Moreover, the maximum number of members of the Commission would in principle be fixed at two-thirds of the number of Member States. The link between the number of Member States and the number of Commissioners would thus still not have relinquished entirely. While in the European Union of 27 the number of Commissioners would in the first instance be reduced to 18, it would paradoxically increase again as a result of enlargement, albeit at a slower rate than under the current arrangements.[65] Eventually, the issue of efficiency would

[63] See, e.g., Part 2 of the House of Lords Select Committee on European Union, Twenty-First Report, Session 2002-2003, where an explanation of this term is demanded.

[64] Art. I-26 TCE.

[65] Note that for the first Commission appointed under the provisions of the TCE, the principle of one Commissioner per Member State would be upheld.

resurface and require yet another adjustment by unanimity decision in the European Council.

4.2 Towards an 'enlargement-proof' institutional structure?

The TCE is not effectively addressing the challenges which the institutional triangle faces in the light of enlargement as it seeks solutions which are in principle confined to today's institutional framework and the inter-institutional balance it creates. Namely the vertical and horizontal distribution of democratic legitimacy and accountability channelled through the composition and decision-making procedures is upheld.

If the aspiration voiced by the Member States, the European Council, the Council and the Commission for a more democratic and efficient European Union that is moreover capable of widening and deepening is taken seriously, those elements of today's institutional structure of the European Union which are most vulnerable to enlargement have to be amended. From the analysis of today's institutional framework it can arguably be concluded that the key lies in a clear demarcation on the European level of the institution(s) representing the Member States and those representing the citizens of the European Union thereby also more clearly differentiating the two strands of legitimacy and accountability on which the European Union is based. This requires a readjustment of the institutional balance which includes the European Parliament and the Council, as well as the Commission. Such a revision would also have the potential to go some way towards enhancing the efficiency of the European Union.

To this end, first of all ways should be explored to remove the negative correlation between the degree of representation in the European Parliament and the number of Member States. In principle this could be achieved by abandoning the system of the distribution of seats to Member States in favour of a uniform electoral system based on a European ballot. This would reinforce the democratic legitimation of the European Parliament as the representation of the citizens of the European Union (rather than of the Member States) and would remove the mounting disproportionate representation which in the present system correlates with enlargement.[66] To be sure, enlargement would still require an adjustment of the number of MEPs in order to ensure that the MEP to European Union population ratio remains at roughly the same levels, but the politically sensitive task of having to readjust the number of seats assigned to a Member State would be removed. If the electoral system was adjusted accordingly, thereby arguably reinforcing the democratic legitimacy of the European Parliament, the latter could become the main pillar on which the representation of the citizens of the European Union rests on the supranational level. The role of such a reinforced EP in the legislative process should then be further strengthened by extending the co-decision procedure to all Community/Union policy areas.

[66] For more details see F. Amtenbrink, 'Continuation or Reorientation', *supra* n. 51.

The strengthening of the direct and proportionate representation of the citizens of the European Union could create the necessary space to explore ways in which the present complicated system of weighted voting in the Council aiming at reconciling the proportionate representation of Member States with the proportionate representation of citizens could be abandoned in favour of the principle of one state, one vote.[67] If all legislative measures would require the consent of the European Parliament, the representation of the citizens of the European Union in all decisions would still be secured. While the Council would lose the power to take decisions without the consent of the European Parliament, its central role in the decision-making procedure could in principle be maintained by requiring that all decisions are subject to consent by the Council. Moreover, the proposed arrangements would in principle not exclude the possibility that the internal decision-making procedure in the Council would still foresee unanimity decisions in some areas.

Yet, in order to increase the efficiency of the legislative procedure in a larger Union, more far-reaching changes to the present decision-making structures would become necessary. In the first instance, abandoning the unanimity requirement in the Council for all remaining policy areas should be discussed as a serious option. Moreover, the possibility to exclude decisions in certain policy areas from the requirement of approval by the Council could be explored. A differentiation between legislative proposals which require the consent of the Council and those on which the ultimate decision rests with the European Parliament would be conceivable.[68] The system of exclusive and shared competencies which is currently applied in defining the vertical distribution of power between the national and supranational level of the European Union could be a starting point for redefining the horizontal distribution of power between the Council and the European Parliament.

A substantial reinforcement of the position of the European Parliament would moreover call for a reform of the composition and tasks of the Commission. Indeed, already today it is rather difficult to explain to European citizens why the only directly democratically elected European institution does not *de jure* have the status of a true legislator that comes with a right of initiative for legislative action. Extending the right of initiative also to the Council could, moreover, open up room for a new consensus on the composition of the Commission. Indeed, the sharing of the right of initiative could help to depoliticize the Commission. Rather than ensuring the equality of Member States through the introduction of a more or less complicated rotation system, the composition of the Commission and namely its number of members could be based on operational needs. In the process the democratic legitimacy streaming from the appointment procedure could be strengthened by

---

67 In fact this principle already applies where the EC Treaty and EU Treaty call for a unanimity decision in the Council.

68 The German federal constitutional system which differentiates between '*Zustimmungsgesetz*' and '*Einspruchsgesetz*' is worth studying in this context. Cf., generally R. Zippelius and T. Würtemberger, *Deutsches Staatsrecht*, 31st edn. (Münich, Verlag C.H. Beck 2005), § 45.

giving the European Parliament the right to reject individual Commissioners-designate.[69]

Despite the improvements that could arguably result from these proposals it cannot be denied that there are limits to the extent to which the institutional framework of the European Union can be made 'enlargement-proof' without touching upon the constitutional foundations of European integration. Article 48 TEU, which requires the consensus of all Member States for any amendments to primary Community law, is based on what may very well be the most fundamental principle governing the relationship between the Member States and the supranational organization they have created. The Community/Union has no competence-competence, as the Member States have to decide whether and to what extent they want to transfer competences to the supranational level. This is the very essence of what Weiler has described as '… European federalism [which] is constructed with a top-to-bottom hierarchy of norms, but with a bottom-to-top hierarchy of authority and real power.'[70] Unless the European Union was to evolve into a full-blown federal system in which the federal rather than the state level can ultimately decide on the allocation of competencies, Member States will retain the role described in Article 48 TEU. As has been highlighted above, the use of *passerelle* clauses does not solve the problem of future blockades, as this simplified treaty amendment procedure relies upon the same principle that underlies Article 48 TEU, that is consensus among all Member States. Considering the currently applicable conditions for its application, enhanced cooperation arguably cannot be utilized as an instrument to circumvent Article 48 TEU either. At the same time it cannot be easily seen how a revised enhanced cooperation provision, which would no longer be confined to the boundaries of today's European constitutional framework, could be applied without the serious risk of a fragmentation of the European Union.

5. Conclusion

It has been suggested that the difficulties which the main European institutions would have as a result of larger membership will evaporate when these institutions are examined individually.[71] However, what becomes clear from the summary examination of the institutional framework offered throughout this contribution is that if based on the current institutional framework further enlargement has every potential to considerably affect the working of the European Union. It may thus only be if one lowers one's sights that the negative effects which enlargement will have in this regard may become neglectable. Indeed, the challenges which the Eu-

---

69 Until now the EP can only reject the whole Commission, including its President, cf., Art. 214(2) TEC.

70 J.H.H. Weiler, 'Federalism and Constitutionalism: Europe's *Sonderweg*', NYU Jean Monnet Working Papers No. 10/00, on-line available at <http://www.jeanmonnetprogram.org/papers/papers00.html> (last visited: 7 May 2007), p. 3. Brackets added.

71 To this end see F. Vibert, *supra* n. 7.

ropean Union faces in the institutional sphere amount to more than mere technicalities which under no circumstances should stand in the way of the historical opportunity which further European unification offers. It has been highlighted that sustainable solutions will require more than minor adjustments to the existing framework. The admittedly provoking proposals made in the previous section, however sketchy and incomplete, may provide a starting point in this regard.

Considering the capacity of the European Union as a *conditio sine qua non* for a further 'widening' of the European Union entails both risks and opportunities. On the one hand, imposing a conditionality principle on parts of the European Union itself introduces boundaries to the political ambitions of the European Union as formulated in Article 49 TEC. It no longer depends solely on the performance of the candidate countries whether accession becomes a reality. In the short term the carrot of EU membership to convince non-EU countries of the desirability of legal and economic reforms would have to be replaced by new incentives. If, on the other hand, the Member States and their citizens(!) are indeed as committed to further enlargement as the majority of their governments claim, the introduction of such a conditionality based on the Union's (institutional) capacity to further enlarge may provide the decision-makers with the necessary incentive to act. It is, after all, the Member States themselves which have the power to construct an institutional framework which provides a sustainable institutional framework for further enlargement.

While concerns about the Union's ability to function with a growing number of Member States are anything but new, this has not resulted in the introduction of a separate precondition for the enlargement of the European Union. Indeed, political considerations always prevailed and enlargement became a reality despite the absence of a sustainable institutional framework. The true reason why in the wake of enlargement the European Union has been muddling from one institutional reform to the next with modest success may be that Member States are not willing to introduce the substantial reforms that will ensure democratic legitimacy and efficiency in a wider European Union. In the past, major announcements were usually followed by little concrete action. This pattern may repeat itself also this time around. Soon after the European Council of June 2006 had emphasized the importance of taking the ability of the European Union to take on new members into account in deciding on future enlargement, an all-clear signal was hastily issued by the Commission and the political leaders of several Member States which vividly stressed that it had never been the intention to introduce a new enlargement criterion and/or to discourage current or future applications for membership. One may wonder what exactly the 'renewed consensus on enlargement' that the European Council of December 2006 referred to in its conclusions actually amounts to.

Tellingly, neither the European Council nor the Commission or the European Parliament elaborate on the process that would have to be applied in reviewing the Union's capacity as part of the pre-accession process. Moreover, no light is shed on the impact that a negative assessment of the EU's capacity would have on the decision to accept new members in the European Union. For some, the latter may of course be rather obvious. Yet, the lack of (open) debate suggests that any repercussions on enlargement are considered inconceivable in terms of the consequences this would undoubtedly have for the ambitious project of European unification. One cannot help being reminded of the poetic words of Christian Morgenstern: '… And he comes to the conclusion: His mishap was an illusion, for, he reasons pointedly, that which must not, can not be.'[72]

[72] From the poem 'The Impossible Fact' by Christian Morgenstern, translated by M. Knight, *The Gallows Songs*. Christian Morgenstern's Galgenlieder. A Selection Translated, with an Introduction, University of California Press 1964.

Chapter 7
A FLEXIBLE FUTURE FOR THE EUROPEAN UNION: THE WAY FORWARD OR A WAY OUT?

Andrea Ott

1. Introduction

The European Union is characterised by its special legal nature which constitutes rights and obligations for Member States and individuals. At the same time, as this structure has developed into a constitutional system with clear objectives, principles and characteristics, it has also developed into an ever-changing and dynamic system which is going through successive Treaty amendments and accessions by new Member States. The original European Economic Community with its six founding members is not recognisable in a European Union of 27 members with political and economic aims and a constitutional project in the form of the Constitutional Treaty in its wake.

As a consequence of the Union's internal complexities and external candidates from Central and Eastern Europe, the Western Balkans and Turkey, the path to accession developed since the EU's last accession of Sweden, Finland and Austria in 1995 into a long and elaborated process which was structured by new policy and legal instruments.[1] The internal capacity to absorb new members became closely linked with the external capacity to implement and apply EU institutional requirements and policies by new members.[2] The characteristics which enable such a complex and ongoing process to work have been found in the elements of flexibility and conditionality whose features can be found in diverse areas of internal and external EU law instruments and policies. As a consequence, certain lines between the EU's ins and outs become blurred as, for instance, the example of the Schengen *acquis* shows. This contribution takes a closer look at the main instrument to reconcile the widening with the deepening, namely flexibility or differentiation with its manifold features and it addresses the risks and limits which lie in the use of such a tool or, in

---

[1] See further K. Inglis, 'EU Enlargement – Membership Conditions Applied to Future and Potential Member States' in K. Inglis and A. Ott (eds.), *The Constitution for Europe and an Enlarging Union: Unity in Diversity?* (Groningen, Europa Law Publishing 2005), p. 225.

[2] Communication from the Commission to the European Parliament and Council, Enlargement Strategy and main challenges 2006-2007 including an annexed special report on the EU's capacity to integrate new members COM (2006) 649, 8.11.2006.

S. Blockmans and S. Prechal, eds., Reconciling the Deepening and Widening of the EU

other words, whether it is the way forward or a way out of the common legal order of the Union.

2. Supranationality versus disintegration?

To understand the Union, its uniqueness and autonomy, supranationality,[3] the primacy of Union law and the law of integration[4] have to be identified as its core characteristics.[5] They translate as such that the members of this Union delegate certain competences to the common constitutional system of the Union constituting independent legal institutions which implement and apply European law uniformly through all its Member States and whose laws and legal principles take precedence over the national law of the Member States protected by an effective legal system.[6] However, the more this special and new legal order has changed through the process of extending its competences and policies beginning with the Single European Act for the area of harmonisation[7] and extending cooperation in the fields of police and justice cooperation and foreign and security policy in the Maastricht Treaty, the more an element of disintegration and differentiation in the internal policies and legal system has been accepted.[8] Important examples are the Schengen regime and the Economic and Monetary Union in which certain Member States permanently or temporarily opted out or decided to join later. But these concentric circles of integration can already be detected in an instrument such as minimum harmonisation in the internal market to accommodate the diverging interests of Member States[9] or international agreements concluded between some EU members within the frame-

---

[3] On supranationality as a sort of genuine principle: H.P. Ipsen, 'Über Supranationalität', in H.P. Ipsen (ed.), *Verfassungsperspektiven der europäischen Integration* (Baden-Baden, Nomos 1984), p. 97; see generally: A. von Bogdandy, 'Constitutional Principles', in A. von Bogdandy and J. Bast (eds.), *Principles of European Constitutional Law* (Oxford, Hart Publishing 2006) p. 59.

[4] Integration as a general guideline can be detected throughout the jurisdiction of the ECJ.

[5] For the development of these principles by the case-law of the ECJ, see J. Weiler, 'The Transformation of Europe', in J. Weiler, *The Constitution of Europe* (Cambridge, Cambridge University Press 1999) p. 19.

[6] On these characteristics: A. Ott, 'Fundamental and Basic Principles of the EC and the EU', in A. Ott and K. Inglis (eds.), *Handbook on European Enlargement* (The Hague, TMC Asser Press 2002) p. 15.

[7] Art. 95(4) TEC allows Member States to retain stricter national measures for reasons of health; these specific enabling clauses have to seen in the light of the changing concept of the Commission, the shift from total harmonisation to minimum harmonisation which is also reflected in the provisions on the environment (Art. 176 TEC), consumer protection (Art. 153(5) TEC) and social policy (Art. 137(5) TEC). On this: E. Vos, 'Differentiation, Harmonisation and Governance' in B. de Witte, D. Hanf and E. Vos (eds.), *The Many Faces of Differentiation in EU Law* (Antwerp, Intersentia 2001) p. 145 (p. 149).

[8] Curtin famously described this after the Maastricht Treaty as the Europe of bits and pieces, D. Curtin, 'The Constitutional Structure of the European Union: A Europe of Bits and Pieces', 30 *CML Rev.* (1993), pp. 17-70.

[9] Introduced by the SEA in 1986, see further: G. de Búrca, 'Differentiation within the Core? The Case of the Common Market', in G. de Búrca and J. Scott (eds.), *Constitutional Change in the EU: From Uniformity to Flexibility?* (Oxford, Hart Publishing 2000) pp. 133-171.

work of the Benelux Economic Union or the Nordic Council.[10] Another effort to prepare for internal diversities arising due to an ongoing enlargement process has been the introduction of a so-called enhanced or closer cooperation, an institutional tool promoted by all the EU members in EC and EU Treaties with the Amsterdam Treaty in 1997.[11]

Diversities among EU members might appear as an internal phenomenon but with an ongoing accession process and privileged cooperation with potential, but unwilling countries such as Switzerland, Iceland, Liechtenstein and Norway and countries participating in the new European Neighbourhood Policy,[12] certain forms of differentiated integration have been extended beyond the EU borders. As a consequence, the lines become more and more blurred between EU insiders and outsiders.[13] In addition to the policy tool of flexibility, the use of conditionality[14] enables and encourages the Union to allow non-EU members to participate in EU policies, programmes and institutional structures such as the EC and EU agencies as long as they do not participate in the supranational, the intergovernmental institutions and decision-making process of the European Union. So the EEA member Norway thereby participates in the internal market through the EEA Agreement in Schengen, in certain external actions such as the Police Mission in Bosnia and Herzegovina and the European Environmental Agency.[15] In contrast to this extension of policies, new EU members do not automatically and fully participate in all policies due to transitional arrangements agreed in the accession treaties but have the right to participate without restrictions in the institutional system of the Union. The last Accession Treaties from 2003 and 2005 for 12 new members provide evidence of a broad extension of the time-limited restriction of the full application of the *acquis communautaire* from the moment of accession.[16]

---

[10] B. de Witte, '"Old-fashioned flexibility": International Agreements between Member States of the European Union', in De Búrca and Scott (eds.), *supra* n. 9, pp. 31-58.

[11] A. Ott, The 'Principle' of Differentiation in an Enlarged European Union, p. 106 in Inglis and Ott, *supra* n. 1.

[12] See on this policy: M. Cremona; 'The European Neighbourhood Policy: Legal and Institutional Issues', *CDDRL Working Papers* No. 25, 2 November 2004, <http://iisdb.stanford.edu/pubs/20738/Cremona-ENP_and_the_Rule_of_Law.pdf>; R. Dannreuther, 'Developing the Alternative to Enlargement: The European Neighbourhood Policy', 11 *EFA Rev.* (2006), pp. 183-201.

[13] N. Wichmann, 'The Participation of the Schengen Associates: Inside or Outside?', 11 *EFA Rev.* (2006), pp. 87-107.

[14] According to Inglis conditionality is prevalent in the Union's external relations with non-candidate countries and include human rights and democracy, good neighbourliness, democratic institutions, the rule of law, market economy principles, the promotion of sustainable development, see K. Inglis, 'EU Enlargement – Membership Conditions Applied to Future and Potential Member States', p. 225 at p. 231 in Inglis and Ott, *supra* n. 1.

[15] Agreement between the EU and Norway on the participation of Norway in the European Union Police Mission (EUPM) in Bosnia and Herzegovina, *OJ* 2003 L 239/32-34. See A. Łazowski, 'EEA Countries' in S. Blockmans and A. Łazowski, *The European Union and its Neighbours – A Legal Appraisal of the EU's Policies of Stabilisation, Partnership and Integration* (The Hague, TMC Asser Press 2006) p. 95.

[16] See further K. Inglis, 'The Accession Treaty and its Transitional Arrangements: A Twilight Zone for the New Members of the Union', in C. Hillion (ed.), *EU Enlargement, a legal approach* (Oxford, Hart Publishing 2004) p. 77.

3. Different forms of flexibility in EU law and policy

Flexibility as a policy tool has gained in importance since the internal development of the constant revision of and amendments to the Treaties unfolded parallel to a constant enlargement process from the 1970s until the enlargements of 2005 and 2007 with up to 12 new Member States. This process found its response in the prolific literature on this subject.[17] It is correctly emphasised that there are many faces of differentiation[18] and a common definition of what it entails is necessarily lacking.[19] One definition characterizes this development as a general mode of integration strategies that try to reconcile heterogeneity within the European Union and allow different groupings of Member States to pursue an array of public policies with different procedural and institutional arrangements.[20] However, this definition excludes new forms of differentiation which also includes non-EU members in EU arrangements with some or all current EU members. This contribution aims to include all different categories of flexibility currently applied in EU law but excluding judicial or administrative flexibility which results from different interpretation and application through judicial and executive authorities. They are divided for this purpose into constitutional flexibility in the form of enhanced cooperation and voluntary withdrawal (section 3.1), differentiation achieved by international agreements (section 3.2) and accession treaties [21] (section 3.3). The former may include third countries or exclude current members of the Union in and from EU policies. These concentric circles of integration adapt to complexities arising in a European Union of 27, however, and create not only legally complex arrangements but are problematic under the aspects of the efficiency of Community law, democracy and the rule of law.

---

[17] F. Tuytschaever, *Differentiation in European Union Law* (Oxford, Hart Publishing 1999); G. de Búrca and J. Scott, *supra* n. 9; B. Witte, D. Hanf and E. Vos, *supra* n. 7; J.A. Usher, 'Variable Geometry or Concentric Circles: Patterns for the EU', 46 *ICLQ* (1997), p. 243, C.-D. Ehlermann, 'Engere Zusammenarbeit nach dem Amsterdamer Vertrag: Ein neues Vertragsprinzip', *Europarecht* (1997), p. 362 (at pp. 366-367); J. Shaw, 'Flexibility in a "Reorganized" and "Simplified" Treaty', 40 *CML Rev.* (2003), pp. 279-311, K. Inglis and A. Ott (eds.), *supra* n. 1.

[18] Witte, Hanf and Vos, *supra* n. 7, p. XI.

[19] A.Ott, 'Unity in Diversity? Differentiation in EU Law and Policy in an Enlarged European Union', *European Centre Natolin, Working Paper* (2004) p. 62 , <http://www.natolin.edu.pl/pdf/zeszyty/NatolinZeszyt15_Ott.pdf>.

[20] A. Stubb, 'A Categorization of Differentiated Integration', 34 *JCMS* (1996), p. 283: G. Glöckler, 'Flexibility and Closer Cooperation', in G. Glöckler, et al., *Guide to EU Policies* (London, Blackstone Press 1998) p. 63, see a similar definition in De Witte, Hanf and Vos ('The facilitation and accommodation of a degree of difference between Member States or regions in relation to what would otherwise be common Community or Union policies').

[21] Accession Treaties are characterised by their double nature as forming international agreements but also the primary law of the Union. See on this A. Ott, *supra* n. 19, p. 58.

3.1 Constitutional flexibility: enhanced cooperation and voluntary withdrawal

The tool of enhanced cooperation is not so much interesting for its practical use because there are no practical experiences to report, but for the state of mind in the Union which furthered at least a minimal consensus among all Member States to include such a tool which sanctioned a differentiated integration from the institutional side. It was born out of the necessity that already in 1996 institutional reforms and the deepening of the integration project moved slowly and happened outside the existing Treaty system as Schengen and the European Social Agreement illustrate.[22] While smaller Member States were and are suspicious of such multi-speed processes, agreement was reached that such an instrument would be suitable for a future enlarged and more heterogenic Union when tamed by certain EU standards which cannot be undermined by such cooperation.[23] Consequently, strict limitations were stipulated for the use of such an instrument which resulted in unclear provisions and a strange mix of procedural and substantial requirements in the Amsterdam EC and EU Treaty for cooperation in the first and third pillar.[24] After further reforms to the instrument with the Nice Treaty, the current enhanced cooperation is found in Articles 11, 11a TEC and Articles 40, 40a, 43-45 TEU. Despite changes such as an extension to foreign policy, lowering the number of participating Member States to eight and eliminating the Luxembourg compromise restriction in the first and third pillar[25] and a softening of the wording in some clauses,[26] such special cooperation among some Member States is still excluded when it falls into an area under the exclusive competence of the Community, undermines the internal market or economic and social cohesion, and does not respect the *acquis communautaire*, the single institutional framework of the Union and the process of integration.[27] While the role of the European Parliament has been strengthened, especially for actions in the first pillar, the legal review by the ECJ is restricted to

---

[22] G. Papagianni, 'Flexibility in Justice and Home Affairs: An Old Phenomenon Taking New Forms', p. 101 in De Witte, Hanf and Vos, *supra* n. 7. In 1989 11 out of 12 Member States concluded a non-binding Social Charter in the form of a resolution which formed the basis for a Protocol and an Agreement on Social Policy among 11 Member States agreed in Maastricht and with the UK 'opting out' which was finally integrated with the Amsterdam Treaty into the EC Treaty. Generally see C. Barnard, 'Flexibility and Social Policy', p. 197, in De Búrca and Scott, *supra* n. 9.

[23] The objective that such cooperation projects have to aim at furthering the objectives of the Union and the Community in order to protect and serve their interests and reinforce their process in integration is especially mentioned (Art. 43a TEU).

[24] A majority of Member States had to participate and Member States could block the application when important and stated reasons of national policy by the opposing member could be invoked.

[25] Non-participating Member States could block when important and stated reasons of national policy were invoked.

[26] Instead of not affecting the competences, rights, obligations and interests of the non-participating Member States which it has to respect, in other cases also effects have been mellowed in certain respects. See Art. 43 TEU.

[27] Art. 43 TEU.

formal and procedural requirements initiating enhanced cooperation.[28] With no practical experience until now, a restricted legal review and the particular wording, enhanced cooperation remains a tool for pressuring reluctant Member States into negotiations which is also exemplified by the practical examples of the European Company Statute and the European Arrest Warrant.[29] In the last case, the European Parliament asked the Council to resort to enhanced cooperation in 2001 before Italy dropped its opposition and enabled all the Member States to adopt this measure.[30] In addition, the list of cooperation examples which was drawn up by the Irish Presidency during the IGC 1996 named such fields as education, vocational training, youth, culture, public health, tourism, energy, civil protection, trans-European networks, industry, research and technology, development cooperation and the fight against social exclusion.[31] These areas are already covered by cooperation with third countries, a form of enhanced cooperation which falls outside the EC and EU Treaties but under the regime of international agreements and involves all EU Member States.[32] As such these cooperations indicate their marginal importance. Apart from difficulties in its practical application, the introduction of such a tool has raised more general questions of whether other forms of closer cooperation among some Member States are still possible on the basis of international law which the majority in the literature confirm[33] and which is also reflected in practice. For the decisive division of competences, it has also been argued that the ERTA doctrine[34] with its consequences on exclusive competences transferred to the Union could be applied when such cooperation takes place.[35] This last argument is denied with the reference that such cooperation is prohibited when it concerns an area of exclusive competences (Art. 43(d) TEU). This argument, however, is based on a misunderstanding of the ERTA doctrine which indicates the dynamic development of moving from shared to exclusive competences through actions of the EC and the example of the Economic and Monetary policy can be mentioned. In this area enhanced

---

[28] See Art. 46c TEU in combination with Arts. 11 and 11a TEC and Art. 40 TEU. However, in the literature it has been argued that Art. 40 para. 3 clarifies that Art. 43 TEU is fully reviewable. H.-J. Cremer in Calliess and Ruffert (eds.), *Commentary*, 3rd edn. (Munich, Beck Publishing 2007).

[29] Another example is the EU Corporate Tax Base, see D. Chalmers, C. Hadjiemmanuil, G. Monti, A. Tomkins, *European Union Law* (Cambridge, Cambridge University Press 2006), p. 158.

[30] J. Wouters and F. Naert, 'The EU's Criminal Law Approach to Terrorism – What has been achieved so far?', *Working Paper*, Leuven University, 2001.

[31] Tuytschaever, *supra* n. 17, p. 55.

[32] Cooperations in the field of research and technology development have already been reflected informally since the SEA by Art. 168 and Art. 172(2) TEC.

[33] See De Witte, 'Chameolonic Member States', p. 238, in De Witte, Hanf and Vos, *supra* n. 7; A. Hatje, 'Article 40, para. 1, and Article 44 para. 28' in J. Schwarze (ed.), *EU-Kommentar* (Baden-Baden, Nomos Publisher 2000), contra B. Martenczuk, 'Die differenzierte Integration nach dem Vertrag von Amsterdam', *ZEuS* (1998), p. 447.

[34] On the ERTA doctrine, see A. Ott and R. Wessel, 'The EU's External Relations Regime: Multilevel Complexity in an Expanding European Union', in S. Blockmans and A. Łazowski, *supra* n. 15.

[35] C.D. Ehlermann, 'Differentiation, Flexibility, Closer Cooperation: The New Provisions of the Amsterdam Treaty', 3 *ELJ* (1995), p. 246 (at p. 258).

cooperation outside the Treaty system was organised and resulted in the exclusive competence of the Union for the countries which have adopted the euro (reflected by Art. I-13(c) of the Constitutional Treaty).[36]

Even though the legal nature of acts taken under enhanced cooperation is disputed, these cooperations have to respect the primacy and institutional structure of the European Union. Article 44 TEU clarifies that they do not form part of the *acquis* but as EC/EU institutions and Member States act within the EC and EU system, these measures amount to a special form of EC and EU secondary law[37] (this includes the basic decision establishing enhanced cooperation and actions falling within the first pillar and the other pillars.[38]) As a consequence, EC secondary law takes precedence over cooperation measures reaching into the first pillar under Article 11 TEC.

Once enacted, the Constitutional Treaty would extend the application of enhanced cooperation. Regulated in Article I-44 and Articles III-416 to 423 of the Constitutional Treaty, it would again raise the threshold of participation in a Union of 27 to nine countries but would include a separate form of structured cooperation for mutual defence[39] and enhanced cooperation in criminal matters.[40] In this context, it is also worth noting the interesting constitutional novelty of differentiation provided by the Constitutional Treaty in Article I-60. This provision, once the Constitutional Treaty is ratified, would for the first time regulate the ability of EU members to leave the European Union. This possibility has been disputed up until now in the literature and a majority of commentators argue from the perspective of the special EU legal order that this withdrawal would only be possible under very exceptional circumstances on the basis of the application of international rules.[41] On the basis of these observations, Article I-60 would simplify the possibility to leave the Union and therefore enable more flexibility. However, a complete separation from the existing integration structures would be neither wise nor manageable for both sides. This is also reflected in Article I-60 TEC which foresees an international agreement negotiated between the Union and the leaving member 'taking into account the framework for its future relationship with the Union.'

---

[36] See the status quo of all the areas of exclusive competences reflected by the Constitutional Treaty in Art. I-13. Generally, see J.-V. Louis, 'Differentiation and the EMU', p. 55, in De Witte, Hanf and Vos, *supra* n. 7.

[37] M. Pechstein, Art. 11 EGV para. 8 in R. Streinz (ed.), *EU Kommentar* (Munich, Beck Publisher 2003); A. Hatje, Art. 11 EGV para. 24 in J. Schwarze (ed.), *supra* n. 33.

[38] Ott, *supra* n. 9, p. 78. Other authors differentiate between the pillars and categorising actions in the third pillar as international agreements: see U. Becker, 'Differenzierungen der Rechtseinheit durch "abgestufte" Integration', in J. Schwarze and P.-C. Müller-Graff (eds.), 'Europäische Rechtseinheit durch einheitliche Rechtsdurchsetzung', *Europarecht Beiheft* 1/1998, p. 53.

[39] Art. I-40(6) in conjunction with Art. III-213.

[40] Art. III-271(4).

[41] T. Oppermann, *Europarecht,* 3rd edn. (Munich, Beck Publisher 2005), p. 73.

3.2 Differentiation through international agreements

Once more, while the classical exercise in EU law is to stress the common constitutional legal order and its decisive differences from any national or international regime, a closer look at the EU institutional arrangements reveals a more complex reality beyond the pillar divisions and EU borders. Three categories cover these complex arrangements, namely either Union/Community policies, legal provisions or institutional participation are extended to current members or to non-members by international agreements (section 3.2.1 and 3.2.2) or the application of certain Community policies and legal previsions is excluded for current members by the accession treaties which will be addressed under section 3.3. This extension of participation for members is based on the fact that they have decided on non-participation with regard to Schengen or intergovernmental policies or they are in a special or privileged relationship as a non-member with the Union and the Union has an interest in allowing them to participate in EU policies and facilitate institutional participation in EU agencies and programmes.

3.2.1 *Extending participation in EU law and policy for EU members*

The countries concerned in this category are Denmark, the United Kingdom and Ireland which negotiated special conditions for participation for the areas of Police and Judicial Cooperation and Common Foreign and Security Policy. Later members, however, are excluded from such arrangements; once new members qualify for Schengen and the EMU, they need to accept and implement these policies as the common *acquis communautaire* among EU members as the Copenhagen accession criteria have clarified.[42] Denmark resisted the introduction of Schengen into the Community framework and, as a consequence, it does not participate in Schengen under Title IV of the TEC but under international law which thereby leads to a restricted effect of the measures under EU law and the exclusion of legal control by the ECJ.[43] The United Kingdom and Ireland also resisted the Schengen communitarisation but have made use of their right to opt in and take part in the application of certain parts of the Schengen *acquis*.[44] Consequently, the legal review under Article 68 TEC does not automatically extend to all Member States. While Ireland and the United Kingdom in the case of opt in are bound by this jurisdiction (Art. 6 of the Protocol on the Position of the UK and Ireland), Denmark falls under the restricted review established by Article 35 TEU.

---

[42] Ott, *supra* n. 11, p. 60 and for the situation with regard to the EMU: B. Dziechciarz, 'Impact of European Union Enlargement on EMU', p. 141 in Inglis and Ott (eds.), *supra* n. 1. For Schengen this is also reflected in Art. 8 of the Schengen Protocol.

[43] Protocol on the Position of Denmark annexed to the Amsterdam Treaty; Art. 3 Schengen Protocol.

[44] Council Decision of 29 May 2000, *OJ* 2000 L 131/43-47; Council Decision of 28 February 2002, *OJ* 2002 L 64/20.

In the area of cooperation in civil and criminal matters Amsterdam also made way for a communitarisation of certain forms of cooperation previously organized under international law among Member States. Originally a legal basis could only be found in Article 293 TEC but later in Article 34(2)(d) TEU for PJCC[45] and now in Articles 61, 65 and 67 TEC legal bases were created to include these Conventions in civil matters into the EC framework. The Union decided, according to Article 65 TEC, to transfer the Brussels Convention on jurisdiction and the recognition and enforcement of judgments in civil and commercial matters (Brussels I) and the Brussels Convention on jurisdiction and the recognition and enforcement of judgments in matrimonial matters and in matters of parental responsibility for children of both spouses based on international law (Brussels II) into EC Regulations.[46] This transferral into the Community system has the main advantage of opening up the jurisdiction of the ECJ by Article 68 TEC[47] while the Conventions either chose to enable the jurisdiction of the ECJ or to leave it outside its range.[48]

Due to the legal situation regarding Denmark, the Community needed to conclude an international agreement with Denmark in order to extend the application of the provisions of the Regulation of Brussels I to Denmark under international law.[49] To insure a uniform application of this Regulation throughout the Union, this agreement introduced in Articles 6 and 7 the possibility to refer a case to the ECJ and the courts in Denmark shall take into due account the rulings contained in the case-law of the ECJ. The obligation under Article 6(2) for Danish courts to take due account of the rulings contained in the case-law of the ECJ mirrors the working homogeneity clause found in Articles 6 and 105 of the EEA Agreement. According to these provisions, the EEA Committee has to maintain a constant review of developments in the ECJ's case-law. However, reflecting its EU Member State status, the ECJ has jurisdiction over this agreement and the Commission can bring a case of non-compliance on the part of Denmark before the ECJ.[50]

As emphasised above, EU members do not lose the right to conclude partial or parallel international agreements among each other[51] and these agreements do not

45 The Europol Convention and the Convention on simplified extradition procedures between the Member States can be named as examples.

46 Council Regulation (EC) No. 1206/2001, *OJ* 2001 L 174/1 and Council Regulation (EC) No. 2201/2003, *OJ* 2003 L 338/1.

47 Though Lenaerts, Arts and Maselis stress the retrograde step of reference to Art. 68 TEC which restricts references more than Art. 234 TEC does, K. Lenaerts, D. Arts and I. Maselis, *Procedural Law of the European Union,* 2nd edn. (London, Sweet and Maxwell 2006) para. 22-002, .

48 See for the jurisdiction of the ECJ: Luxembourg Protocol, *OJ* 1978 L 304/1 and where no jurisdiction of the ECJ has been enabled: Brussels Convention on the elimination of double taxation in connection with the adjustment of profits of associated enterprises *OJ* 1990 L 225/10. Also the Europol Convention is excluded from a legal review by the ECJ.

49 Council Decision of 20 September 2005 and Agreement, *OJ* 2005 L 299/61.

50 Agreement between the EC and Denmark on the jurisdicion and the recognition and enforcement of judgments in civil and commercial matters, *OJ* 2005 L 299/62-70, see Art. 6 on the jurisdiction of the ECJ in relation to the interpretation of the Agreement. According to Art. 7 the Commission can also bring cases before the ECJ involving Denmark's non-compliance with this Agreement.

51 B. de Witte, 'Chameleonic Member States: Differentiation by Means of Partial and Parallel International Agreements', p. 231, *supra* n. 7.

become an automatic integral part of Community law and trigger the jurisdiction of the ECJ.[52] However, certain *modi vivendi* can be introduced to enable a homogeneous interpretation, especially when it concerns an EU member and as long as the primacy and effectiveness of EC law is respected. This primacy works not only in the direction of national Member States' legal orders in line with the sincere cooperation obligation (Art. 10 TEC) but also in the direction of EU law as the interpretation of Article 47 TEU in the case of ECJ environmental crimes implies.[53] As a result, such special arrangements only add to the already existing cumbersome legal review structures under Title IV and in the third pillar.[54]

3.2.2 *Extending participation in EU law and policy to non-EU members*

The other category of extending EU policies concerns the EU's interest in extending its influence on third countries by offering the incentive of participation in policies and subinstitutional levels to non-EU members. The main candidates are potential members such as the EEA countries of Norway, Iceland and Liechtenstein, but also Switzerland and the current candidate countries from the Western Balkans and Turkey. In addition, also falling within this group are countries which participate in the European Neighbourhood Policy, a policy concept developed by the Union which offers these countries in the Euromed area and Eastern Europe an alternative to accession by in the future extending certain policies, possibly the internal market, to these countries without membership.[55]

So far, the ENP policy is only in its infancy and current forms of cooperation include the extension of internal market freedoms to the EEA countries,[56] certain policies such as education and training to EU candidates,[57] the Schengen regime to the EEA and Switzerland[58] and actions under the Common Foreign and Security Policy[59]

---

[52] ECJ, Case C-162/98, *Hartmann* [1998] *ECR* I-7083. See further K. Lenaerts and P. van Nuffel, *Constitutional Law of the European Union*, 2nd edn. (London, Sweet and Maxwell 2005), para. 18-007; Lenaerts, Arts and Maselis, *supra* n. 47, para. 21-002.

[53] ECJ, Case C-176/03, *Commission* v. *Council* [2005] *ECR* I-7879; critical are D. Chalmers, et al., *supra* n. 29, p. 140.

[54] See Chalmers, et al., *supra* n. 29.

[55] See generally A. Ott and R. Wessel, 'The EU's External Relations Regime: Multilevel Complexity in an Expanding European Union', in Blockmans and Łazowski (eds.), *supra* n. 15.

[56] Currently only practised with the EEA area.

[57] Agreement between the EEC and the Republic of Iceland establishing cooperation in the field of education and training within the framework of the ERASMUS programme, *OJ* 1991 L 332/22-30; Framework Agreement on Scientific and Technical Cooperation between the European Communities and the Republic of Iceland.

[58] Agreement with the Republic of Iceland and the Kingdom of Norway concerning the latter's association with the implementation, application and development of the Schengen *acquis*; Council Decision of 25 October 2004 on the signing, on behalf of the European Community, and on the provisional application of certain provisions of the Agreement between the European Union, the European Community and the Swiss Confederation, concerning the Swiss Confederation's association with the implementation, application and development of the Schengen *acquis*, *OJ* L 2004 L 370/ 78-79.

[59] Agreement between the European Union and the Republic of Bulgaria establishing a framework for the participation of the Republic of Bulgaria in the EU crisis management operations,

and Police and Judicial Cooperation to countries even beyond the EEA or ENP borders.[60] The sharing of policies without the institutions does not necessarily exclude the participation of institutions which were especially set-up to manage and implement EU policies such as the EC and EU agencies which are growing in number and are also spread over other pillars.[61] Depending on the form of the agency, whether it concerns a regulatory or executive agency, the participation might differ but this also creates problems of implementation for non-EU members. While an executive agency is involved in the management of Community policy and the distribution of information in support of the European Commission, other regulatory agencies regulate economic and social policies, such as the preparation and adoption of the regulatory framework; the preparation and adoption of legislative acts for implementing the regulatory framework; and monitoring the implementation of the regulatory and legislative framework.[62] So far, the participation of third countries in the European Environment Agency which is responsible for management and information has been based on international agreements and cooperation will be extended to other agencies in the future.[63] In such a way this participation is complete in that it includes contributing to the budget and participation in the Management Board, but without the right to vote (Art. 3 of the Agreement).[64] Currently this agency has 31 members; the 27 EU Member States and Iceland, Liechtenstein, Norway and Turkey. The non-EU members of Switzerland, Albania, Serbia and Montenegro, Bosnia-Herzegovina, Croatia and Macedonia have applied for membership.

Another example concerns the newly established European Border Agency.[65] Through the association of the EEA countries in the implementation, application and development of the Schengen *acquis* their participation in the agency is a necessary precondition.[66] The agreement foresees a unique limited voting participa-

---

OJ 2005, L 46/50–56; Agreement between the European Union and the Kingdom of Norway establishing a framework for the participation of the Kingdom of Norway in the European Union crisis-management operations – Declarations, *OJ* 2005 L 67/8-13.

60 Agreement between the European Union and the Republic of Iceland and the Kingdom of Norway on the application of certain provisions of the Convention of 29 May 2000 on Mutual Assistance in Criminal Matters between the Member States of the European Union and the 2001 Protocol thereto, *OJ* 2004, L 26/3-9; Agreement between the European Union and the Republic of Iceland and the Kingdom of Norway on the application of certain provisions of the Convention of 29 May 2000 on Mutual Assistance in Criminal Matters between the Member States of the European Union and the 2001 Protocol thereto; *OJ* 2004 L 26/3-9; Agreement between the European Union and the Russian Federation on the participation of the Russian Federation in the European Union Police Mission (EUPM) in Bosnia and Herzegovina (BiH), *OJ* 2003 L 197/38-41.

61 A list of all existing EC/EU agencies is provided on the website of the European Union, <www.europa.eu.int>.

62 See on this E. Vos, 'Agencies and the European Union', in T. Zwart and L.Verhey (eds.), *Agencies in European and Comparative Law* (Antwerp, Intersentia Publishing 2003) p. 113.

63 See example the Agreement between the EC and Turkey, *OJ* 2001 L 213/112.

64 See also Art. 24 of the Draft Interinstitutional Agreement.

65 European Agency for the Management of Operational Cooperation at the External Borders of the Member States of the European Union, *OJ* 2004 L 349/1.

66 Proposal for a Council Decision on the conclusion, on behalf of the European Community, of an Arrangement between the European Community and the Republic of Iceland and the Kingdom of

tion in the Agency, but the EU has already clarified that this of an exceptional nature attributable to the specific nature of Schengen cooperation and the special position of Norway and Iceland. Another new example which implies new flexible solutions in the future is the establishment of a European Defence Agency under the second pillar. This agency establishes flexibility on a different level, namely with regard to membership which is voluntary for EU members and voluntary participation in individual programmes and projects is a possibility. [67]

One of the primary tasks of the EU legal system with the European courts is to ensure legal homogeneity and legal review, especially with regard to the supranational pillar. These tasks are also of importance when policies or measures are extended to third countries. EEA Opinions 1/91 and 1/92 by the ECJ clarified to a certain extent under what circumstances the supranational and special legal order of the Union can ensure legal homogeneity when policies are extended.[68] The original concept of cooperation between EFTA and EC members envisaged a dynamic and homogeneous European Economic Space by extending the internal market and other policy areas such as the environment and education,[69] as well as creating common decision-making and administrative institutions with joint organs in the form of an EEA Council and EEA Joint Committee. A EEA Court was envisaged to be functionally integrated into the ECJ and national courts of the EFTA countries would also be given the opportunity to refer questions to the ECJ on the interpretation of the EEA provisions. However, the extent and modalities of the procedure's application were left to the discretion of EFTA countries. The ECJ came to the conclusion that such voluntary reference by EFTA courts would change the nature of the function of the ECJ as foreseen in Article 220 TEC. In the revised version, the Joint Committee was charged with ensuring an homogeneous interpretation and the ECJ accepted this with the argument that once the ECJ is mandated to give a ruling, the Joint Committee is bound by it. Consequently, voluntary jurisdiction involving third countries is in line with the Community legal order as long as it is agreed in international agreements that in the case of a voluntary reference leading to judgments, these judgments are binding and not merely advisory.[70]

Such ECJ 'arbitration' was in the past also agreed in the Association Agreement with Greece and the still applicable Association Agreement with Turkey so that the road to the ECJ is opened when the Association Council cannot settle the conflict.[71]

Norway on the modalities of those states' participation in the European Agency for the Management of Operational Cooperation at the External Borders of the Member States of the European Union, COM (2006) 0178 final.

[67] M. Trybus, 'The New European Defence Agency: A Contribution to a Common European Security and Defence Policy and a Challenge to the Community Acquis?', 43 *CML Rev.* (2006), pp. 667-703.

[68] ECJ, Opinion 1/91, *EEA* I [1991] *ECR* I-6079; Opinion 1/92, *EEA* II [1992] *ECR* I-2821; see on these opinions: B. Brandtner, 'The Drama of the EEA: Comments on the Opinions 1/91 and 1/92', 13 *EJIL* (1992), p. 300.

[69] Lenaerts calls this a selective duplicate of the Community: Lenaerts and van Nuffel, *supra* n. 52, para. 23-007.

[70] See *supra* n. 65.

[71] Art. 25 of the Ankara Agreement. See further A. Weber in H. von der Groeben and J. Schwarze (eds), *Kommentar zum EU und EG-Vertrag,* 6th edn. (Baden-Baden, Nomos 2004) Art. 310, para. 38.

However, it should be noted that this possibility has not so far been used in practice and in fact later accession association agreements such as the Europe Agreements do not include such a clause, which is in contrast to other forms of arbitration or the resolution of conflicts by the association committees is only foreseen in other Association Agreements.[72] In addition, Art. 20 of the Agreement between the EC and the Swiss Confederation on Air Transport is notable in that it states that all questions concerning the validity of decisions of the Community institutions taken on the basis of their competences under this Agreement shall be the exclusive competence of the ECJ.[73] As a consequence, no experience with the jurisdiction of the ECJ over non-EU members exists and the EEA example of consistent interpretation in which the EEA Joint Committee is able to settle the dispute by referring it to the ECJ has so far not been used and this role is rather fulfilled by the EFTA court and its jurisdiction. For other non-EU members such as Norway or Iceland other ways of dispute settlement have been agreed upon. So the Agreement between the EU and Iceland and Norway on the application of certain provisions on Mutual Assistance in Criminal Matters regulates that disputes need to be addressed between the Contracting parties (Art. 4).[74]

In sum, it is left to the legal creativity of the Union and its contracting parties to find long-term solutions for EU members and third countries as long as certain standards elaborated by the case-law of the ECJ are respected. This namely includes respect for the primacy of EC law[75] and EEA law[76] in conflicting situations, respect for the independence of the European courts and the non-involvement of third countries in the decision-making of supranational institutions of the Union. Especially the Schengen regime is an example of existing complexities. While Norway and Iceland apply the Schengen agreement on the basis of an international

[72] See Art. 98 Cotonou Agreement.

[73] On 14 July 2005 the CFI decided Case C-70/04 where the Swiss confederation asked for an act of annulment against a Commission Decision on measures relating to the approaches to Zürich airport. The case, however, has not yet been decided because Switzerland first disputed whether the Court of First Instance was responsible for this judgment; this was affirmed by the ECJ in its judgment on 14.7.2005, Order of the Court of 14.7.2005, in Case C-70/04, *Swiss Confederation* v. *Commission*, *OJ* 2004 C 94.

[74] Agreement between the EU and Iceland and Norway on the application of certain provisions of the Convention of 29 May 2000 on Mutual Assistance in Criminal Matters, *OJ* 2004 L 26/3-9; Art. 3 of the Agreement concluded by the Council and Iceland and Norway concerning the latter's association with the implementation, application and development of the Schengen *acquis*, *OJ* 1999 L 176/36-62; Art. 4 of the Protocol to the Agreement between the EC and Iceland and Norway concerning the criteria and mechanisms for establishing the State responsible for examining a request for asylum lodged in a Member State or in Iceland and Norway, *OJ* 2006 L 57/16-18 which involves a Joint Committee. Art. 4 of the Agreement between the EU and Iceland and Norway on the application of certain provisions of the Convention of 29 May 2000 on Mutual Assistance in Criminal Matters, *OJ* 2004 L 26/3-9; Art.4 of the Protocol to the Agreement between the EC and Iceland and Norway concerning the criteria and mechanisms for establishing the State responsible for examining a request for asylum lodged in a Member State or in Iceland and Norway, *OJ* 2006 L 57/16-18.

[75] De Witte, *supra* n. 7, p. 243.

[76] Protocol 35 of the EEA Agreement and EFTA Court, Case E-1/94, *Restmark*, EFTA Court Rep. [1994-1995] 15.

agreement with the European Union, the relations with the United Kingdom, Ireland and Denmark which either apply or opt into the Schengen regime under special circumstances also required a separate agreement between the Council and Iceland and Norway on the establishment of rights and obligations between Ireland and the United Kingdom and Norway in the areas of the Schengen *acquis* which apply to these States.[77] However, not only are complex regimes created which, to a certain extent, lack consistent legal control, but they also suffer from the disadvantages of the application of international law with inconsistent implementation, the lack of direct effect and supremacy. A way to resolve some but not all of these problems, without changing the nature of the legal system, is found in the mandate of national courts to interpret their decisions in the light of the case-law of the ECJ to ensure homogeneity or even to enable reference to the ECJ on a voluntary basis or reference to a mixed committee between the participating sides.[78]

3.3 Differentiation through accession treaties

3.3.1 *Excluding participation in EU law and policy for EU members*

The accession treaties from 2003 and 2005 reflect the political realities of a complex and diverse European Union with countries joining which have been going through substantial societal, political and economic changes. Former Communist regimes have been prepared through an elaborate pre-accession process to fulfil the requirements of Copenhagen with a stable political environment, a functioning market economy and the ability to fulfil the conditions of being a full member of the European Union including the policies of the monetary union and the internal market.[79] While the current members saw these formal criteria as a litmus test for the ability to join, they did not trust the ability to measure the effectiveness of and the actual capacity to apply and maintain the *acquis*. In response, the accession treaties include a number of derogations and safeguard measures which result in gradual accession steps. Half of the *acquis* areas include derogations for new Member States in such policy areas as the free movement of goods, the movement of persons, company law, competition policy, agriculture and the environment.[80] In sum, the accession treaties create complicated forms of differentiation which can be divided into temporary derogations from the *acquis* involving the Schengen *acquis* and the internal market *acquis*, a derogation from the EMU, transitional regimes and, in addition, optional derogations through safeguard clauses which guard the

[77] *OJ* 2000 L 15/1.

[78] For an example for this see Art. 4 of Agreement between the EU and the Republic of Iceland and the Kingdom of Norway on the application of certain provisions of the Convention of 29 May 2000 on Mutual Assistance in Criminal Matters between the Member States of the European Union and the 2001 Protocol thereto, *OJ* 2004 L 26/1.

[79] Copenhagen criteria: Ott and Inglis, *supra* n. 6, p. 4.

[80] See further: A. Ott, *supra* n. 19, p. 62.

internal market, sectoral policies,[81] criminal and civil matters[82] and even the ability before accession to accede to and insufficiently adopt and implement the *acquis*.[83]

It needs to be emphasized that such derogations and exclusions from EU policies for EU members can only be done on a temporary basis. The main examples of the price to be paid by the new members are the temporary derogations from the internal market *acquis* in the area of the movement or workers and new forms of safeguard clauses. The movement of workers provision in the act of accession and its annexes enable the EU-15 to derogate from the free movement of workers and their families for the first two years after 2004. Except for Sweden, the United Kingdom and Ireland, all other members retained their national regime at the moment of accession. A second phase was reached in 2006 in which the EU-12 had to notify the Commission whether they would keep these national arrangements in place. Germany, Austria, the Netherlands, Belgium, France, Luxembourg and Denmark decided to keep them until 2009. At most, they can be extended until 2011 when the preconditions for an exceptional safeguard clause are fulfilled. These restrictions on the free movement of workers will also be extended to the new members Romania and Bulgaria from 1 January 2007 onwards.[84]

In addition, previously unknown safeguard clauses extend wide-reaching monitoring functions to the Commission.[85] Firstly, Article 38 of the Accession Treaty 2003 applies in the event of a failure by new Member States to implement commitments undertaken in the accession negotiations which result in a serious breach or an imminent risk of a breach in the functioning of the internal market, including any commitments in all sectoral policies which concern economic activities with cross-border effect. They may be applied for a period of at least three years but with no clear end in sight as they can be applied as long as the relevant commitment has not been fulfilled. This commitment entails any commitment of the core part of the European Union *acquis*.[86] Article 39 includes a safeguard clause on relevant com-

[81] Art. 37 of the Accession Treaty 2003, Art. 37 of the Accession Treaty 2005, *OJ* 2005 L 157/29.

[82] Art. 38 of the Accession Treaties 2003 and 2005.

[83] New safeguard clause introduced by the Accession Treaty 2005, Art. 39, *OJ* 2005 L 157/29.

[84] See Annex XI, the List referred to in Art. 20 of the Protocol, *OJ* 2005 L 157/104.

[85] See also F. Bigami, 'The Challenge of Cooperative Regulatory Relations after Enlargement', Conference Paper, Columbia University, April 2003, p. 22 and K. Inglis, 'The Accession Treaties and Transitional Arrangements: A Twilight Zone for the New Member States', in Hillion, *supra* n. 16.

[86] Art. 38: 'If a new Member State has failed to implement commitments undertaken in the context of the accession negotiations, causing a serious breach of the functioning of the internal market, including any commitments in all sectoral policies which concern economic activities with cross-border effect, or an imminent risk of such breach the Commission may, until the end of a period of up to three years after the date of entry into force of this Act, upon motivated request of a Member State or on its own initiative, take appropriate measures. Measures shall be proportional and priority shall be given to measures which disturb least the functioning of the internal market and, where appropriate, to the application of the existing sectoral safeguard mechanisms. Such safeguard measures shall not be invoked as a means of arbitrary discrimination or a disguised restriction on trade between Member States. The safeguard clause may be invoked even before accession on the basis of the monitoring findings and enter into force as of the date of accession. The measures shall be maintained no longer than strictly necessary, and, in any case, will be lifted when the relevant commitment is implemented.'

mitments undertaken regarding the Justice and Home Affairs *acquis*, namely all measures relating to mutual recognition regarding the area of criminal law under Title VI of the TEU and directives and regulations relating to mutual recognition in civil matters under Title IV of the TEC.[87] While the conditions laid down in Article 39 could be justified as equal treatment, when the situation in the current Member States is kept in mind where their respective mutual trust of each other in these areas is limited, the conditions established in Article 38 manifest a substantial post-accession process of monitoring and compliance control. These safeguard clauses extend pre-accession conditionality which was previously only applied by the European Union and current Member States according to the Accession Partnerships and its Article 4 of Regulation (EC) No. 622/98[88] into the post-accession phase and in a legally binding form. They also give the Commission a new tool of compliance which extends beyond the existing infringement procedure according to Articles 226 and 228 TEC towards the EU-15.

In practice, before accession the Commission had already threatened to use safeguard measures against Poland if that country failed to meet its commitments and would not speed up its accession commitments.[89] According to warning letters sent out by the Commission on 11 March 2003, Poland was singled out as the biggest

---

They may however be applied beyond the period specified in the first paragraph as long as the relevant commitments have not been fulfilled. In response to progress made by the new Member State concerned in fulfilling its commitments, the Commission may adapt the measures as appropriate. The Commission will inform the Council in good time before revoking safeguard measures, and it will take duly into account any observations of the Council in this respect.

[87] Art. 39: 'If there are serious shortcomings or any imminent risks of such shortcomings in the transposition, state of implementation, or the application of the framework decisions or any other relevant commitments, instruments of cooperation and decisions relating to mutual recognition in the area of criminal law under Title VI of the EU Treaty and Directives and Regulations relating to mutual recognition in civil matters under Title IV of the EC Treaty in a new Member State, the Commission may, until the end of a period of up to three years after the date of entry into force of this Act, upon motivated request of a Member State or on its own initiative and after consulting the Member States, take appropriate measures and specify the conditions and modalities under which these measures are put into effect. These measures may take the form of temporary suspension of the application of relevant provisions and decisions in the relations between a new Member State and any other Member State or Member States, without prejudice to the continuation of close judicial cooperation. The safeguard clause may be invoked even before accession on the basis of the monitoring findings and enter into force as of the date of accession. The measures shall be maintained no longer than strictly necessary, and, in any case, will be lifted when the shortcomings are remedied. They may however be applied beyond the period specified in the first paragraph as long as these shortcomings persist. In response to progress made by the new Member State concerned in rectifying the identified shortcomings, the Commission may adapt the measures as appropriate after consulting the Member States. The Commission will inform the Council in good time before revoking safeguard measures, and it will take duly into account any observations of the Council in this respect.'

[88] According to which if a candidate fails with respect to certain essential elements the European Union may take appropriate steps with regard to any pre-accession assistance; see K. Inglis, 'Enlargement', p. 110, in Ott and Inglis (eds.), *supra* n. 6.

[89] On this see E. Landaburu from the DG Enlargement on 29 April 2003 in a joint committee of the Polish and European Parliament in Warsaw. See further: K. Inglis, 'The Union's Fifth Accession Treaty: New Means to Enlargement', 41 *CML Rev.* (2004), pp. 20-22.

offender, with deficiencies noted in nine areas of EU law, including the internal market rules, competition rules, audio-visual policy, the customs union and financial control.[90] The strict approach by the Commission towards deficiencies in the implementation is emphasised in the Comprehensive Monitoring Reports by the Commission on the state of preparedness of the incoming Member States which were published in November 2003.[91] Especially the internal market safeguard clause monitoring incoming Member States is problematic in relation to the record of implementation of the internal market *acquis* by the old Member States, the EU-15.[92] In addition, uncertainties arise when failed commitments can trigger the countermeasures and concerning the question of which measures are appropriate in reaction to serious breaches. In a Joint Declaration by the Czech Republic, Estonia, Lithuania, Poland, Slovenia and the Slovak Republic on Article 38 of the Act of Accession annexed to the Final Act of the Accession Treaty, these countries declared that the implementation failures relate only to obligations arising from the Treaties.[93] This interpretation is, however, on the one hand not binding because it is not mutual and, on the other, it is disputable in the light of the drafting of this safeguard clause whether the Commission and the EU-15 Member States wanted to include special monitoring on the capacity to apply the *acquis communautaire*. This administrative capacity is known as the Madrid criterion which supplements the Copenhagen criteria and emphasises the capacity of institution-building.[94] Additionally, the character of appropriate measures to counter these deficiencies is not specified, only that it has to be proportional and shall not lead to arbitrary discrimination. No parallels can be drawn between the safeguard clause and Article 7 TEU which restricts certain rights of Member States when violating the fundamental principles of the European Union specified in Article 6 TEU. Instead, this safeguard must be seen in the light of the infringement procedure of Articles 226 and 228 TEC and can only result in comparable remedies. According to Article 228 TEC the remedies include an obligation to act or to stop infringements.

---

[90] Commission threatens Poland with safeguard measures, 30.4.2003, <www.euractiv.com>.

[91] See <http://www.europa.eu.int/comm/enlargement/report_2003/index.htm>.

[92] See on this the Internal Market Scoreboard from July 2004, singling out the founding members France and Germany, next to Greece, as the biggest offenders of the Internal Market *acquis*, Internal *Market Scoreboard*, DG Internal Market, July 2004, No. 13.

[93] 'The Czech Republic, the Republic of Estonia, the Republic of Lithuania, the Republic of Poland, the Republic of Slovenia and the Slovak Republic understand that the notion "has failed to implement commitments undertaken in the context of the accession negotiations" only covers the obligations that are arising from the original Treaties applicable to the Czech Republic, the Republic of Estonia, the Republic of Lithuania, the Republic of Poland, the Republic of Slovenia and the Slovak Republic, under the conditions laid down in the Act of Accession, and the obligations defined in this Act. Therefore the Czech Republic, the Republic of Estonia, the Republic of Lithuania, the Republic of Poland, the Republic of Slovenia and the Slovak Republic understand that the Commission will consider application of Article 38 only in cases of alleged violations of the obligations referred to in the preceding paragraph.'

[94] See on this P. Nicolaides, 'Preparing for Accession to the European Union: How to Establish Capacity to Effective and Credible Application of EU Rules', in M. Cremona (ed.), *The Enlargement of the European Union* (Oxford, Oxford University Press 2003), p. 43.

The Union went one step further in the accession treaties with Bulgaria and Romania which include an additive postponement clause in the form that accession can be excluded for another year when the Commission's monitoring reports detect clear evidence that the stage of preparation for the adoption and implementation of the *acquis* is such that there is a serious risk of being unprepared to meet the requirements of membership. Subsequently, the Council will act unanimously on the basis of a Commission recommendation.[95] This safeguard clause creates a new tool of conditionality which is especially directed at the potential Turkish perspective for accession and strengthens the existing monitoring rights of the Commission by a new form of a legally binding clause previously unknown in Community law.

3.3.2 *Constitutional principles limiting exclusion?*

This extensive use of derogations, transitional arrangements and safeguard clauses results in different legal regimes applying between Member States which question the common application of EU law, legal certainty but also become questionable in the light of EU practice concerning certain policies towards non-EU-members described under section 3.2.2. Icelandic, Liechtenstein, Norwegian and Swiss citizens, while not being EU citizens but EEA and EFTA nationals, enjoy a better labour market access for the forthcoming years and consequently better treatment than EU citizens from new Member States. An EEA Enlargement Agreement incorporates all amendments and derogations introduced by the accession treaties. Concerning Swiss-EU relations and due to the non-participation of Switzerland in the EEA, bilateral relations between the EU and Switzerland have since 1999 been based on seven sectoral agreements. One of the Swiss Sectoral Agreements which came into force in 2002 concerns the free movement of Swiss and EU citizens.[96] Different to the EEA Agreements, the *acquis* is not automatically extended but the Swiss labour market will open gradually over twelve years; after seven years the Swiss will make use of a referendum to ask their population whether to continue with this sectoral agreement for an indefinite time period. From its entry into force, EU citizens lawfully resident in Switzerland have a right to non-discriminatory treatment (Art. 2 of the sectoral agreement) and after two years the priority given to Swiss nationals will be abolished and after five years the quota for Community workers shall be abolished. Thus, it will take 12 years to accomplish complete free movement.[97] In the first half of 2004, the EU negotiated with Switzerland to extend this agreement on the incoming Member States. While the EU insisted at the beginning of the negotiations on the same treatment of current and incoming EU citizens by the Swiss government, Switzerland referred to the announcement by current

---

[95] According to the Commission, this is considered as a 'nuclear deterrence button', 'Bulgaria, Romania face safeguard from Commission', 17.6.2004, <www.euractiv.com>.

[96] See S.Breitenmoser, 'Sectoral Agreements between the EC and Switzerland: Content and Context', 40 *CML Rev.* (2003), p. 1137.

[97] In case of serious economic of social difficulties, a Joint Committee shall examine appropriate measures to remedy the situation, see Art. 14 para. 2 Swiss Sectoral Agreement.

Member States to retain current national measures which would have meant that Switzerland would have possibly opened its labour market earlier than current Member States. Switzerland and the EU consequently agreed that Switzerland can keep a seven-year transitional year period until 30 April 2011 with a quota system and it is able to differentiate between current Member States' citizens who will get full access to the Swiss labour market by 2007 while incoming EU citizens are restricted until 2011.[98] Other legal collisions have been identified with balancing the broadly interpreted right of EU citizens which also includes a general non-discrimination principle with restrictions in the application of social benefits and the rights of family members of EU-8 nationals in relation to Bulgarian and Romanian family members falling still under the Association Agreements.[99]

As discussed, EU law and its special nature implies restrictions on extending EU structures to third countries. The same question needs to be asked when EU members are excluded from certain policies. One clear precondition seems to be that such derogations cannot be extended indefinitely. However, is there a general principle which restricts Member States from deviating from common standards through accession treaty law? The EU/EC Treaties do not clarify this and until now the only indications in a rather cryptic manner have been given by the ECJ in the EEA opinion in such a way that Article 300 TEC does not provide any basis for setting up, under an international agreement, a system of courts which conflicts with Article 220 TEC and, more generally, with the very foundation of the Community. For the same reasons, an amendment to Article 300 could not rectify the incompatibility with Community law.[100] The literature is divided on this question. While a majority of commentators believe in fundamental or supraconstititutional principles which cannot be altered by Member States, especially not by an accession treaty,[101] several authors see this as the inherent right of the founding fathers of the Treaties to change their content by consensus.[102] The former view is supported by several

[98] In addition, a general safeguard clause will be applicable until 2014, see generally Neuerungen beim freien Personenverkehr Schweiz – EU ab 1. Juni 2004, *Medienmitteilung Staatssekretariat für Wirtschaft.*

[99] See M. Dougan, 'A Spectre is Haunting Europe … Free Movement of Persons and the Eastern Enlargement', in Hillion, *supra* n. 16; A. Ott, *supra* n. 19, p. 66.

[100] The ECJ spelt out in Opinion 1/91 that Art. 300 TEC does not provide any basis for setting up a system of courts under an international agreement which conflicts with Art. 220 TEC and, more generally, with the very foundations of the Community. For the same reasons, an amendment of Art. 300 could not rectify the incompatibility with Community Law of the system of courts to be set-up by the agreement.

[101] On supraconstitutional principles: F. Snyder, 'General Course on Constitutional Law of the European Union', *Academy of European Law* (ed.) (Vol. VI, Book I, 1998), p. 76; J.L. Cruz Vilaca and N. Picarra, 'Y a-t-il des Limites Matérielles à la Révision des Traités Instituant les CE?', *CDE* (1993), p. 29; J. Wouters, 'Constitutional Limits of Differentiation: the Principle of Equality', p. 326, in De Witte, Hanf and Vos, *supra* n. 7.

[102] M. Pechstein, Art. 48 EUV, para. 2, in Streinz, *supra* n. 37; B. de Witte, 'Rules of Change in International Law: How special is the European Community?', *NYIL* (1994), p. 321; B. de Witte, 'The Semi/Permanent Treaty Revision Process', in P. Beaumont, C. Lyons and N. Walker (eds.), *Conver-*

arguments.[103] First, it becomes obvious from the Treaty provisions that a differentiation between Treaty amendment according to Article 48 TEU and accession according to Article 49 TEU has to be made; changes to the Treaties which go beyond mere adjustments need to follow the amendment procedure.[104] This is underlined by the case-law of the ECJ on accession treaties.[105] And the idea of minimum principles, which remain out of reach for change within a constitutional system such as the European Union, are reflected in national constitutions, like the German one and the Maastricht decision by the German Bundesverfassungsgericht,[106] and when the minimum standard is identified as the minimum common constitutional standards which are common among Member States. But even when such minimum supraconstitutional standards are acknowledged as forming the very foundations of the Community, it is more difficult to work out which principles could form these core elements of the legal order. Such principles as the obligation of coherence and the unity of law, solidarity and equality among Member States, the principle of democracy and the rule of law could be named. While the obligation of coherence among Member States is explicitly mentioned in Article 1 TEU and coherence or consistency, as a guiding criteria for the Union's measures, is mentioned in detail in Article 3 TEU, it is not clear how far this is a judiciable principle. Some authors stress, instead, that the unity of law (Rechtseinheit) as a principle is defined by the unified or consistent application of EU law.[107] This is a general principle that is not explicitly defined or named in the Treaties but shines through in Article 2 TEU ('maintaining in full the *acquis communautaire*') and is primarily an overarching principle of the judicial system of the European Union. Even though Article 220 TEC mentions only the interpretation and application of the Treaty, the uniform application of EU law becomes evident from the interpretation of the European Union as a special legal order and from the function of supervision through the preliminary ruling system (Art. 234 TEC). However, the concentric circles of integration created for different EU members, as discussed above, also question whether such a unity of EU law is applicable as the scope of application agreed between the EU members is determined. Another principle is solidarity which needs to be analysed

---

gence and Divergence in European Public Law (Oxford, Hart Publishing 2002), p. 51; M. Pechstein and C. Koenig, *Die Europäische Union*, 2nd edn. (Tübingen, Mohr 1998) pp. 251-252.

[103] In the literature also the EEA Opinion is seen as an indication of this view: ECJ, Opinion 1/91, *EEA* I [1991] *ECR* 6084.

[104] See also Becker, *supra* n. 38, p. 9; G. Nicolaysen, *Europarecht I*, 2nd edn. (Baden-Baden, Nomos, 2002); contra: De Witte, *supra* n. 102, p. 321; De Witte, *supra* n. 102, p. 51; Pechstein and Koenig, *Die Europäische Union*, 2nd edn. (Tübingen, Mohr 1998), pp. 251-252.

[105] See Case 185/73, *Hauptzollamt Bielefeld* v. *OHG König* [1974] *ECR* 607: 'No Provision in the Treaty of Accession or in the Act accompanying can be construed as validating measures, whatever their form, which are incompatible with the Treaties establishing the Communities.'

[106] Maastricht decision: BVerfGE 89, 155, 31 *CML Rev.* (1994), p. 57.

[107] On this see especially T. Oppermann, 'Die Dritte Gewalt in der Europäischen Union', *Deutsche Verwaltungsblatt* (1994), p. 901; and further A. Hatje, 'Europäische Rechtseinheit durch einheitliche Rechtsdurchsetzung', p. 7, in J. Schwarze and P.-C. Müller-Graff (eds.), 'Europäische Rechtseinheit durch einheitliche Rechtsdurchsetzung', *Europarecht Beiheft* 1/1998; see also Becker, *supra* n. 38, p. 29.

in the context of equality among Member States and the sincere cooperation principle of Article 10 TEC.[108] The Court confirmed as such that Article 10 TEC imposes mutual duties of genuine cooperation and assistance.[109] Furthermore, this principle finds its special expression in the inclusion of cohesion in Articles 158 to 162 TEC and is generally reflected in Article 2 TEC.[110] There are even indications that a clear definition as to what it entails and how far it extends is difficult to extract and has not as yet been specified by the Treaties or the Court.[111] Solidarity as a legal term is rather fuzzy; specific references to solidarity can also be found in the provisions on structural funding and economic and social cohesion in Articles 158 to 162 TEC, where the reduction of disparities in economic and social development is the policy aim.[112] There have been few judgments of relevance for interpreting solidarity in recent years. In comparison to subsidiarity, Community solidarity has kept a low profile.[113] In the 1970s the ECJ stated that, in permitting Member States to profit from the advantages of the Community, the Treaty also imposes on them the obligation to respect its rules. For a state to break unilaterally or to profit from, according to its own conception of national interest, the equilibrium between advantages and obligations flowing from its adherence to the Community would bring into question the equality of Member States.[114] The judges clarified that a failure in the duty of solidarity accepted by Member States strikes the fundamental basis of the Community legal order but this interpretation is strongly connected with equality among Member States which underpins the constitutional legal order of the Union. This legal entity is not built on power politics but on equal treatment of Member States ensuring support for a weaker Member State by regional policies and structural funding, and the achievement of common policies and goals in spite of the size and strength of the respective Member State. The principle of equal treatment or non-discrimination is mainly used in the relationship between the individual and the European Union but as a separate notion is relevant in relations among Member States. Again, the legal point of reference is the principle of sincere cooperation stipulated in Article 10 TEC. However, one has to keep in mind that this principle has a clearer image. A general principle of equality of states and there-

[108] This was confirmed by the jurisdiction of the court as early as 1973: ECJ, Case 49/72, *Commission* v. *Italy* [1973] *ECR* 101; ECJ Joined cases 6 and 11/69, *Commission* v. *France* [1969] *ECR* 523.

[109] ECJ, Case 44/84, *Hurd* v. *Jones* [1986] *ECR* 29, especially with regard to solidarity: ECJ, Joined cases C-63/90 and C-67/90, *Portugal and Spain* v. *Council* [1992] *ECR* I-5073.

[110] See further C. Calliess, 'Art. 1 EU-Vertrag', in C. Calliess and M. Ruffert, *Kommentar zum EU-Vertrag und EG-Vertrag* (Neuwied, Luchterhand 1999), paras. 44 to 49.

[111] C. Stumpf, 'Artikel 1 EUV', para. 47, in Schwarze, *supra* n. 33.

[112] This includes the fair financial transfer among Member States: see for the European Union, Peace, Freedom and Solidarity, Communication of the Commission on the institutional Architecture, COM (2002) 728 final, p. 14.

[113] See E.A. Marias, 'Solidarity as an Objective of the European Union and the European Community', *Legal Issues of European Integration* (1994/2), p. 85 and it becomes especially manifest when looking at the British EU law literature and the lack of consideration given to solidarity.

[114] ECJ, Case 39-72, *Commission* v. *Italy* [1973] *ECR* 101; ECJ, Case 128/78, *Commission* v. *UK and Northern Ireland* [1979] *ECR* 419 (para. 12).

fore Member States can be already derived from international law.[115] This equality of sovereign states is one of the major principles of international law and is reflected in the way the accession negotiations were conducted. The ECJ has interpreted this principle in connection with the above-mentioned solidarity principle when Member States were not completely implementing Community law or only implementing it in respect of those parts of the *acquis* which were advantageous to them.[116]

Whether these constitutional principles limit temporary differentiation among Member States is debatable. Not so much for the reason that they cannot be identified but for the lack of any case-law, the clear restrictions of legal review in this area[117] and due to the novelty of substantial derogations introduced in the accession treaties. Further investigation of these restrictions is necessary as they will characterise any further enlargement process.

4. Flexibility in an enlarging Union: the way forward or a way out?

A closer look at the current set-up of the internal and external structures of the Union reveal that differences between EU insiders and outsiders become blurred and make it difficult to speak about one single European legal order when certain core elements of the internal market are extended to third countries while EU members are confronted with restrictions. Without doubt, to be an insider in the system is more attractive for weaker and poorer states because the slight but decisive difference between the ins and outs is the ability to take part in institutional and constitutional decision-making and the equality among Member States ensures that different interests between smaller and bigger members are considered and balanced. However, the more the Union extends and fails in amending its institutional structures to a Union of a possible 30 or more members, the less effective, successful and attractive the decision-making will be. The introduction of an instrument of enhanced cooperation which allows the Union to resort to institutional flexibility is of no help as the selective inclusion cannot lead to a complete exclusion of unwilling Member States. Experiences with this instrument so far have shown that it is political rather than legal and is used as an instrument to put pressure on unwilling Member States. And the extensive use of differential treatment and safeguard clauses introduced in

[115] See, for instance, J. Wouters, 'Constitutional Limits of Differentiation. The Principle of Equality', p. 301 (at p. 319), in De Witte, Hanf and Vos, *supra* n. 7. He refers to Art. 2(1) of the Charter of the United Nations and the Helsinki Final Act.

[116] ECJ, Case 39/72, *Commission* v. *Italy* [1973] *ECR* 101; ECJ, Case 128/78, *Commission* v. *UK* [1979] *ECR* 419.

[117] The ECJ is also not in a position to declare an accession treaty or an act of accession null and void, but only has a limited review to analyse whether the act of accession has been infringed or secondary law has been modified with respect to the act of accession.

the accession treaties prevent the use, on a larger scale, of constitutional flexibility in the form of enhanced cooperation.

Despite this situation, differentiation or flexibility is still seen as a remedy for institutional pitfalls connected with a growing heterogeneity and complexity of the existing European Union. This can be highlighted by the discussion following the possible accession of Turkey. Due to the size of the country, it is obvious that accession to the Union will mean that the Union has already gone through substantial reforms internally before Turkey can accede under extensive restrictions to the full application of the *acquis*.[118] The concept of a privileged partnership which was presented by conservative parties in the discussion surrounding the candidate status of Turkey in 2004 and 2005 as an alternative to accession sounds, however, rather peculiar. A privileged partnership going beyond the current association status only exists in the EEA which creates a twin pillar of a special legal order in Europe which is streamlined with the EU legal order and participates in internal market and core policy areas. Whether this arrangement can be considered a role model for other cooperation models outside the EU needs to be seen as the backdrop for future internal and external EU developments.[119] Especially when the lines between insiders and outsiders become blurred and the institutional and legal dynamics of the Union slow down through an incapacity to reform the Union, other forms of flexible cooperations become more attractive. The ENP which might follow this path is still in its infancy and is not comparable due to the heterogeneity of participating third countries. In the long run, the Union needs to develop alternative concepts to accession, forms of privileged partnerships which are tested by different forms of cooperation with outsiders in different policy fields. A concept of gradual integration which consists of incremental integration in the form of joint decision-making powers for already integrated areas and the sectoral adoption of the *acquis* sounds innovative[120] but would be questionable with regard to standards set by the ECJ and in light of such fundamental principles as equality among Member States, the principle of unity and the coherence of the law.

5. Conclusion

Differentiation or the fact that the Union is growing into a more heterogeneous entity with differences in the scope and effect of the application of EU law and policy is an unavoidable development in the current and future fabric of the European Union. While the Constitutional Treaty's main aim was to simplify and structure the existing Treaties and other legal sources, a parallel development is to restrict the application of the EC/EU policies to members or to extend them to EU mem-

---

[118] See further C. Karakas, 'Gradual Integration: An Attractive Alternative Integration Process for Turkey and the EU', 11 *EFA Rev.* (2006), pp. 311-331.

[119] Łazowski, *supra* n. 15, p. 146.

[120] Karakas, *supra* n. 118, p. 322.

bers as well as to third countries. However, for EU members as well as for non-members flexible constructions which accommodate differences within the Union but which also encourage cooperation outside the Union are confronted with the deficiencies of differentiation: The lack of unity, legal control and efficiency which pose challenges to the rule of law and democracy.

Flexibility can be characterised as a by-product of the complexities of this evolving organisation. While the uniform application and effect of the supranational legal order is underpinning the constitutional system of the European Union, a flexible approach is necessary to achieve further accession (widening) and to further the integration process with heterogeneous groups of Member States (deepening). In addition, with renewed attention to the 'absorption capacity' of the Union, new and attractive alternatives to full accession need to be outlined which also create a differentiation including outsiders. Therefore, neither special cooperation among some EU members nor the extension of EU policies to third countries are discouraged. To prevent that EU policies and measures change into simple arrangements of international law, certain institutional structures of committees and homogeneity clauses are created as safeguard mechanisms. However, here a distinction between EU members and non-EU members is necessary; only those legal solutions to integration without full participation have so far been successfully adopted for the insiders such as Denmark and the United Kingdom or the special associated EEA members, but not for other third countries. It is true that institutional or budgetary difficulties can be easily bridged even with non-EU members, but the more difficult questions arise when legal effect and legal control by the ECJ is concerned. How can the homogeneous interpretation of similar provisions deriving from different legal sources be ensured, how can the primacy and effectiveness of Community law be secured as well as the independence of Community and especially EU law and its legal system? This is especially important when supranational law-making in the fields of the third pillar widens and the Court of Justice's jurisdiction in this area is strengthened. The answers to these questions determine whether differentiation is the way forward or a way out for the European Union.

Chapter 8
WIDEN TO DEEPEN? THE POTENTIAL AND LIMITS OF ACCESSION TREATIES TO ACHIEVE EU CONSTITUTIONAL REFORM

Christophe Hillion

1. Introduction

The widening of the European Communities/Union has often been used as a vehicle for the deepening of the European integration process, although not specifically through accession treaties. While there might be good reasons for introducing reforms to the Union's constitutional order on the basis of a treaty of admission, it may also have to be done within certain limits. The argument which is central to this paper is that constitutional reform through accession treaties is circumscribed notably by the Member States' and institutions' duty to observe fundamental principles underpinning the EU's legal order. The paper also examines the role which the Court of Justice could play to ensure that such limits are observed.

Further to the semantic clarifications introduced in Chapter 1 of this volume, it should be pointed out that the notion of 'widening' refers here to the enlargement of the European Union in the strict sense, i.e., based on the provisions of Article 49 TEU, instead of the widening of EU governance through, e.g., policies through which the Union exports its standards (EEA, ENP, etc.).[1] As to the concept of 'deepening', it traditionally relates to the idea of furthering the European integration process by increasing the scope and intensity of the Community method, as foreseen in Article 2 TEU. This paper goes beyond this restrictive classical connotation when examining the potential and limits of the use of accession treaties to achieve constitutional reforms. 'Reform' is conceived here as revisiting the institutions' powers, the constitutional organisation/distribution of powers, as opposed to quantitative adjustments (e.g., the allocation of seats in the different EU bodies, voting rights in the Council, etc.). Indeed, reform does not necessarily entail deepening in the sense of furthering the integration process, but may go the other way, as will become apparent in the paper.

---

[1] See S. Lavenex, 'EU External Governance in Wider Europe', 11 *Journal of European Public Policy* (2004), p. 680; S. Lavenex and F. Schimmelfennig, 'Relations with the Wider Europe', 45 *JCMS* (2007), p. 143.

S. Blockmans and S. Prechal, eds., Reconciling the Deepening and Widening of the EU

2. Can widening serve as a vehicle for deepening?

The question is of course rhetorical. There is a close, almost causal link between widening and deepening. As was pointed out in Chapter 1 of this volume, each accession process has triggered constitutional discussion and reform. In this sense, the Commission's numerous reports on the implications of enlargement almost systematically contain sections on the need to reform the Community/Union in the context of the latter's expansion.

Indeed, widening has often been used as an *incentive*, if not a *justification* for deepening. To put it differently, old Member States, or at least some of them, have often required deepening as a trade-off for widening.[2] New Member States, too, have generated additional demands in terms of EC/EU policy or constitutional functioning, based on their national interests or culture. For example, the development of the ENP and the inclusion of a specific Article I-57 in the Treaty establishing a Constitution for Europe – Article 7a in the Reform Treaty – are partly the result of the EU's eastward enlargement, and of countries, like Poland and Lithuania, promoting the development of an EU eastern policy/dimension.[3] In the same vain, the EU accession of Nordic EFTAs, triggered a greater concern for transparency and openness in the decision-making process. It has been suggested that the revised Article 1 TEU has to do with the 1995 accession: 'This Treaty marks a new stage in the process of creating an ever closer union among the peoples of Europe, in which decisions are taken *as openly as possible* and as closely as possible to the citizen.'[4]

The *prospect* of widening also has an impact on the institutional functioning of the European Union. The development and progressive codification of accession conditions by the European Council, typified by the Copenhagen criteria, is a case in point. Those criteria anticipated the introduction in the TEU of a new formulation of Article 49.[5] Furthermore, the so-called 'pre-accession strategy', aimed to prepare the entry of the CEECs, involved new institutional interactions and routines which have since then partly been introduced in the governance of EU external relations. For instance, the Commission's monitoring of the candidates' progress in meeting EU accession conditions can also be found in the context of the ENP.

Arguably, the Convention on the Future of Europe magnified the impact that the prospect of an EU enlargement has on the functioning and policies of the European Union. The Convention was established to envisage the 'Future of Europe', in the context of the upcoming 'big bang' enlargement of the Union. Not only was the convention method a novelty in the EU treaty revision procedure, it was also novel

---

[2] See, in this regard, the conclusions of the Conference of Heads of State or Government of the EEC Member States, The Hague, 1-2 December 1969.

[3] See M. Cremona and C. Hillion, 'L'Union fait la Force? Potential and Limitations of the European Neighbourhood Policy as an Integrated EU Foreign and Security Policy', *EUI LAW Working papers* (2006).

[4] Emphasis added. Further: L. Miles, 'Sweden and the Intergovernmental Conference', 33 *Co-operation and Conflict* (1998), p. 339.

[5] See Chapter 4 of this volume and the references contained therein.

in its inclusion of non-members in the drafting of the Constitutional text. Widening thus has an influence on the constitutional shaping of the Community/Union, beyond the mere arithmetic adaptation in the composition of the institutions.

Moreover, deepening has progressively become a *requirement* in the context of widening as clearly expressed in the so-called 'fourth Copenhagen criterion', whereby enlargement should be subject to 'the Union's capacity to absorb new Members, while maintaining the momentum of European integration.'[6] The Luxembourg European Council of 1997 further articulated this requirement, by establishing that enlargement would not take place before prior institutional reform of the European Union. The celebrated Amsterdam 'left-overs' first had to be tackled adequately to ensure that the Union could function with additional states. Institutional reform, in the form of an additional treaty, thereby became a *conditio sine qua non* for widening. This triggered a new IGC, which led to the painful birth of the Treaty of Nice. The latter was then considered to bring about the necessary reforms for the Union to open up.[7] Indeed, the Nice Treaty contains a protocol on enlargement, which foresees the institutional adaptations thereby required, albeit organised in several sequences (e.g., the Commission would not contain as many members as Member States as soon as the Union includes more than 27 Member States). The Nice Treaty also contained a Declaration including adaptations to the composition of the institutions entailed by the accession of new states.[8]

To be sure, Commission President Barroso's address before the European Parliament, on the occasion of the presentation of the Commission's report on Bulgaria and Romania, offered a further illustration of how deepening has become a condition for widening. The President declared that 'after the completion of the 5th enlargement, with the accession of Bulgaria and Romania, I believe that an institutional settlement should precede any future enlargement. This is the way to ensure that our enlarged Union will function in an efficient and harmonious way.'[9]

---

[6] See Chapter 6 of this volume.

[7] See G. Verheugen, 'Speech', in A.E. Kellermann, J.W. de Zwaan and J. Czuczai (eds.), *EU Enlargement: The Constitutional Impact at EU and National Level* (The Hague, T.M.C. Asser Press 2001), pp. 511-515.

[8] Here, we have an interesting scheme whereby what ought to have been negotiated in the context of accession negotiations and ultimately included in the accession treaty, was foreshadowed in the Treaty of Nice. What we are witnessing is a confusion/convergence between the Treaty revisions based on Art. 48 TEU and the Admission agreement based on Art. 49 TEU.

[9] SPEECH/06/535 of 26 September 2006. In the same vain, at a meeting with the then French Prime Minister de Villepin, Mr Barroso said: 'Nous avons ... évoqué la question de l'élargissement qui est un des grands objectifs de l'Europe mais ceux-ci doivent être réalisé (sic) dans le respect de nos conditions, de nos critères et de notre capacité à intégrer les nouveaux Etats membres. Pour la suite, il n'y a pas de décision formelle mais en temps que Président de la Commission européenne, je considère qu'il serait imprudent d'avoir d'autres membres dans l'Union – à part la Bulgarie et la Roumanie qui le deviendront prochainement avant un règlement institutionnel. Après le prochain élargissement à la Bulgarie et la Roumanie qui constitue la dernière phase de la réunification de l'Europe, nous ne sommes pas en condition pour accueillir de nouveaux Etat membre. Il faut que les pays candidats respectent les conditions et les critères pour devenir membres de l'Union européenne mais il faut que l'Europe soit préparé à les recevoir.' Speaking points President Barroso; Rencontre avec Dominique de Villepin,

In short, widening has in many respects been a vehicle for deepening. Indeed, more than a justification, widening has progressively been conditional upon deepening. The next question is to see what role, if any, accession treaties have played in bringing about constitutional reform (and deepening).

3. The role of accession treaties in bringing about institutional reform

3.1 Legal potential

According to Article 49 TEU, a treaty of admission is negotiated, concluded and ratified by the Member States and the candidate state(s) concerned. In other words, it is an intergovernmental treaty, like revision treaties foreseen in Article 48 TEU. In the EU's legal order, an accession treaty has a primary law nature, on a par with the founding treaties. Its provisions can only be repealed, suspended or amended in accordance with the review procedure established by Article 48 TEU. Indeed, an accession treaty is not an act of the institutions in the sense of Article 230 TEC, that is to say it cannot, in principle, be challenged by the institutions, or by the Member States.[10]

As recalled by Article 49 TEU, it is the *purpose* of the accession treaty to set out the 'conditions of admission and the adjustments to the Treaties on which the Union is founded, which such admission entails.' Hence, a treaty of accession must have the same legal status as founding treaties, for if the former were to have an inferior legal ranking to that of the latter, they could not introduce the 'adjustments' envisaged in Article 49 TEU. Of course, the key question here is what the term 'adjustments' (and indeed 'conditions of admission') essentially means, and in particular how far constitutional reforms can be seen as 'adjustments to the treaties' entailed by accession. It has been argued that a functional interpretation of Article 49 TEU could support constitutional reforms for the purpose of achieving one of the goals for which the Union was set-up, namely ensuring the effectiveness of the mechanisms and the institutions (Art. 2 TEU).[11]

Premier ministre de la France; Commission européenne, Bruxelles, 25/09/2006. See also in this regard the 2006 Strategy paper of the Commission and the December 2006 European Council; see Chapter 6 in this volume.

[10] Further support for this proposition can indeed be found in the European Court of Justice's case-law: Joined Cases 31/86 and 35/86, *LAISA et al.* v. *Council* [1988] *ECR* 2285; Case C-445/00 R, *Austria* v. *Council* [2003] *ECR* I-8549.

[11] See S. Blockmans, 'Reconciling Widening and Deepening: Enlargement as a Vehicle to Break the Union's Constitutional Deadlock', in A. Albi and J. Ziller (eds.), *The European Constitution and National Constitutions: Ratification and Beyond* (The Hague, Kluwer Law International 2007), pp. 249-259.

3.2 Advantages in introducing reforms through accession treaties

Given the usual parallel processes of widening and deepening, using the accession treaties to introduce institutional reforms would simplify and streamline the overall endeavour. In effect, instead of two intergovernmental processes, two ratification procedures running in parallel, there would be an overall constitutional package which could have the effect of avoiding ratification 'fatigue'. It could also be a way to tackle the increasing risk of a ratification failure stemming from the increasing number of Member States.

One could also use the accession treaty as a way out of a constitutional *impasse*. This possibility was mooted following the Irish 'no' to the Treaty of Nice. Many authors speculated about the political expediency and the legal feasibility of such a scenario.[12] In this particular case, it would have avoided creating the feeling that people are asked the same question several times if they do not give the right answer.

Indeed, using the accession treaty to introduce changes would also be an acknowledgement that enlarging the Union is not simply an arithmetic exercise and an extension of the *acquis* to other new participants. It would make it clear that enlargement is an important constitutional event, and a process which involves profound consequences for the Union, be that in its functioning or because it entails granting European citizenship to new nationals. Moreover, using the accession negotiations to reflect upon new constitutional arrangements with future Member States would arguably bring about more legitimacy to the constitutional reform. Of course, this degree of legitimacy can be achieved, either by waiting until after the accession of a new state to involve the latter in the constitutional discussion, or by conducting the process in parallel with the participation of the candidates, as illustrated by the Convention on the Future of Europe.

Depending on where one stands, using the treaty of accession to introduce reforms is also a means to involve the EU institutions in the constitutional process, in contrast to what is foreseen when the classical (intergovernmental) procedure of Article 48 TEU is followed, though it would be less dramatically different if the Convention model was to be retained as the usual treaty reform model.[13]

One could however posit that deepening through accession treaties may blur the distinction between constitutional change (the object of Art. 48 TEU) and enlarging the application of the EU *acquis* (which appears to be the object of an accession treaty envisaged in Art. 49 TEU). Blurring that distinction might tempt Member States to hold referenda that may well be legitimate in relation to constitutional change based on Article 48 TEU, but arguably less so in relation to the admission of new states.

---

[12] See in this regard, e.g., G. Edwards, 'Reforming the Union Institutional Framework, a New EU Obligation?' in C. Hillion (ed.), *EU Enlargement – A Legal Approach* (Oxford, Hart Publishing 2004) p. 23.

[13] See Art. 33 of the revised TEU; CIG 1/1/07, 5 October 2007.

Conversely, Member States should be careful about using accession treaties for introducing constitutional reform. Such treaties are, both *de jure* and *de facto*, much less intergovernmental than the treaties envisaged in Article 48 TEU. Accession Treaties require an opinion of the Commission, a unanimous decision in the Council and the assent of the European Parliament. One may wonder whether the Member States are thus willing to give the European Parliament a veto right on constitutional reform.

3.3 **Practice**

One may recall that accession of new states, in itself, entails constitutional change. Beyond the increased number of Commissioners, judges, reshuffled voting figures in the Council, and the redistribution of seats in the European Parliament and other institutions, the functioning of the EU organs is more fundamentally affected. Think of a *tour de table* in the Council with 15 ministers and a *tour de table* with 25 ministers, or the functioning of the Courts. The increase in numbers obviously leads to a different ambiance and a different functioning.[14] Think also of the additional official languages introduced by the accession treaty. Obviously, the number of jokes has to be drastically reduced in the Council proceedings. Thus, accession treaties almost by definition introduce institutional change, beyond the arithmetic 'adjustments'. Increasing the number of Member States means change in the functioning of the European Union, and the more new states are involved, the more this will affect the functioning of the institutions.

Alongside this first institutional change, the contracting states have occasionally chosen to introduce significant change in the functioning of the Union. One may evoke that the 1972 Accession Treaty did more than adjusting the composition of the institutions: it introduced a fundamental change in the EC fisheries policy, as recalled by the Court decision in its *Kramer* judgment.[15] It should be noted that this reform further *communitarised* the fisheries policy. In other words, this reform entailed further integration.

More recently, new institutional mechanisms have also been introduced in the functioning of the Union by accession treaties, under the guise of 'adjustments entailed by accession'. This creeping constitutional change is epitomised by Articles 38 and 39 of the Act of Accession 2003 (as well as Arts. 37 and 38 of AA 2005) on specific safeguard clauses. These clauses contain a number of innovations in the EU institutions powers, inspired by the routines of the pre-accession strategy.[16] In a nutshell, these provisions endow the Commission with an unprecedented

---

[14] With respect to the Courts, see, e.g., H. Rasmussen, 'Present and Future European Judicial Problems after Enlargement and the Post-2005 Ideological Revolt', 44 *CML Rev.* (2007) pp. 1661-1687.

[15] Cases 3, 4 and 6/76, *Cornelis Kramer and others (Biological resources of the sea)* [1976] *ECR* 1279.

[16] See K. Inglis, 'The Accession Treaty and its Transitional Arrangements: A Twilight Zone for the New Members of the Union', in C. Hillion (ed.), *EU Enlargement: A Legal Approach* (Oxford, Hart Publishing 2004), pp. 77-109; C. Hillion, 'The European Union is dead. Long live the European Union … A Commentary on the Accession Treaty 2003', 29 *European Law Review* (2004), p. 583.

power to monitor new Member States' compliance with not only EC internal market legislation, but also with some parts of EU law, namely third pillar rules.[17] This novel system of redress is inspired by the pre-accession strategy institutional arrangements, but foreign to the powers conferred upon the Commission by the Treaties.

4. Limits to the introduction of institutional reforms through accession treaties

Far from deepening the European integration process, the novelties evoked in the previous section appear to undermine some of the key principles underpinning the Union's constitutional order, e.g., the equality of states and the principle of legitimate expectations. Indeed, the new institutions' powers conflict with key provisions of the treaty of accession that include them. An example is provided by Article 1(3) Treaty of Accession 2003, which stipulates that: 'the provisions concerning the rights and obligations of the Member States and the *powers and jurisdiction of the institutions of the Union as set out in the* ... Treaties [on which the Union is founded as amended or supplemented] ... shall apply in respect of this Treaty [of accession].'[18]

Allegedly, such atypical arrangements may be considered as necessary 'adjustments' to the Treaty entailed by enlargement, as envisaged in Article 49 TEU. Indeed, the purpose of such arrangements is to ensure a smooth reception of the new states. More importantly, these arrangements are tolerable 'adjustments' because they are *temporary*. In other words, one could argue that an accession treaty could include extensive constitutional alteration, even if it does not sit easily with the basic organisation established by the founding treaties. The proviso would however be that such institutional change is a *necessary* adjustment to the Treaty in the sense that it is *entailed by enlargement*, and that its distorting effects on the functioning of the Union are *limited in time*, in that they are temporary derogations from the normal functioning of the EU constitutional order. This proposition has indeed been made by the Commission in the *Doego* v. *Mattheus* case,[19] and is supported by the *EEA* jurisprudence of the Court of Justice.[20]

---

[17] See A. Łazowski, 'And Then They Were Twenty-Seven ... A Legal Appraisal of the Sixth Accession Treaty', 44 *CML Rev.* (2007), pp. 401-430.

[18] Emphasis added. See, e.g., Art. 1(3) of the Treaty of Accession 2003; Art. 3 of the Treaty of Accession 2005; Art. 1(3) of the Treaty of Accession 1994; see also the decision of the Council of 22 January 1972 concerning the accession of Denmark, Ireland, Norway and the UK, *OJ* 1972 L 73. The Opinion of the Commission with respect to the accession of ten states in 2004 says the following: 'In so far as the Treaty of Accession *transposes the principles governing the institutional balance of the Union of 15 to a Union of 25*, these provisions are acceptable for the period up until the enforcement of the provisions which will follow the Intergovernmental Conference provided for in the Declaration on the future of the Union attached to the Treaty of Nice.' Emphasis added. *OJ* 2003 L 236/3, at p. 4 (pt. 8).

[19] Case 98/73, *Mattheus* v. *Doego* [1978] *ECR* 2203.

[20] Opinion 1/91, *EEA* [1991] *ECR* I-6079.

Arguably, the future accession treaty with Turkey could fail to meet this general requirement. Various elements contained in the negotiating framework for Turkey, adopted by the Member States in October 2005 to start accession negotiations, could lead to a profound change in the functioning of the Union.[21] In particular, the negotiating framework mentions that '[l]ong transitional periods, derogations, specific arrangements or permanent safeguard clauses … may be considered' in areas such as freedom of movement of persons, structural policies or agriculture. In this author's view, the permanent possibility for EU institutions, on the basis of an accession treaty, to limit notably the free movement of persons related to particular Member States, would not constitute an 'adjustment to the founding treaties justified by accession'. Instead, it would be an erosion of the fundamental principles on which the Union is based, notably the principle of non-discrimination on the basis of nationality. This principle is a well-established cornerstone of the internal market and an inherent right to European citizenship that is destined to be the fundamental status of EC nationals. The novelty contained in the negotiating framework for Turkey would amount to a profound constitutional revision, which goes beyond the framework established by Article 49 TEU, and arguably violates its provisions.[22]

In other words, while there may be advantages in using accession treaties for the purpose of introducing reform; there may also be a risk that such treaties are abused to introduce fundamental change in the EU constitutional order. Although, in principle, accession treaties are negotiated by Member States and are of a primary law nature, Member States do not have unfettered discretion to introduce whatever reform they wish through accession treaties. Legally, if reforms may be introduced through accession treaties, they may not, in any event, have the intent or effect of undermining the foundations of the European integration process. There are legal – if not constitutional – limits to the type of institutional reform that can be introduced through accession treaties under the guise of adjustments to the Treaties.

One thing is to establish the limits to the use of accession treaties to introduce institutional reforms, for instance to prevent them revising the foundations of the Union or altering the core functions of the institutions (the Court, for example). The next step is to envisage the means to ensure that this does not happen.

5. Role of the Court

According to Article 46 TEU,

> '[t]he provisions of the Treaty establishing the European Community, the Treaty establishing the European Coal and Steel Community and the Treaty establishing the European Atomic Energy Community concerning the powers of the Court of Justice of

[21] Negotiating Framework, Luxembourg, 3 October, 2005.

[22] See C. Hillion, 'Negotiating Turkey's Membership to the European Union. Can the Member States Do As They Please?', 3 *EuConst* (2007), pp. 269-284.

the European Communities and the exercise of those powers shall apply (...) to the following provisions of this Treaty: (…) (f) Articles 46 to 53 [TEU]'.

Hence, the European Court of Justice has jurisdiction on the provisions governing the admission of new Member States, contained in Article 49 TEU. It also has jurisdiction concerning the provisions of Article 48 TEU.

Indeed, the preliminary provisions of Article 46 TEU suggest that the full range of remedies established by the EC Treaty apply in relation to, *inter alia*, the provisions of Articles 48 and 49 TEU. This means, for instance, that the signature of a treaty of accession by the Council could be subject to judicial review (procedure of Article 230 TEC). The Court may also exercise its power to deliver an opinion under the procedure established by Article 300(6) TEC to control the compatibility of the envisaged treaty of accession with the provisions of Articles 48 and 49 TEU. In this context, the Court's jurisdiction is not restricted merely to ensuring adherence to the procedural stipulations of Articles 48 and 49 TEU, it may also ascertain that its substantive requirements are fulfilled.[23] In other words, the Court has jurisdiction to ascertain that the Member States do not introduce fundamental changes to the EU founding Treaties in the guise of adjustments that enlargement entails.

6. Conclusion

Widening has often been used as a vehicle for deepening, though not specifically through accession treaties. While there might be good reasons for introducing reform on the basis of a treaty of admission, various arguments suggest that it should be done within limits. Institutional reform through accession treaties has to be justified by enlargement and cannot have the effect of undermining the foundations of the Union's constitutional order. As this paper suggests, the Court of Justice has jurisdiction to guarantee that these limits are observed. Where that jurisdiction would be exercised in practice remains to be seen.

[23] Art. 46(f) TEU. Compare with Art. 46(e) TEU which expressly limits the Court's jurisdiction to the 'purely procedural stipulations of Article 7 TEU'.

KEYNOTE SPEECH

Piet-Hein Donner

1. Introduction

Ladies and Gentlemen, it is a pleasure and an honour to be able to address you in the familiar surroundings of the Asser Institute. I was asked to attend and accepted as a Minister of Justice; the request was transferred to the present Minister of Justice but he asked me to fulfil this pleasant commitment as a former Minister of Justice, although he would very much have liked to be with you today.

For Dutch lawyers the Asser Institute is a venerable institution with regard to questions concerning the future of European law. The present surroundings are equally respectable in that regard, considering that tomorrow it will be two years ago that the EU Ministers of Justice and Home Affairs met here for two days to deliberate on the steps and multi-annual approach of justice and police cooperation in the Union, since then referred to as the Hague Programme.

A discussion on the future of the law of the European Union is timely and important. Community law serves as the basis for European integration and cooperation. It is clear that the process of integration and cooperation has run into trouble since the rejection of the European Constitutional Convention in two Member States that were founding members of the European project. It is of course a paradox that recent polls indicate that European citizens, in particular Dutch citizens, although they rejected the Constitutional treaty, still have high expectations of legal cooperation within the Union. This ambiguous attitude within the population demands a great deal from policy-makers and legislation in political and legal terms. Thus it is useful and opportune to meet here to discuss the question of how to proceed and to reconcile the need to deepen and to widen European cooperation. It is clear, of course, that progress in this regard is not primarily a question of law and of legal debate, but of political will. And that political will seems to be lacking. Yesterday the European Commission announced that it intended to freeze the process of enlargement for the time being. And last week the Ministers of Justice and the Interior could not agree on any further practical progress in the area of police and justice. Considering the legal nature of the European structure and integration process, the political will could however be effectively strengthened if new juridical and legal approaches could be developed.

S. Blockmans and S. Prechal, eds., Reconciling the Deepening and Widening of the EU

This is particularly true with regard to the fight against cross-border criminality, organised crime and terrorism. These are currently some of the most daunting challenges facing our national societies. Almost all Member States have been confronted in the past few decades with an increase in crime and illegality. In the Netherlands we are at the moment engaged in prosecuting some of the leading actors in the field of organised crime and find it extremely difficult to convince people to become witness for the prosecution, simply because of the threatening atmosphere surrounding the prime suspects. If, however, governments appear to be unable to protect society and individuals from the threats of terrorism and organised crime, it will erode public confidence in the capacity of governments in general to protect public interests and private security, and thereby threaten the very fundaments of our social systems. At the end of the day it could threaten European unity – and not only in the area of justice and home affairs – if Member States would be driven apart by the fear of external threats of terrorism, organised crime, cross-border criminality and social insecurity.

2. General remarks

As I understand, you will be discussing the future of European Union law in three separate sessions. The first will focus on the question of deepening the Union, the second on widening and the third on new ways forward. All three sessions deal with issues that, if handled separately, could keep you busy for days, weeks or even years. Especially a group of learned people as has gathered here today.

Allow me therefore to limit my observations to the subjects of the first and last session: the question of deepening European integration and of new ways forward. Moreover, I will focus my remarks on the area of police and justice cooperation. Although I am no longer a Minister of the Crown and have thereby regained some measure of academic freedom, I still think that if I would venture into other areas of European integration, it would not endear me with my former colleagues.

For the same reason I fear to tread on the subject of the second session, the widening of European integration. But be assured that it is not due to a lack of interest. Although the Commission decision for a respite after the coming enlargement is understandable, it is a form of procrastination on a question that is extremely important for the future development of European society, both within the Member States as well as among the Member States. Europe will have to settle the question of enlargement in a satisfactory way, one way or the other. Personally, I prefer one way, but it is not for me in my present position to take a firm stance and to elaborate which one. That does not mean that the increasing legal diversity of the EU and all its legal implications should not be discussed as of now. Given the assistance here today of many representatives from new Member States and countries with a European perspective, I think it particularly opportune to do so in the coming session.

3. Deepening

With regard to the question of deepening European cooperation, things are somewhat simpler. Everybody is in favour and supports further progress, but nobody really knows how. The Hague Programme mapped the road. The steps that have since been taken were discussed last week in Tampere in Finland. I was not present as I had other things to attend to, but – as has since become public – there was not much support for the institutional approach proposed by the Commission for improving the decision-making process in the third pillar. Especially in the area of Justice and Home Affairs it is often not simply a question of finding a common position between divergent political positions, but between 25 (soon 27) divergent legal systems and underlying traditions. At present decision-making in the third pillar is often more effective, even with the unanimity requirement, than decision-making in other areas of European Union policy. Decision-making in the area of asylum policy has not progressed very much even though the unanimity requirement was abolished two years ago.

A major obstacle in the area of Justice and Home Affairs is the predominant legal approach in solving problems of cooperation. This is of course the approach that has proven effective in creating the internal market and in harmonising environmental policies and other administrative and competitive obstacles to the free movement of persons, goods and services. But in the area of police and justice the main obstacles are often of a practical and jurisdictional nature. Even if the whole of the criminal code would be uniform in all of the Member States, a police officer crossing the border would thereby lose all his authority and powers. Similarly courts, even though their judgments are mutually recognised, have only a territorially restricted jurisdiction. Law and legislation in the field of justice and public order is moreover not a product of the past fifty years, like in areas of administrative or economic legislation, but is the result of an age-old process closely associated with national social and political history. Thus approaches to common problems that require uniform or harmonised legislation will always meet with strong resistance.

It is precisely for these reasons that a pragmatic approach was chosen in The Hague Programme that focussed more on questions of practical cooperation than on an increasing number of legislative measures. Developments since then have justified that approach, considering that most progress has been made in finding specific solutions to specific problems especially in the field of cross-border cooperation in border areas.

Crime in border areas merits particular attention precisely because of the jurisdictional problems. The fact that by crossing the border one moves from one legal system into another creates all kinds of special problems. Thus in negotiating the Treaty of Enschede on police cooperation in border areas with the Federal Republic of Germany, we found that at a particular place an industrial site had been developed in the Netherlands that could only be accessed by road over German territory, which posed almost insolvable questions with regard to the applicable law. More often the situation of contiguous legal systems attracts individuals without respect for any law and who are looking to take advantage of differences in legislation and police systems. Thus we have all developed information systems that allow our police forces to have immediate access to car licence registrations or personal registrations, but the moment a police officer is confronted with persons or vehicles from just across the border information requests have to go by way of the capital and take days or weeks to be answered. For that reason the Benelux countries have negotiated a treaty that allows direct access to some registrations and has simplified the access to other police registrations. It moreover allows for common police operations on both sides of the border and provides the possibility for police officers to cross the border on their own initiative in order to intervene in criminal acts, even if it requires the use of firearms.

Solving such practical problems with Union-wide measures is often not feasible or useful given the specific nature and problems of border areas. Seeking cooperation and agreement on a smaller scale also proves to be a method to advance on a wider scale, as has been the case with the Prüm Treaty. It was originally negotiated between the Netherlands, Germany, Belgium, Luxembourg and Austria, but from the outset it was made clear that others could join. Eventually France and Spain joined and became signatory partners right from the start, while other Member States have since indicated that they wish to join. Similarly the Schengen agreements were originally negotiated and concluded between France, Germany and the Benelux, but subsequently almost all other Member States joined and they have since been included in the European Union Treaty.

The example of the Treaty of Prüm goes to show that substantial progress in the area of police and justice is possible by focussing on practical problems with a restricted number of partners, without being exclusive. This approach is adequate for cross-border criminality in border areas, but it is not the solution for fighting international organised crime. And yet it could show us the way.

4. New solutions

As I have just argued, Member States have to increase their capacity to combat international organised crime and terrorism. None of the Member States, not even the largest, is any longer capable of repressing on its own these forms of criminality that make use of global markets and international means of communication. In order to strengthen our capacity to compensate for the loss of national enforcement capability, European countries have to develop new common strategies for coordinating policy and operations where it is needed. We have been removing almost all obstacles to cross-border movements for our citizens, but at the same time our police and judicial services still remain locked in their national jurisdictions. A discrepancy that has been skilfully exploited by criminals and organised crime.

The harmonisation of legislation is not an effective answer to this problem. As I argued earlier, the harmonisation of legislation in the area of criminal law and public order is apt to run into fierce resistance given its historic and traditional roots. The diversity of national systems reflects the diversity of Europe, and should therefore be respected as much as possible. Moreover, it is not a question of focusing on a limited number of crimes and procedures, because national criminal legislation is a unified, integrated system. Harmonising one aspect has effects on the system as a whole and is often not feasible in isolation. Dealing with a part will therefore eventually involve the whole of the criminal system and even then it will not have solved the jurisdictional limitations of national courts and police forces. For the same reasons the attempt to realise more uniform penalties came to nothing. It was concluded that European-wide equivalent levels of penalties would be almost impossible to impose, as penalties must also be proportional to the penalties for other criminal offences within the national justice systems and that uniform penalties will still have a different effect because of the divergent national systems of parole. The same holds true for uniform penal provisions that have to be interpreted in national courts in correspondence with the terminology used in national legislation.

Maybe we should therefore start at the other end and try to solve the jurisdictional problem. Fighting international cross-border organised crime requires a police force that can as easily move from one country to another, as can the criminals and criminal activities they are investigating. Such a police force would imply not only an integrated command structure, but also a common judicial supervision by the public prosecution and the judiciary. This would imply the creation of a separate jurisdiction for dealing with certain forms of serious, cross-border crime and organised crime, that would cover the whole of the Union territory and that would operate alongside the national legal order, with its own specific standards and procedures. It would not only facilitate investigation and prosecution, but would also allow for the uniform adjudication and enforcement of any punishments imposed. Although this jurisdiction would operate alongside national jurisdictions, it need not be completely separate. Cooperation and integration with national authorities and services could be achieved by a personal union of certain functions in both the national and the European jurisdiction. Authorities and officials of the national legal system could be working in both jurisdictions in different capacities.

I realise that a solution of this kind would require the development of a large amount of legislation and regulations. It would however require just as much legislation to achieve the same goal by way of harmonisation of national legislation which would require much more effort and would eventually affect the whole of national criminal law and procedure. And although this alternative appears to be a radical innovation, it is the application of a concept that has been in use since the start of the Community. The EEC Treaty invested the European Commission with its own competence to investigate, prosecute and punish cartels and abuses of dominant positions, while national authorities remained competent in all cases that fell within the boundaries of national law. It is a solution that has also been practiced in the United Sates to solve a similar problem. Up to the 1920s the system to cope with cross-border crime in the United States was based on state law and judicial and police cooperation. Eventually it proved inadequate to cope with the mobility of criminals and the ever increasing intensity of cross-border criminality. The abduction and murder of Lindbergh's son eventually triggered the change to a system in which a federal criminal law system operates alongside the criminal legislation of the separate states. It started out as a system that only covered a limited number of crimes with a cross-border dimension. Since the 1970s the scope of federal law has increased in relation to the growing intensity of interstate movement and commerce. This has also resulted in a natural alignment in terms of legislation, without any obligatory harmonisation.

5. The judicial system

Whatever the solutions that are to be found, there is one absolute precondition for any enlargement or deepening of European cooperation in the area of Justice and Home Affairs, and that is the improvement of the European judicial system. It should be realised that by extending the scope of European regulation in the field of immigration law and criminal law, European law is entering an area of government policy in which almost each decision has to be submitted to a judicial review. As the number of directives or framework decisions regulating national policy in these areas increase, the situations in which questions on compatibility arise will also increase. The sheer number of immigration and criminal cases in the national courts will generate a workload for the Court of Justice that would completely overwhelm it. And even if the Court could cope with the increased workload, the present length of procedures would be prohibitive for national policy. National asylum or immigration policy cannot function adequately if major questions require two to three years to be answered. The same holds true for criminal prosecutions that would take a similar length of time for preliminary questions to be answered. Any lawyer for the defence would have an overriding interest in finding questions of compatibility with European law, because the length of time required to answer these questions would in itself constitute a breach of Article 6 of the European Convention on Human Rights.

A separate jurisdiction with its own system of judicial review would provide a solution to this problem as well. In the same way the administrative decision to admit a refugee could also be transformed into a proper Community decision with its own system of judicial review. But whatever the solutions for the principal questions, first these questions of the resulting workload and the length of procedures have to be solved if we want to deepen or to enlarge European cooperation in the field of justice and home affairs.

6. Conclusion

Ladies and Gentlemen, I have come to a conclusion. Reconciling the European development and the different criminal law systems not merely requires a more in-depth and a practical approach. If we really wish to deal with the increasing problems of international crime and terrorism, we must seek to find fundamental new approaches.

Effective action to combat crime (and terrorism) will require a jurisdiction that is not limited by national borders with regard to either the investigation, the prosecution or the judgment of specific crimes. I have argued for a solution of this question by instituting a separate jurisdiction, with its own criminal statutes, procedures and powers. It would be a parallel jurisdiction that could however be coordinated with national jurisdictions by way of a personal union of authorities, functions and officials. In this way the coordination and integration of national and European operations can be ensured.

It is a direction in which we should be moving if we are to arrive at balanced and effective solutions. This idea is not a directly applicable blueprint, but merely a concept. It is also an invitation to join in efforts to try and find a solution. I hope that all those involved in the law of the European Union will contribute to developing such a solution.

Thank you for your attention.

REPORT OF THE DISCUSSIONS

Karolien Pieters, Leonardo Massai and Tamara Takács

1. Deepening

Prof. Dr. Monica den Boer and Prof. Dr. Norbert Reich talked about the 'deepening' process of the European Union. Prof. den Boer presented a paper on the reform in the domains of immigration, terrorism and security and Prof. Reich looked at the internal market for services and establishment.

Prof. Dr. T. Varady (Central European University in Budapest) added some remarks to the lecture presented by Prof. den Boer. Prof. Varady confirmed that the 'fight against terrorism' is part of the European area of freedom, security and justice, but questioned whether this is the case in reality. Prof. Varady referred to Guantanamo Bay where it is obvious that dealing with terrorism is not always an element of freedom, security and justice. Although in Europe there are no such extreme examples as Guantanamo Bay, Prof. Varady emphasized some problems on European soil. He mentioned that the notion of 'terrorism' and the notion of 'actions against terrorism' have emerged under a quite unusual intensity, have an ideological flavour and have been given enormous media attention. Prof. Varady explained why this resulted in problems in Europe. During the enlargement process, the signals from the European Union towards Central and Eastern Europe were those of freedom, rights of privacy, human rights … These rights were imposed on the Central and Eastern European countries in the light of the enlargement process. These days, however, the Central and Eastern European countries receive opposite signals from the European Union through the notion of 'war on terror'. The power of the notion of 'war on terror' resulted in building a structure around the strong idea of facing terrorism by those who have a vested interest. Those with an interest are tempted to show that terrorism is huge, to say that every incident belongs to Al-Qaeda and to show how efficient they are in facing terrorism, because they would lose their function without terrorism. Prof. Varady is convinced that protection against the terrorist threat is required, but needs to be balanced.

Prof. Dr. K. Sajko (University of Zagreb) commented on the paper presented by Prof. Reich concerning the industrial disputes between the free movement rights of new Member States versus collective action rights in old Member States. Prof. Sajko

S. Blockmans and S. Prechal, eds., Reconciling the Deepening and Widening of the EU

was of the opinion that the pending *Laval* and *Viking* cases, discussed by Prof. Reich, are two very interesting cases and he hoped that the European Court of Justice will take balanced decisions. He also referred to the *Daily Mail* case (case 81/87, Judgment of 27/09/1988, The Queen/ Treasury and Commissioners of Inland Revenue, ex parte Daily Mail and General Trust PLC, *ECR* 1988 p. 5483) where the question was asked whether it is possible to transfer the seat of a company from one Member State to another without consequences for the Member States. Prof. Reich, however, argued that the *Daily Mail* case did not apply in this context, because it only concerns company law and private international law.

Prof. Dr. M. KEPINSKI (Adam Mickiewicz University, Poland) strongly supported the conclusions of Prof. Reich concerning the *Laval* case and added one observation. The labour force in Central and Eastern Europe is cheaper compared to that in Sweden. As a consequence the application of Swedish rules to Central and Eastern European companies would result in the loss of the competitive advantage for Central and Eastern European companies. Therefore, Prof. Kepinski supported all the arguments by Prof. Reich and the former case-law, such as the *Rush Portuguesa* case (C-113/89, Judgment of the ECJ of 27 March 1990, Rush Portuguesa Ld[a] v Office national d'immigration, *ECR* 1990 I-1417). The *Rush Portuguesa* case is about Portuguese labour imported into France, in which the ECJ decided against the application of French rules to the imported Portuguese labour force. Prof. Reich agreed with the 'competitive advantage' argument, but had one remark concerning the *Rush Portuguesa* case. He stated that this case-law does not exclude the host state from imposing restrictions, such as minimum wages. Prof. Reich referred to the *Laval* case where Swedish law is not clear about imposing minimum wages and the overall wage level, which is not the same.

Mr B. FIBBE (Law Office Nauta Dutilh) had a question for Prof. den Boer. The police in the Netherlands, Belgium, France, etc. are confronted with an enormous amount of work as a result of the enlargement of the European Union. The police in the different Member States do not meet the standards which are required to work successfully together on international criminal matters and they also lack the motivation of acting on an international level. The national police forces prefer to operate in their own Member States, for which they are trained and which they are used to. Mr Fibbe asked Prof. den Boer whether there is anything like a concept of a European standard which should be met by the police in the Member States, because all international rules remain ineffective as long as the police forces are not able to work with these rules. Prof. den Boer recognised that the police forces of the different Member States are not very willing to cooperate more closely on criminal matters. 'Police professionalism', such as better education, training seminars and information about the police systems abroad would provide a solution to this problem. But there is also the 'strategic leadership' issue. Last year the Board of Chief Officers released a report in the Netherlands entitled 'Politie in Ontwikkeling'. This report was not welcomed by the police because this meant extra work. It still remains very difficult for the top police echelons to motivate the lower echelons. A precondition for this change is the coordination between the different police layers. The national police felt that they were completely marginalised in the Police Working Group and the diplomatic negotiations at the European level. There should be a circulation of ideas between the top and the lower echelons of the police so that they do not feel totally neglected and are rather a part of enacting the European legislation.

Prof. Dr. L. VÉKÁS (Eötvös Loránd University, Budapest) asked for Prof. Reich's opinion on the preparatory acts of the Directive on Services in the Internal Market (Directive 2006/123/EC of the European Parliament and the Council of 12 December 2006 on services in the internal market, *OJ* L 376, 17.12.2006, pp. 36-68). Prof. Reich thought that the 'Common Position on this Services Directive' of 17 July 2006 with its 110 pages is too extensive and complicated to be presented to the public. The positive result of the Services Directive, however, is that it totally exempts the Posted Workers Directive (Directive 96/71/EC of the European Parliament and the Council of 16 December 1996 concerning the posting of workers in the framework of the provision of services, *OJ* L 18, 21.1.1997, pp. 1-6). Prof. Reich finally remarked that the rules concerning services are also applicable to association countries (countries which concluded an Association Agreement with the EC), since the freedom of association is guaranteed without restriction to the Association countries.

2. WIDENING

Drs. Steven Blockmans and Dr. Wybe Douma presented the topic of the EU borders and the process of 'widening' the Union, respectively looking at the current EU commitments towards South Eastern Europe (Blockmans) and at the limits of EU enlargement in view of the relations with eastern European neighbours, Belarus, Moldova and Russia in particular (Douma).

Prof. Dr. B. BORDAS (University of Novi Sad), commented on Blockmans' paper 'The "consolidated" enlargement agenda of the EU. Prof. Bordas started by considering the position of Serbia in the system of Community pre-accession assistance, namely the position determined in the Instrument for the Pre-Accession Assistance (IPA) and its qualification as a *potential* candidate country. She recognised the importance of this assistance relation which has contributed to making Serbia less isolated in Europe, although European Union accession is still rather distant. Prof. Bordas highlighted the importance of the role of education in the dissemination of the ideas and values of the European Union, especially in the light of Serbia's accession and the acceptance of this change by a rather sceptical public opinion.

Finally, on the relationship between Serbia and the European Union, Prof. Bordas emphasized the following current dilemmas:

- the role of ordinary people in third countries;
- the status of third-country nationals and the issue of residence in the European Union;
- the problems of the applicability of national and/or Community law to private relationships;
- the issue of tourism and the excessive length of time for obtaining a visa.

On the effect of compulsory visas for third-country citizens entering EU territory, she criticized the long-term procedures and difficulties met by Serbian citizens by mentioning the restrictions to the *principle of the free movement of persons* due to reasons of combating organised crime, corruption, illegal immigration, etc. According to Prof. Bordas, such a complicated visa regime for entering the European Union is an obstacle both for the position of Serbia in the accession process and for the acceptance of EU integration by the Serbian people. Prof. Bordas concluded her comments by questioning the future of the relationship between the European Union and Serbia in the next ten years.

Prof. Dr. V. Astapenka (Belarus State University, Minsk) commented on Douma's paper 'The final frontier and beyond: Ukraine, Moldova, Belarus, ENP, Russia'. Prof. Astapenka focused his comments on the issue of the EU's borders. At first, he considered the relationship between Belarus and the European Union. Although Belarus is not involved in the process of EU accession, the 2004 enlargement affected the geopolitical position of Belarus in Europe since Poland, Lithuania and Latvia are now its new EU neighbours. However, the status of the dialogue between Belarus and the European Union is still at the same point as in 1997 when the European Union suspended the ratification process of the Partnership and Cooperation Agreement with Belarus and restricted contacts at the ministerial level due to the lack of democratic reforms in the country. The EU enlargement process and the extension of the EU's borders may have significant effects for Belarus, both in a positive and a negative way. For instance, foreign trade substantially increased in Belarus after the 2004 enlargement. Moreover, the widening of the European Union towards Eastern Europe and the creation of new borders contributed to the strengthening of policies in the field of the EU third pillar, namely in the areas of freedom, security and justice. Prof. Astapenka recognised that the changing EU borders affects cross-border trade, relations and the way of life for many, as well as contributing to a certain level of uncertainty as far as aspects like identity, traditions and community belonging are concerned. He expressed his concern with regard to the establishment of a new final frontier in Eastern Europe. He finally stressed the need for more integration and collaboration between the European Union and its neighbouring countries, in order to promote a more effective political dialogue and economic cooperation.

Prof. Dr. V. Pavić (University of Novi Sad) asked the panel whether it could provide more information on the financial and technical assistance provided by the

European Union to the candidate and potential candidate countries. In particular, he highlighted the strong need for capacity building in Serbia and he criticized the waste of funding from the European Union. According to Blockmans, the decline in funds is not the solution, although he acknowledged the need to spend the money allocated to the Western Balkans in a more efficient way, especially in respect of technical assistance. The issue is not only the quantity of the funding, but also the quality thereof, in other words how this money is actually spent on project implementation in the field. Douma answered that, in fact, a large part of the funding for technical assistance goes to Western Europeans (consultancy and advice) and therefore the European Union should be more careful concerning the spending of the money in a more efficient way. He also mentioned the problem of local corruption in many candidate and future candidate countries. Pavić mentioned the issue of European companies investing in Eastern Europe and emphasized the fact that the European Union should put more emphasis on monitoring the activities of EU companies in third countries. He pointed out the case of Shell investing in Georgia and Azerbaijan. Douma emphasized the fact that the European Union usually requires companies to apply EU legislation correctly, although the issue of double standards is sometimes very real, especially in respect of big companies.

Prof. Dr. N. REICH (Bremen University) asked Douma about the issue of Kaliningrad and whether EU membership is foreseen for this territory in the future. According to Douma, the European Union is not pressing very hard in this respect and the current agreement with Russia is going to remain in place in the near future.

3. RECONCILING DEEPENING AND WIDENING

Prof. Dr. J.W. DE ZWAAN (Erasmus University, Rotterdam) presented categories of modalities for variations of full membership and alternatives to full membership. He recalled that variations of full membership had in the past taken place as transitional mechanisms, and temporary forms of cooperation can be used as enhanced cooperation and permanent mechanisms. On the subject of enhanced cooperation, Prof. de Zwaan referred to the Prüm Treaty mentioned in Prof. den Boer's presentation earlier that day, and he expressed the view that the participating countries should have made better use of an arrangement of enhanced cooperation, if only the requirements had been met, in order to promote police cooperation in the third pillar. As for alternatives to membership, he mentioned mechanisms similar to European Economic Area, the European Neighbourhood Policy and the tailor-made Partnership and Cooperation Agreements.

He urged the acceptance of further Member States and offered options for mechanisms to accommodate them within the European Union: either in the form of 'concentric circles' or by involving new Member States in a gradual manner, first in the intergovernmental pillars and eventually arriving at full-fledged cooperation within a regional context. He also recalled the necessity of returning to the Constitutional

Treaty and its institutional reforms, the abolition of the pillars, and the enhancement of democracy, legitimacy and efficiency.

Prof. Dr. R.A. Wessel (University of Twente) asked Prof. de Zwaan whether it would be possible to separate the partial participation of Member States within the pillars without jeopardizing the unity of the Union, and could it be possible to involve countries separately in the intergovernmental pillars without a view on ongoing developments in the Community? Prof. Wessel suggested that the debate should concentrate on the possibilities of participation in relation to certain issues, projects or operations, rather than differentiating between the pillars. Prof. de Zwaan, in his answer, pointed out that the situation is very difficult, and enlargement is highly politicized. He emphasized that the pillars are to date separate, and we have to incorporate new challenges and tasks within this complicated structure. He saw that the cooperation within the areas of peace and stability could be a good start for involving newcomers and later on the participation would gradually extend to other areas of policies.

Prof. Dr. N. Reich claimed, with regard to the transitional periods laid down in accession treaties, that the time periods are so short that they *de facto* cannot be reviewed within two years. This, in his view, is a *de facto* denial of justice which has been deliberately placed in the accession treaties. He also referred to the *Rush Portuguesa* case, where there were restrictions on the free movement of workers, but, instead, the provision on the free movement of services was employed, so that the Portuguese provider could bring its own workforce to France, and thus, the transitional arrangements were circumvented.

Dr. A. Łazowski (University of Westminster) referred to the safeguard clauses in the accession treaties of the 2004 enlargement and recalled that the Polish legislator could be subject to monitoring and sanctions under the safeguard clause based on the Accession Treaty, taking into account the fact that the Polish Constitutional Court had found the EAW to be incompatible with the Polish Constitution; however, Germany cannot be relied upon for a similar decision by the Bundesverfassungsgericht. He also reminded us that the Enlargement Protocols of the same enlargement round specify that only nationals of Cyprus and Malta will be seen as 'old Member State nationals' *vis-à-vis* Switzerland, having a full right of free movement of persons.

According to Dr. A. Ott (University of Maastricht), privileged partnership, as has been suggested for the case of Turkey, can only be acceptable in intergovernmental pillars. She also reflected on the comments of Dr. Łazowski and the double standards, and agreed that these are unfair and potentially morally incorrect, but in the Union's current situation they are legally justifiable, without any legal remedy.

Prof. Dr. F. Amtenbrink (Erasmus University, Rotterdam) wondered whether it was possible to sell newcomers second and third class citizenship. Prof. de Zwaan again emphasized the gradual involvement of these countries in the integration process.

Dr. A. FARCAS (former Minister of European Integration of Romania), reflected on the presentations of the panel by depicting the fifth enlargement of the European Union as a historical achievement with major global strategic significance. He also recalled the importance that the Commission in its country reports had assigned to the membership of Romania and Bulgaria, being situated at a strategic location with potentially positive implications for the EU's international security and stability argument. He recalled the diverging factors that occurred in the late 1990s and were widespread amongst the CEECs, emphasizing the merits of the leaders of Europe in placing these countries back in Europe in a politically, socially, economically more coherent entity. The manifold challenges that these countries had to struggle with revolved around the transformation into democratic systems and liberalised economies. The gradual achievements resulted in an easier adjustment and responsiveness to the process of Europeanization and EU membership capacity. He considered the reunification of Europe as a process which is not yet complete, highlighting the challenges that are imposed on the European Union in its relations with the post-Soviet Easter European countries.

Dr. A. Ott addressed Prof. Dr. C. HILLION (Leiden University) and his comment on how individuals could invoke a legal review of accession treaties as international agreements, expressing her doubts as to whether primary law can be actively annulled.

Drs. S. BLOCKMANS also addressed Prof. Hillion asking how far the liberal interpretation of Article 49(2) allowing for minimal institutional adjustments by virtue of an accession treaty can be stretched for the situation when Croatia wishes to join the European Union and the Constitutional Treaty is still not in force. Can the accession treaty of Croatia serve as a means for dramatic amendments and institutional reform? He also recalled that all Member States must ratify the accession treaties and that they can potentially have an impact on future enlargements and candidates.

Dr. F. GOUDAPPEL (Erasmus University, Rotterdam) addressed Prof. Hillion, and she considered that accession agreements are different from those signed under Article 300(6), as the former are international agreements between the acceding country and each Member State and not the European Union. She referred to the *Solange* case-law of the Bundesverfassungsgericht, namely that it is a national issue, having ratification as its centrepiece. She also claimed that an accession treaty is not an international treaty, but that the result is an internal text.

Prof. Dr. T. EIJSBOUTS (University of Amsterdam) also addressed Prof. Hillion, expressing his surprise that the speaker had sought refuge at the European Court of Justice and pointed out that Article 48 TEU includes the European Parliament as well, and this involvement of the European Parliament has a serious impact on the behaviour of the Member States.

Prof. Dr. C. Hillion, in his response, underlined that he had not sought to set the European Parliament aside, as he considered this institution to be very important, but, in his view, the ECJ's complimentary role should be equally emphasized. He underlined the fact that the European Parliament might have a strange influence on the accession process, as during the discussions populist opinions, unrelated to the European Union itself, may emerge; nevertheless, at the end of the day, it all comes down to the EP's approval, and, as such, the use of the veto power can halt the process itself. Prof. Hillion emphasized that what he was calling for is an ultimate judicial guarantee.

He further claimed that it is not the accession treaty as such that would be challenged and consequently reviewed by the European Court of Justice, but the decision of the Council to conclude the accession treaty. This as a legal act which can be challenged under the ERTA doctrine. He contended that Article 230 TEC is applicable *mutatis mutandis* to whatever might be challenged under Articles 46-53 TEU. Relating to individual standing, he considered that a Council decision for a permanent derogation from the free movement of workers laid down in an accession treaty does individually and directly concern a Turkish worker permanently deprived of this right. Other participants at the colloquium seemed to challenge Prof. Hillion's position on this point, recalling the *Plaumann principle*. But Prof. Hillion viewed the existence of the 'closed group' requirement laid down in the *Plaumann principle* as being fulfilled in this case. Furthermore, he argued that a permanent derogatory mechanism, as in the case of Turkey, would imply second-class membership, and such a treaty is not exactly an accession treaty, as a genuine accession treaty has to cover all assets of membership.

He also added that the Court had the power to review the content of an accession Treaty, if it is a genuine accession treaty, as an 'envisaged agreement', as provided for in Article 300(6) TEC; or if it is not a genuine accession treaty, then the Court reviews it as an external agreement of the Community in disguise, concluded in contravention of Article 47 TEU.

Regarding Article 49(2) TEU and how far accession treaties can modify the institutional structure, Prof. Hillion upheld a liberal point of view, but reminded those present that the Member States may not depart from the founding principles underlying the EU legal order. On this point, he recalled that when Ireland voted against the Nice Treaty, various institutional reforms were mooted in the Nice Treaty in order to tackle the forthcoming enlargement. He pointed out that the EU institutions had different procedural roles related to an accession treaty, or to a revision of founding treaties. Furthermore, he argued in favour of a referendum when accession introduces profound institutional reform.

Mr. D. Labin (MGIMO University, Moscow) added his remarks to the general discussion related to this panel, by recalling that Ukraine has several free trade agreements with Russia. One of the regional trade agreements is an economic agreement, which provides for the free movement of persons and is open to countries in Central Asia. Therefore, if the European Union establishes a system with Ukraine similar to that of the European Economic Area, then those workers from Central Asia would use the free movement provided by that regional cooperation as a bridge to the European Union by virtue of the most favoured nation clause.

LIST OF CONTRIBUTORS

Fabian Amtenbrink is Professor of European Union Law at the School of Law of the Erasmus University in Rotterdam.

Steven Blockmans is senior research fellow in EU law and deputy head of research at the T.M.C. Asser Institute in The Hague.

Monica den Boer is Professor of Comparative Public Administration, in particular the internationalisation of the police function at the Faculty of Social Sciences of the Vrije Universiteit in Amsterdam, and Academic Dean at the Police Academy of the Netherlands, Apeldoorn.

Piet-Hein Donner is currently Minister of Social Affairs and Employment of the Netherlands.

Christophe Hillion is Professor of European institutional law at the University of Leiden, and Visiting Professor at the College of Europe (Bruges/Natolin-Warsaw).

Adam Łazowski is senior lecturer at the School of Law at the University of Westminster in London.

Leonardo Massai is junior research fellow in EU law at the T.M.C. Asser Institute in The Hague.

Frans Nelissen is Professor of international environmental law at the Faculty of Law of Groningen University and Director of the T.M.C. Asser Institute in The Hague.

Andrea Ott is university lecturer in European Law at the Faculty of Law of Maastricht University.

Karolien Pieters is junior researcher in EU law at the T.M.C. Asser Institute in The Hague.

Sacha Prechal is Professor of European Law at the Faculty of Law of Utrecht University and one of the directors of the Europa Institute.

Norbert Reich is Professor Emeritus at the School of Law of the University of Bremen and Visiting Professor (Extraordinarius) at the Faculty of Law of the University of Tartu.

Tamara Takács is Ph.D. researcher at the T.M.C. Asser Institute in The Hague and junior lecturer in European law and international economic law at the School of Law of Utrecht University.

INDEX

A
absorption capacity, EU V, 11, 73, 87, 111-115, 156
see also integration capacity, EU
see also enlargement, EU
see also European, membership, conditionality
see also post-accession monitoring
accession negotiations 69-73 77, 81-86, 109, 111, 147, 149 n. 86, 154, 159 n. 8, 161, 164
benchmarking 83-85
chapters of accession negotiation 63-64, 70 n. 50, 71, 83-84
revised procedure 71, 82-84
screening process 70, 77
suspension of 84-85, 100
see also enlargement, EU
accession treaties 3, 12, 31, 82, 121, 135-136, 146-147, 150-157, 160-165, 180-182
Act of Accession 63 n. 19, 64, 119, 147, 149, 154, 162
as a vehicle for introducing institutional reform 12, 161-162
limits of 163-164
ratification of 160-161, 181
safeguard clauses 64, 82-83, 117, 146-150, 151 n. 98, 154, 162, 164, 180
status in EU legal hierarchy 160
transition periods 64, 82
see also enlargement, EU
see also flexibility, differentiation through accession treaties
see also post-accession monitoring
agencies (EC/EU) 16, 143-144
Albania 5, 60, 73-74, 79-80, 86, 143
Albany case, ECJ [1999] 33, 36, 54 n. 65
Alcan case, ECJ [1997] 54
Angonese case, ECJ [2000] 40
Ankara Agreement 61-63, 144 n. 71
approximation of national legislation to EU's *acquis* 24, 89, 109
Area of Freedom, Security and Justice (AFSJ) 6, 13, 18, 20, 25-26, 28
Armenia 5-6
Asser College Europe VI
asylum, visa and migration policy, EU 14, 18, 23, 169,
see also immigration
Austria 2-3, 14, 34 n. 16, 38-39, 55, 69-70, 82, 133, 147, 160, 170
Azerbaijan 5-6, 179

B
Barcelona Process 5
Barroso, José Manuel 71 n. 52, 159
see also, European Commission, President of
Belarus V, 4-6, 178
Belgium 101 n. 49, 147, 170, 176
benchmarking
see accession negotiations
Benelux 101 n. 48, 135, 170
Black Sea Economic Cooperation 78
border controls 14-16, 18, 22-23
see also FRONTEX
Bosman case, ECJ [1995] 40, 55
Bosnia and Herzegovina (BiH) 5, 60, 73-74, 79-80, 85-86, 135, 143 n. 60
Brussels Convention 51, 141
Bulgaria 4, 9, 14, 60, 79-83, 111, 119, 142 n. 59, 147, 150-151, 159, 181
Bundesverfassungsgericht 152, 180-181
Maastricht Urteil 119 n. 33, 152
Solange doctrine 180
Byggnads (Laval case), ECJ 30, 32-34, 37-46, 49-55

C
candidate countries V-VI, 1, 3-5, 11, 19, 28, 60-65, 67, 73-77, 83-86, 113-116, 130, 135 n. 14, 142, 179
see also accession negotiations
see also Copenhagen criteria
see also enlargement, EU
see European Union, membership conditionality
see also Instrument for Pre-accession Assistance (IPA)
see also potential candidate countries
see also pre-accession conditionality, EU
Caucasus 5-6
Central and Eastern European Countries (CEEC) 3, 5, 8-9, 18, 62-67, 80, 86, 158, 175-176, 181

Central European Initiative 78
Central European University V, 175
Central European Free Trade Agreement (CEFTA) 13, 80-81, 85
see also regional cooperation (as EU membership conditionality)
Charlemagne 59
Charter of Fundamental Rights of the EU 3, 7-8, 15, 26, 35-36, 52
citizenship of the EU 2, 29, 83 n. 111, 96 n. 26, 161, 164
Clingendael Institute VI
closer cooperation 2-3, 9, 135-138
see also enhanced cooperation
see also flexibility
cohesion (principle of) V, 2, 153
Commission v. France [1997] 39, 153 n. 108
Commission v. Luxembourg [2004] 38 n. 26, 44
Committee of the Regions 2
Committee on Internal Security (COSI) 27
Common Foreign and Security Policy (CFSP) 2-3, 66, 73-74, 124-125, 140, 142
see also European Political Cooperation (EPC)
see also European Security Strategy (ESS)
see also High Representative for the Common Foreign and Security Policy
see also High Representative of the Union for Foreign Affairs and Security Policy
see also Second Pillar
Common Security and Defence Policy (CSDP) 144 n. 67
concentric circles of integration 134, 136, 152, 179
see also flexibility
constitutional traditions in EU Member States 29, 35
constitutional principles of the EU 134 n. 3, 150, 154
constitutional reform of the EU 157, 160-162
Constitutional Treaty, EU 4, 7-8, 10, 21 n. 26, 22 n. 30, 23-26, 85, 116, 124, 133, 139, 167, 181
see also Treaty establishing a Constitution for Europe
Convention on the Future of Europe 3, 158, 161
Copenhagen criteria 9, 76-77, 83, 146. n. 49, 149, 158
see also absorption capacity, EU
see also enlargement, EU
see also European Union, membership, conditionality
COREPER 20, 120-121
see also Council of Ministers, EU
corruption (anti-corruption policy) 5, 9, 19
Costa v. ENEL, ECJ [1964] 95 n. 24
Council of Europe 26, 67
Council of Ministers, EU 69-71
General Affairs and External Relations Council (GAERC) 63, 71 n. 53
voting systems (representation of Member States) 117-119, 126, 128
see also COREPER
see also decision-making, EU
see also qualified majority voting (QMV)
Court of First Instance (CFI) 79, 107, 145 n. 73
Court of Justice (ECJ) 7, 11-12, 25, 29-35, 39-51, 79, 89-98, 102-108, 118, 134 n. 4-5, 137, 140-146, 151-156, 160, 165, 176, 181-182
annulment procedure (Art. 230 TEC) 94 n. 22, 145 n. 73, 181
infraction procedures (Artt. 226 and 228 TEC) 95, 100-103
see also 'policing the boundaries'
see also uniform application and interpretation of EU law
Croatia V, 4, 60, 68-71, 77-83, 88 n. 3, 143, 181
see also candidate countries
Cyprus 5, 9, 60-64, 69 n. 41, 82, 180
Czech Republic 62, 69 n. 41, 80, 149

D

Daily Mail case, ECJ [1988] 176
data protection (data exchange) 23, 26
decision-making, EU 2, 6, 9, 13-28, 73, 79, 82, 91, 99-100, 112-128, 135, 144-145, 154, 158, 169
assent procedure 3, 68, 72, 122, 162
co-decision procedure 24-25, 122, 127
see efficiency, EU
deepening of the European Union V, 1-12, 14-19, 29, 59-60, 87, 109, 121, 127, 133, 137, 156-175, 179
Delors, Jacques 3
del Ponte, Carla 70 n. 47, 81
Denmark 2, 35, 72, 140-141, 146-147, 156, 163 n. 18
differentiation, EU 12-13, 19, 78, 133-141, 146, 151 n. 101, 154-156
see also flexibility
direct effect (principle of) 39, 95-98, 116, 146
Directive 96/71/EEC 30
directoire(s) 9
see also flexibility
see also pioneer groups
disintegration of the EU 8, 134

E

effet utile (doctrine of) 41
Energy Community Treaty 79-80, 85, 88
see also enhanced multilateralism
see also regional cooperation (as EU membership conditionality)

enhanced bilateralism 11, 79, 85, 88-91, 108-110
see also European, membership, alternatives to full membership
enhanced cooperation 3, 9, 19, 66, 93, 121-122, 129, 136-139, 154-155, 179
see also closer cooperation
see also flexibility
enhanced multilateralism 79, 85, 88-89, 93-96, 108-110
see also European, membership, alternatives to full membership
enlargement, EU V, 1-15, 19, 24, 29, 59-88, 111-136, 140 n. 42, 147-168, 172-182
borders of the EU V, 4-5, 14-21, 59, 85-86, 96, 101, 135, 140, 143-144, 173, 177-178
see also European Union, membership, conditionality, Art. 49 TEU, geography
enlargement agenda for South Eastern Europe 59-86
history of V, 1-6, 85, 114 n. 13
opposition to V, 60
see also accession negotiations
see also candidate countries
see also Copenhagen criteria
see European Union, membership, conditionality
see also Instrument for Pre-accession Assistance (IPA)
see also post-accession monitoring
see also pre-accession conditionality, EU
see also widening of the European Union
environmental protection 2, 6, 7, 48 n. 51, 79, 84, 95, 134 n. 7, 142-146, 169
equal treatment (principle of) 52, 104 n. 60, 153
see also prohibition of discrimination (principle of)
Estonia 31, 69 n. 41, 149
Euro(zone) 9
Eurojust 15-16, 23-27
Europe Agreement (EA) 65 n. 30, 67, 77, 89, 109 n. 79, 145
European Arrest Warrant (EAW) 138, 180
European Central Bank 7
European Coal and Steel Community (ECSC) 59, 76, 80, 94, 164
European Commission 3-5, 12, 15-18, 24, 20-27, 49-86, 92-93, 107, 112-118, 122-130, 133 n. 7, 141, 147-150, 158, 163, 167-17
size and composition of 3
decision-making by 20-21
President of 3, 113, 125, 129 n. 69, 159
see also Barroso, José Manuel
member of 3, 68 n. 34, 75, 99, 122-129, 162
European Common Aviation Area (ECAA) 79-80
see also regional cooperation (as EU membership conditionality)
European Communities (EC) 2, 12, 29, 32-36, 40-41, 47 n. 46, 56, 59, 61, 69, 76, 87-108, 134-139, 142-144, 155-158, 162-165, 177
see also European Union
European Constitution V, 29, 35, 117 n. 26, 133-134, 160 n. 11
see also Treaty establishing a Constitution for Europe
European Convention for the Protection of Human Rights (ECHR) 34-35, 39, 45, 52-53
European Council 1, 4, 17, 26, 62-76, 82-86, 111-115, 124-130, 159-160
President of 4
European Court of Human Rights 34
see also Gustafsson judgment
see also Rasmussen judgment
European Court of Justice
see Court of Justice (ECJ)
European Drugs Monitoring Agency for Drugs Addiction 16
European Economic Area (EEA) 11, 87-110, 135, 141-145, 150-157, 163, 179, 183
EEA Council 92, 144
EEA Joint Committee 92, 99-100, 107, 144-145
EEA Opinion [1991] 144, 151-152
EEA Opinion [1992] 144
European Free Trade Area (EFTA) 88-109, 144-145, 150
EFTA Court 91-109, 145
Akoeruvaldio v. Asgeirsson et al. [2003] 97, 106
CIBA v. Norway [2002] 106-107
Einarsson v. Iceland [2002] 98
Karlsson hf. v. Iceland [2002] 98, 107 n. 75
Paolo Pizza v. Paul Schurte AG [2005] 106
Sveinbjörnsdottir v. Iceland [1998] 96, 98, 107 n. 75
EFTA Surveillance Authority 92-94, 100-105
EFTA Surveillance Authority v. Iceland [2003] 104
EFTA Surveillance Authority v. Liechtenstein [2005] 104
EFTA Surveillance Authority v. Norway [2003] 103
European integration process V, 1-12, 157, 163-164
see also Intergovernmental Conference (IGC)
European Monetary Union (EMU) 6, 139-140, 146

European Neighbourhood Policy (ENP) VI, 5, 11, 13, 56, 87, 135, 142-143, 155-158, 178-179
  see also European Union, membership, alternatives to full membership
European Parliament (EP) 2-3, 12, 15-16, 24-26, 68, 71-72, 84, 96 n. 26, 112-138, 148 n. 89, 159, 162, 177, 181-182
  Brok Report 113-116, 123-124
  composition and competences 24-25, 68, 114-137, 157-162
  reform of electoral systems in Member States 127
  Stubb Report 113-118
European Police College (CEPOL) 15
European Political Cooperation (EPC) 2
European Public Prosecutor 13
European Road Transport Agreement (ERTA) 138, 182
European Security Strategy (ESS) 13
European Union (EU) 1-35, 43, 55-183
  institutional structure and reform V, 2-12, 59, 111-131, 135-137, 154-165, 180-182
    accountability 7, 27, 117-118, 125-127
    institutional balance (principle of) 116, 127, 163 n. 18
    democratic legitimacy 2, 11, 22, 112, 115-118, 123, 127-130
    efficiency 7, 11, 27, 112-127, 130, 136, 156, 180
    institutional capacity 111-131
    through accession treaties 12, 157-165
    transparency 3, 8, 11, 20, 27, 48, 57, 115, 158
    see also pillar structure, EU
  membership 2-6, 11, 60-88, 95, 108-122, 129-135, 142-144, 150, 164 n. 22, 179-182
    alternatives to full membership 156, 179
      privileged partnerships 155, 180
      second-class membership 110, 182
      see also enhanced bilateralism
      see also enhanced multilateralism
      see also European Neighbourhood Policy (ENP)
    conditionality 60, 65 n. 28, 66-67, 73-85, 130-135, 148-150
      Art. 49 TEU 4, 76, 87, 152, 157-165
        European identity 5-6
        Geography 4-5, 10-15, 49, 59, 87-89, 104, 108, 120, 123
      Art. 6 TEU (human rights, democracy, rule of law) 3, 8, 149, 164-165
      see also Copenhagen criteria
      see also absorption capacity

European Union (EU)...
  membership...
    conditionality (cont.)
      see also International Criminal Tribunal for the former Yugoslavia, ICTY conditionality
      see also regional cooperation (as EU membership conditionality)
  as reform promoter, exporter of standards 11
  see also European Communities (EC)
  see also European integration process
Europol 14, 16, 22-27, 141 n. 45 and 48
European Policy Mission in Bosnia-Herzegovina (EUPM) 135 n. 15, 143 n 60
External Borders Convention 14

F

Finalarte case, ECJ [2001] 44
Finland 2, 3, 14, 21 n. 29, 31, 37, 48, 120, 133, 169
flexibility (in EU law and policy) 8-9, 12, 125, 133-139, 154-156
  constitutional flexibility 136-137, 155
  different forms of 136
  differentiation 12, 136-141, 146, 151-156
    constitutional principles limiting differentiation 150-154
    through accession treaties 136, 146-154
    through international agreements 140-146
  opt-in/out 2-3, 8-9, 19-20, 26, 134, 137 n. 22, 140, 146
  see also concentric circles of integration
  see also closer/enhanced cooperation
  see also directoire(s)
  see also multi-speed Europe
  see also variable geometry
  see also voluntary withdrawal from the EU
Former Yugoslav Republic of Macedonia (FYROM) 4-5, 60, 72-73, 79-80, 86, 88 n. 33, 143
  see candidate countries
France 4, 39-40, 47, 59, 65, 72, 82, 85, 120, 123-124, 147, 149 n. 92, 153 n. 108, 159 n. 9, 170, 176, 180
Francovich and Bonifaci cases, ECJ [1991] 39
freedom of contract 33
freedom of establishment 10, 39, 55, 104
freedom to provide services 18 n. 17, 30-56, 64
  Directive 2006/123/EC (Services directive) 177
free movement of workers 8, 38-40, 61, 64, 83 n. 112, 109, 147, 180-182
Friedenspflicht 36, 42-46
FRONTEX 16
  see also border controls

G

Georgia 5-6, 88 n. 3, 109, 179

Germany 38, 47, 50, 55, 101 n. 48-49, 120 n. 34, 124, 147, 149 n. 92, 169, 170, 180
Gotovina, Ante 68 n. 38, 69-70, 81
Gustafsson judgment, ECtHR [1996] 34-35, 42, 44

H

(The) Hague programme 13-14, 19-22, 28, 167, 169
High Representative for the Common Foreign and Security Policy 3, 73 n. 65
  see also Common Foreign and Security Policy
High Representative of the Union for Foreign Affairs and Security Policy 7
  see also Minister for Foreign Affairs, EU
homogeneity (principle of) 89, 93, 95-102, 107-108, 141, 144-146, 156
Hungary 62, 69 n. 42, 80

I

Iceland 80 n. 96, 90 n. 8, 96-99, 104, 107 n. 75, 108, 135, 142-146, 150
institutional balance (principle of) 116, 127, 163 n.18
  see also European Union, institutional structure and reform
International Criminal Tribunal for the former Yugoslavia (ICTY) 66, 70, 75, 77, 81-82
  ICTY conditionality 81-82
  see also European Union, membership, conditionality
immigration 6-7, 13-14, 18-19, 21-22, 172, 175-176, 178
  see also asylum, visa and migration policy, EU
industrial action 30-42
Instrument for Pre-accession Assistance (IPA) 177
  see enlargement, EU
  see also pre-accession conditionality
integration capacity, EU V, 11, 112 -115
  see also absorption capacity, EU
  see also European Union, membership, conditionality
Intergovernmental Conference (IGC) 3-4, 7-8, 23, 63, 84, 138, 158 n. 4, 159, 163 n. 18
  see also European integration process
International Monetary Fund (IMF) 72
Ioannina compromise 8
Ireland 2, 19, 140, 146-147, 153 n. 114, 163 n. 18, 182
Italy 39 n. 33, 68, 82, 120, 138, 153-154

J

Justice and Home Affairs (JHA) 2, 13, 16-17, 21 n. 29, 22, 65, 137 n. 22, 148, 167-169, 172
  see also Police and Judicial Cooperation in Criminal Matters (PJCC)
  see also security (AFSJ)
  see also Third Pillar

K

Kaliningrad 179
Karadžić, Radovan 74-75, 81
Kosovo 60, 66, 74, 79-81, 85-86
Kramer case, ECJ [1976] 162

L

Laeken Declaration 115
Latvia 29-30, 34, 37-38, 44-46, 50-57, 69, 178
Latvian Construction Workers Association (LCWA) 37, 45
Laval case, ECJ [2007] 11, 29-57, 176
legal personality, EU 8
Lex Britannia 30, 36, 40-56
Liechtenstein 99, 104, 106, 135, 142-143, 150
Lisbon Treaty
  see Reform Treaty
Lithuania 69 n. 41, 149, 158, 178
loyal cooperation (principle of) 95
Luxembourg 1, 38, 44, 62, 69-70, 101, 107, 137, 141, 147, 159, 164, 170

M

Macedonia
  see Former Yugoslav Republic of Macedonia (FYROM)
Malta 5, 9, 69, 180
MATRA programme VI
Mattheus v. Doego case, ECJ [1978] 163
Mengozzi, Advocate General, ECJ 29-30, 55
membership of the EU 2-6, 11, 60-88, 95, 108-122, 129-135, 142-144, 150, 164 n. 22, 179-182
  see also Copenhagen criteria
  see also European Union, membership
Milošević, Slobodan 75
Minister for Foreign Affairs, EU 7, 64, 69
  see High Representative of the Union for Foreign Affairs and Security Policy
Mladić, Ratko 74-75, 81
Moldova 4-6, 80, 177-178
Monnet, Jean 17, 63, 83, 119-120, 129 n. 70
Montenegro 60, 74-75, 79-80, 86, 143
Morgenstern, Christian 131
multi-speed Europe 2, 8-10
  see also flexibility

N

NATO 62, 67

national parliaments 7-8, 24-26, 118, 125-126
Netherlands 1, 4, 12-13, 18, 22, 29, 59, 68, 81-87, 101, 111, 118, 120, 123, 125, 133, 147, 157, 167-170, 175, 176, 185
Nordic Council 135
Norway 80, 90, 97, 99, 103-104, 108, 135, 142-143

O
OECD 72
Omega Spielhallen case, ECJ [2004] 52
opt-outs 2, 8
  see also flexibility
organised crime (tackling of) 5, 13, 15, 22 n. 32, 78, 168, 170-171, 178
OSCE 67

P
partial agreements 141
participation in EU law and policy for EU members 141
participation in EU law and policy for non-EU members 142-146
Partnership and Cooperation Agreement 178-179
pillar structure, EU 3, 7-8, 20, 139 n. 38
  disappearance of 8
  see also 'policing the boundaries'
  see also Second Pillar
  see also Third Pillar
pioneer groups 19
  see also directoire(s)
  see also flexibility
Poaires Maduro, Advocate General, ECJ 31 n. 6
Poland 62, 69, 80, 148-149
Police and Judicial Cooperation in Criminal Matters (PJCC) 3, 8, 21, 24-26
  see also Justice and Home Affairs (JHA)
'policing the boundaries' (Artt. 46-47 TEU) 17 n. 14, 18 n. 16, 25
Portugaia Construcoes case, ECJ [2002] 44 n. 43, 50
posting of workers 30 n. 5, 37-38, 56, 177
post-accession monitoring 148
potential candidate countries VI, 5, 11, 60, 65, 73-74, 77, 85-86, 113, 177, 179
pre-accession conditionality 67, 76, 148
  see also European Union, membership conditionality
  see also Instrument for Pre-accession Assistance (IPA)
primacy of Community law principle 53
privileged partnership 155, 180
  see also European Union, membership, alternatives to full membership
prohibition of discrimination (principle of) 12, 83
  see also equal treatment (principle of)
proportionality (principle of) 36, 55, 57, 118, 125
public policy exceptions 51

Q
qualified majority voting (QMV) 2, 7, 21, 23, 115, 117, 120, 124
  see also Council of Ministers

R
Rasmussen judgment, ECtHR [2006] 34-35, 162
reconciling the deepening and widening of the EU V, 4, 29, 109, 179
Reform Treaty 7, 8, 13, 19 n. 22, 23-25, 27, 158
regional cooperation (as EU membership conditionality) 77-78 81
  see also Central European Free Trade Agreement (CEFTA)
  see also European Common Aviation Area
  see also Energy Community Treaty
  see also European Union, membership, conditionality
Romania 4, 9, 14, 60, 79-80, 82-83, 111, 119 n. 31, 147, 150-151, 159, 181
Rush Portuguesa case, ECJ [1990] 38, 43-46, 176, 180
Russia V, 5, 92, 143, 177-179, 183

S
Schengen (Agreement, *acquis*) 2-3, 8-9, 12, 15-16, 18-19, 22, 90 n. 8 and 11
Schmidberger case, ECJ [2003] 34 n. 16, 39
Schuman, Robert 17
Second Pillar 122 n. 41, 144
  see also Common Foreign and Security Policy
security (AFSJ) 6, 10, 12-28, 175, 178, 181
  see also Police and Judicial Cooperation in Criminal Matters (PJCC)
Serbia 60, 74-75, 78 n. 90, 8082, 86, 143, 177-179
Serbia and Montenegro 74-75, 80, 143
Single European Act 2, 109, 134
Slovak Republic 69, 80, 149
Slovenia 9, 69, 71, 80, 149
Social Protocol 2-3
social dumping 11, 30-31, 47 n. 45, 51-52, 55-57
social rights 10-11, 29-59
  minimum pay, collective bargaining, industrial action 47, 50, 53
  labour unions 29-35, 39-45, 52, 54-55, 57
  non-statutory exemptions for 33
Solana, Javier
  see High Representative for the Common Foreign and Security Policy
solidarity (principle of) 20, 152-154
Southeast Europe Cooperation Initiative 78
South East Europe Cooperation Process 78

Spain 2, 32 n. 13, 64 n. 26, 153 n. 109, 170
Stabilisation and Association Agreement (SAA) 65-69, 72-78, 81, 86
Stabilisation and Association Process (SAP) 65-68, 73, 77-78, 87
Stability Pact for South Eastern Europe 77, 78 n. 89
(member) state liability (principle of) 39, 95-98, 107
subsidiarity (principle of) 2, 7-8, 24-25, 125-126, 153
supranationalism / supranationality 8, 134
Sweden 2-3, 14, 34-38, 42-50, 55-57, 120, 133, 147, 158 n. 4, 176
Switzerland 11, 19, 88-95, 99-102, 108, 110, 135, 142, 143, 145, 150-151, 180
  Bilateral I agreement 94, 100-102
  Bilateral II agreement 90, 92
  EC-Swiss Agreement on Air Transport 90, 93, 95-96, 101
  EU-Swiss Agreement on Schengen 90 n. 11, 92 n. 18, 93 n. 20, 95, 99, 101-102, 108
  guillotine clause 110

T

Tampere programme 14-15, 20
  see also Justice and Home Affairs (JHA)
  see also security (AFSJ)
Third Pillar 3, 7, 14, 20, 121, 137, 139 n. 38, 142, 156, 163, 169, 178-179
  see also Justice and Home Affairs (JHA)
  see also Police and Judicial Cooperation in Criminal Matters (PJCC)
T.M.C. Asser Institute V-VI, 167, 185-186
terrorism (counter-terrorism) 13-22, 28, 66, 138 n. 30, 168-175
transition periods 64, 82
  see also accession treaties
Treaty establishing a Constitution for Europe V, 4, 59, 111, 117 n. 24, 123, 158
  French and Dutch referenda on V, 4, 59
  name and symbols 7
  see also European Constitution
Treaty of Amsterdam 3, 13-14, 16, 23, 109, 122 n. 44, 135, 137, 137 n. 22, 138 n. 33 and 35, 140 n. 43, 141, 159
Treaty of Enschede 169
Treaty of Lisbon
  see Reform Treaty
Treaty of Maastricht 2-3, 7, 13-14, 103, 109, 115, 134, 137 n. 22
Treaty of Nice V
Treaty of Prüm 9, 19, 170, 179
Treaty of Rome 117 n. 26
treaty revision procedure 151 n. 186, 158, 159 n. 8
  Art. 48 TEU 121, 125, 129, 152, 160-161, 162, 165, 181
  simplification of 129
Turkey V, 4-5, 59-67, 70 n. 47, 81 n. 99, 82-83, 86-88, 109-111, 118-120, 133, 142-144, 155, 164, 180, 182
  see also candidate countries
two-speed Europe
  see flexibility

U

Überseering case, ECJ [2002] 39
United Kingdom 2, 8-9, 19, 26, 68, 81-82, 120, 124, 140, 146-147, 156
Ukraine V, 4-6, 88, 92, 109, 178, 182-183
uniform application and interpretation of EU law 93-95
United Nations Security Council 61, 66, 79
United States 4, 19, 171
Utrecht University VI, 185

V

Van Gend and Loos case, ECJ [1963] 95 n. 24
variable geometry 9-10, 20, 91 n. 12, 136 n. 17
  see also flexibility
Viking case, ECJ [2007] 11, 30-31, 55, 176
voluntary withdrawal from the EU 136-137, 139
  see also flexibility

W

Walrave case, ECJ [1974] 40, 55
Werhof case, ECJ [2006] 35
Western Balkans 60, 65-68, 7374, 76-77, 78-79, 81, 85, 87-88, 133, 142, 179
  EU-Western Balkans summit in Zagreb 65, 74
  EU-Western Balkans summit in Thessaloniki 65
  European Partnerships 66
widening of the European Union 1-2, 10-15, 19, 29, 60, 67, 85-87, 111-113, 117, 120-121, 126, 127, 130, 133, 156-161, 165, 168, 177-179
  see also enlargement, EU
Wolff case, ECJ [2004] 51
Wouters case, ECJ [2002] 40
WTO VI, 80

Z

Zagreb University V, 175